SEVEN BIG AUSTRALIANS

SEVEN BIG AUSTRALIANS

Adventures with Comic Actors

ANNE PENDER

Seven Big Australians: Adventures with Comic Actors
© Copyright 2019 Anne Pender
All rights reserved. Apart from any uses permitted by Australia's Copyright Act 1968, no part of this book may be reproduced by any process without prior written permission from the copyright owner. Inquiries should be directed to the publisher.

Monash University Publishing
Matheson Library and Information Services Building
40 Exhibition Walk
Monash University
Clayton, Victoria 3800, Australia
www.publishing.monash.edu

Monash University Publishing brings to the world publications which advance the best traditions of humane and enlightened thought.

Monash University Publishing titles pass through a rigorous process of independent peer review.

ISBN: 9781925835212 (paperback)
ISBN: 9781925835229 (pdf)
ISBN: 9781925835236 (epub)

www.publishing.monash.edu/books/sba-9781925835212.html

Series: Biography

Internal design: Les Thomas

Cover design: Jeenee Lee

Front cover images: Carol Raye – courtesy Fairfax Media; photograph by Victor Sumner. Barry Humphries – courtesy Alamy; photograph by Neil Spence. Noeline Brown – courtesy Getty Images Entertainment. Max Gillies – courtesy Ponch Hawkes; photograph by Ponch Hawkes. John Clarke – courtesy Fairfax Media, photograph by Neil Newitt. Tony Sheldon – courtesy of Tony Sheldon; photograph by Kurt Sneddon. Denise Scott – courtesy Token Artists; photograph by James Penlidis.

Back cover image: Anne Pender – photograph by David Elkins.

A catalogue record for this book is available from the National Library of Australia.

This research was supported fully by the Australian Government through the Australian Research Council's Future Fellowship funding scheme (project FT110100256). The views expressed herein are those of the authors and are not necessarily those of the Australian Government or Australian Research Council.

Printed in Australia by Griffin Press an Accredited ISO AS/NZS 14001:2004 Environmental Management System printer.

The paper this book is printed on is certified against the Forest Stewardship Council ® Standards. Griffin Press holds FSC chain of custody certification SGS-COC-005088. FSC promotes environmentally responsible, socially beneficial and economically viable management of the world's forests.

CONTENTS

Introduction vii

Chapter 1 **Carol Raye**: Living on Champagne. 1

Chapter 2 **Barry Humphries**: 'A Bit of Psychic Nudity?'. 38

Chapter 3 **Noeline Brown**: 'I'm Not Afraid of the Audience' . . . 72

Chapter 4 **Max Gillies**: Marvellous Max. 101

Chapter 5 **John Clarke**: Bat On. 154

Chapter 6 **Tony Sheldon**: Do You Believe in Angels? 192

Chapter 7 **Denise Scott**: Comedy is Not Pretty. 238

References 273

Acknowledgements 276

About the Author 277

To the actors who shared their life stories.

In memory of John Clarke,
1948–2017

INTRODUCTION

The Australian theatre, television and film industries are dynamic in ways that could never have been imagined half a century ago. Since the 1950s these industries have expanded and demonstrated extraordinary vitality. The vibrant Australian performing arts industry would not exist in its current form without the creative contribution of actors. Actors are the public face of the performing arts, carrying the immediate responsibility for the success of each show. In spite of this they are frequently left out of theatre history. Yet, it is the actors, and often the characters they play, that we remember when we recall a favourite television program, film or play, long after we have seen it. It is the actors who make a play or a television program credible, enjoyable and memorable.

Comic actors have made a particularly strong contribution to cultural life in Australia over the last 60 years. They have brought a range of memorable characters to the stage, television and film; they have transformed our image of ourselves, helped to overturn the crippling cultural cringe, and they have brought Australian humour and satire to the world.

The biographical essays in this book offer portraits of the lives of seven significant Australian comic actors whose careers span the period from the Second World War until the present. Each essay offers the story of one actor's family origins, background, childhood, training, career and artistic achievements, drawing on extended interviews I conducted over five years with each actor. The lengthy life interviews have allowed me to develop a rapport that has facilitated the creation of a full portrait of the individual actor, each of whom has contributed immensely to the cultural life of millions of ordinary Australians.

Until the mid-1950s and early 1960s Australian actors were a minority on the stage in their own country. Actors who were trained in the United Kingdom dominated the industry and the big touring companies brought performers to Australia from overseas rather than employing local actors. Australian actors also departed for London to gain experience in the West End and in repertory companies all over the UK, wherever they could find work. This situation changed in the 1950s as a result of the production of new Australian plays by small but significant companies and the vision of a range of actors, playwrights and directors such as Doris Fitton, Sumner Locke Elliott, Hayes Gordon, Barry Humphries, Ray Lawler, John Sumner, Bill Orr, George Ogilvie and many others. For example the Independent Theatre, the Ensemble and the Phillip Street Theatre Companies in Sydney, and the University Theatre Repertory Company in Melbourne, began to stage Australian plays in the 1950s, and to offer popular satirical revue theatre that provided employment for Australian performers in extended seasons. Australian actors at last spoke in the vernacular when they performed Australian plays and revues, and did not have to worry so much about their accents, although the preference for a cultivated accent persisted for many years and well into the 1970s.

The actors whose lives are profiled in this book: Carol Raye, Barry Humphries, Noeline Brown, Max Gillies, John Clarke, Tony Sheldon and Denise Scott, represent high calibre performance and the full range of comic forms in Australia, the pioneering of new forms and a contribution to the transformation of comic performance in multiple

INTRODUCTION

genres in their work. This set of actors also reveals the fact that Australian comic performance was dominated by white Anglo-Celtic Australians for at least forty years after the War. It was not until the late 1980s and 1990s that comic performers of Indigenous heritage and from non-English speaking backgrounds came to prominence and transformed Australian comedy once more. The actors profiled here however are members of the first generations of actors to have made their careers primarily in Australia and their careers predate these later transformations. They seized the opportunities that developed in Australia on stage and then on television. Television allowed Australian actors to pursue their careers at home and to avail themselves of opportunities that simply did not exist prior to the introduction of the medium in 1956.

Actors often gain recognition for the ways in which they excel at either tragic or comic roles. In Australia, however, actors have had to be versatile and able to work across both serious drama and comedy. In some instances, actors become celebrated because they can perform across all the genres of theatre with emotional virtuosity. The actors in this book have worked across the genres and have distinguished themselves in comedy. Four of the seven actors, Carol Raye, Noeline Brown, Max Gillies and Tony Sheldon, are recognized for their contributions to comedy and to musical theatre, in addition to their work in other genres. All of the actors profiled here have appeared on the main stages of Australia and in community theatres throughout the country. Six of the seven actors have appeared on stage, television and in film. Of the seven, Tony Sheldon is the only one to have exclusively dedicated his life to stage performance. As he told me, he is an 'unrepentant theatre animal'. Sheldon, the son of Toni Lamond and Frank Sheldon, and nephew of Helen Reddy, is also the only performer in this collective biography to emerge from a family of entertainers.

Carol Raye, who was brought up in the UK, started her professional career during the War on the stages of the West End as a teenager. Raye arrived in Australia in 1964, and immediately set about producing and appearing in the first Australian satirical revue program on television, *The Mavis Bramston Show*. She brought her considerable experience as a dancer and as an actor on stage, television and film, as well as her expertise as a television producer to the fledgling Australian television industry. She also brought her knowledge of popular British television satire to Australian television.

Barry Humphries is recognised around the world for his signature character, Dame Edna Everage, who savaged and enchanted audiences for more than 60 years. He is an outlandish man from an ordinary family in Melbourne who propelled Australia into the international spotlight through his stage and television extravaganzas. Humphries has contributed to the transformation of popular theatre in Australia, the UK and the US, and achieved a powerful reversal of the cultural cringe at home. Humphries transformed popular entertainment in his one-man shows and contributed to a major innovation in television through his highly successful parodic chat shows on British television during the 1980s and 1990s. He is a provocateur who is happiest alone on stage performing his one-man show.

Noeline Brown began her career in the amateur theatres of suburban Sydney and appeared briefly as the eponymous Mavis on *The Mavis Bramston Show*. Her career in television comedy and as a quiz show personality alongside Graham Kennedy brought her to national attention. She has contributed to a number of landmark comic stage

INTRODUCTION

productions and appeared in musicals and highly successful stage shows that blend the comic and dramatic in innovative ways.

Max Gillies began his career in Melbourne directing youth theatre productions and teaching theatre studies at tertiary level. He achieved success as a member of the Australian Performing Group and went on to perform popular stage shows in which he impersonated politicians. Eventually his success with these productions led to his acclaimed satirical television sketch comedy show *The Gillies Report*, which made him a household name in Australia.

John Clarke, who died in 2017, created a character called Fred Dagg in his native New Zealand before moving to Australia where he wrote and performed sketches that gently satirised Australian politicians of all varieties. He created a new style of television comedy called 'mockumentary' with his popular series *The Games*. Clarke appeared in and wrote screenplays for films in various genres, wrote numerous literary satirical columns, poetry and books, and created the longest running satirical sketch show on television in Australia with *Clarke and Dawe*.

Tony Sheldon has appeared on stage in a variety of genres, including straight plays and a range of Australian premieres throughout his career. He has excelled in comic and musical theatre, making his name internationally for his role as Bernadette in *Priscilla Queen of the Desert*, playing in Sydney, London and on Broadway in this Australian musical.

Denise Scott is one of the pioneers of stand-up comedy in Australia and has created a distinctive, highly theatrical performance style that blends comic forms and borrows on traditions of stand-up comedy that come from the United States, although her performance style and the content of her routines is stridently Australian. Her career demonstrates remarkable resilience and commitment to breaking through the barriers for women in comedy.

These seven comic actors are also known for their ability to write scripts for performance. Each actor profiled in this book has also collaborated on script writing ventures with writers and other actors. In fact, one of the seven, John Clarke, considered himself to be a writer foremost in spite of his extraordinary career as an actor. Each of them has contributed material to the shows in which they have appeared on stage and on television. Humphries, Gillies and Scott have appeared in highly successful full-scale, one-person shows in which they blend comic genres. These one-person shows are fully scripted, curated theatrical events and bear the hallmarks of a distinctively Australian sense of humour.

Traditionally it is possible to observe a darkness in Australian comedy and a subversive celebration of anarchic or even bad behaviour. Michael Sharkey observes that Australian comedy 'often seems to endorse the "wrong thing" in its mocking treatment of sacred cows').[1] Australian comedy also frequently includes slapstick, vaudevillian clowning, the tall story, black humour, raw or confronting material and a highly energetic, physical style. The profiles in this book demonstrate however that Australian comedy and satire is not homogenous, but is varied and highly idiosyncratic. For example, the signature styles of John Clarke and Max Gillies, are completely different, even though they have both contributed to astute, highly nuanced political satire throughout their careers.

In addition to their long and varied careers in entertainment, each of these actors share a similar history in that none of them

---

1   Michael Sharkey, 1988, *The Illustrated Treasury of Australian Humour*, Melbourne: Oxford University Press, p. 14.

INTRODUCTION

had formal qualifications in a studio or actor-training school. For example, Barry Humphries did not undergo any formal training as an actor: he worked with leading Australian directors such as John Sumner, Ray Lawler and Peter O'Shaughnessy at the Melbourne Theatre Repertory Company, Phillip Street Theatre and with independent directors before he began to write, devise and perform his one-man shows in the early 1960s. Carol Raye, a dancer, learned to act on the job as well on the main stages of the West End. Noeline Brown worked in amateur theatre and then at the Phillip Street Theatre in Sydney and at the Neutral Bay Music Hall before making her television debut in the early 1960s. John Clarke started out in university revue theatre in Wellington, New Zealand. Max Gillies auditioned unsuccessfully for the new National Academy for Performing Art; he learned through performing in the small theatres of Melbourne and through teaching before his baptism of fire as a member of the innovative Australian Performing Group. This group transformed Australian theatre through its experiments in theatre making and its positioning of the performer as central to the making of theatre. The APG also pursued collaborative opportunities with local playwrights such as John Romeril, Jack Hibberd and David Williamson. Tony Sheldon learned through 'osmosis', by working with directors such as John Bell and Terence Clarke in Sydney in the 1970s. Denise Scott studied to be a teacher and apart from taking some classes in improvisation with the Canadian David Lander, she also learned to perform on the job in children's theatre, a small regional clowning troupe, cabaret acts with Judith Lucy and Lynda Gibson, and on her own, in her forays into the emerging world of stand-up in Melbourne during the 1980s.

Although these actors have the fact of their learning to perform on the job in common, and several of them have occasionally worked together, (Carol and Noeline; John and Max; Tony and Max) their styles, preferred forms and specific achievements are varied and highly individual. The essays on each actor document the opportunities and the difficulties faced by each performer throughout his or her career. All of them have experienced difficulties that are common to many actors but each actor's specific difficulties are different. The actors profiled in this book share the fact of having to find their way in an industry for which they had no formal training and for which there is no clear career path. They had to negotiate the range of directorial rehearsal styles they encountered, to manage the challenges of leaving behind a particular comic style or character at regular intervals; each had to counter the tyranny of typecasting, and had to learn to sustain themselves during long seasons and tours. Several of the actors had to learn to sing; each of them had to change direction in order to develop, manage collaborative enterprises, develop and maintain rapport with other actors, negotiate the uncertainties of employment, and work away from home for long periods, sometimes overseas. Some of the actors have also self-produced their work, enduring financial hardship and stress as a result, and others have managed their careers independently without the help of agents or mentors. The precarious circumstances surrounding the work of actors, particularly before the advent of rehearsal pay in the early 1970s, and the Dickensian conditions of employment that the actors described to me in my interviews with them, make their achievements all the more impressive.

Of course, the actors have also had to manage their off-stage lives and family responsibilities, caring for sick and aging parents, looking after spouses and bringing up children. The challenges for each

INTRODUCTION

actor have been enormous and each one of them in the interviews generously reflected on their own particular experiences of major life events and the daily reality of pursuing the life of a performer. Their recollections offer insights into their own creative lives, to the profession, Australian cultural life and to comedy itself. In most cases I conducted the interviews at the home of each actor, and they responded to questions in writing at times as well. I am privileged to have had this opportunity to spend extended periods listening to the life stories of each of the actors. They were all more than generous with their time and their recollections.

The Australian Research Council provided me with generous funding to undertake a major research project on the lives and work of Australian actors, under the auspices of a Future Fellowship. This book on comic actors is one of the outcomes of the research project. I am also grateful to the National Film and Sound Archive for granting me a fellowship to allow me to view hundreds of hours of television programs from the earliest periods of broadcasting in Australia and to peruse scripts and other materials that have informed my biographical portraits of actors.

It is often said that a biographer must surrender to his or her subject: my method of interviewing does this, allowing the individual to take the lead in the process. The actors who are the subjects of this book are artists who have given up their lives to entertain others in an industry that has undergone immense changes during their careers. It is important for the historical record and for the future of the performing arts that their experiences are documented and understood. It is also important that the individual is celebrated, remembered and accorded the significant place in cultural history that they deserve.

Chapter 1

CAROL RAYE: LIVING ON CHAMPAGNE

(B. 1923)

Carol Raye lives on an organic garlic farm south west of Kempsey on the Macleay River, near Sherwood not far from Dongdingalong. Her daughter Sally Ayre-Smith (one-time film producer) runs the farm with her husband, sculptor Marcus Skipper (of Montsalvat fame). It was harvest at the farm when I visited Carol, and sixteen strapping young backpackers greeted me from the back of a ute as they jolted up the muddy driveway for lunch. The smell of garlic from the verandah was intoxicating in the stinging November sun.

At 95 Carol Raye is enjoying active retirement after a long career in the theatre that began when she was a girl. She celebrated her 15th birthday as the lead in an amateur performance of *No, No Nanette* in Portsmouth. She turned 16 during a professional tour of the musical comedy *Bobby Get Your Gun in Birmingham*, chaperoned by her parents. Her 17th birthday saw her in the West End at His Majesty's Theatre playing a lead role in *Funny Side Up*. At 18, she was principal girl in the pantomime of *Robinson Crusoe* at the Manchester Palace Theatre, and she made her film debut in 1944.

Carol performed on stage, television and film for sixty years. She came to Australia with her husband and children because her husband took up a job with CSIRO in 1964. Carol joined Channel 7 soon after arriving and within months she was producing and starring in the *Mavis Bramston Show*, the most popular television program in Australia at the time, and the first locally made satirical show. Carol's career is in fact three careers: dancer in musical comedy, a screen actress and producer, and in the later stages of her working life, once again as a stage actress. She is a celebrated comic actress and has also appeared in a range of plays that transcend their comedy. Every performer's life is shaped by other people, by patrons and mentors, by circumstance, chance and luck. In her life Carol had to make difficult choices, but particularly when she married. Her own career was interrupted for ten years, and she began all over again in Australia where nobody knew of her London achievements, let alone her work in the US and Kenya. In moving from the UK, to Kenya, to Australia, to the UK and back again, Carol suffered again and again as an outsider. In spite of her extraordinary success as an actress in Australia she never attained full insider status.

Carol's memory for detail is exquisite, her ability to mimic as sharp as it was when she arrived in Australia in 1964, and she has an agile, whimsical sense of humour. She still has her petite dancer's erect posture and grace, and she radiates warmth. When her husband died in 2016 after 65 years of marriage, Carol seriously considered moving back to England. She told me on one of my visits in 2018 that she had given up the idea and that she and her daughter had bought another farm.

A Child in the West End

Carol Raye was born Kathleen Mary Corkrey. As an only child, she was close to her father, Reuben, a Lieutenant Paymaster in the Royal Navy, to her mother Ethel, who filled their many houses with music as an accomplished pianist, and to her only cousin Toni. Her paternal grandparents were influential on her, and during the war came to live with Carol and her parents. Carol still carries her grandfather's whistle in her handbag – the one he used for work with the Thames Water Police. Carol's grandmother was a determined woman, a fine seamstress who kept an intriguing collection of Victorian buttons, lace and other trimmings. On visits to her house in Bermondsey, London, she would wrap Carol's tiny feet with newspaper that she had warmed by the fire.

Throughout her life Carol has wandered the globe. As a child, there were two stints in Malta (due to her father's naval postings), and one in Bermuda, where Carol recalls the shade of the towering pepper trees in the school yard, and a few years at Purbrook Park County High School in rural Hampshire near Portsmouth. She learned to ride a horse and loved to swim, draw and read. Carol took dancing lessons at least twice week throughout her childhood; the horse riding did not last because of the risk of injury to her precious dancer's limbs. Carol pleaded with her parents to allow her to leave school as soon as she could. Her father was doubtful. He thought she should push on and go to university, even though it would involve financial hardship for them. But at 15 all Carol wanted to do was dance. She took her first ballet lessons in Portsmouth when she was four years of age and had completed the schedule of exams set out by the Royal Academy of Dance by the time she was ready to leave school. She quickly qualified in ballroom, receiving a coveted certificate signed by Victor Sylvester, also gaining proficiency in tap dancing.

When Carol read in the *Dancing Times* that an Australian choreographer-dancer called Freddy Carpenter had opened a new school in London she convinced her mother Ethel to take her to audition for him in his Soho studio. Carol had in her mind that she might get further instruction with the Australian choreographer, and she yearned to learn modern dancing and swing – the dance she imagined would be essential to know in order to perform in musical comedy. A fine boned redhead from Adelaide, Freddy

Carol Raye aged 16.
Courtesy of Carol Raye.

Carpenter made his name in London as a dancer, and later turned to choreography. Dressed in a brown chiffon frock, with her mother playing the piano, Carol sang a Jessie Matthews song and confidently showed Carpenter a dance routine. She made a strong impression and the following week he telegrammed Ethel Corkrey: 'Bring the child to London next week to meet Stanley Lupino'. It was the summer of 1939.

Carol danced her audition routine for the diminutive comic revue writer and performer Stanley Lupino and he immediately offered her the ingénue lead role in his new musical revue *Funny Side Up*. Ethel accompanied Carol who was sixteen, to Manchester for the rehearsals and try out season. Carpenter decided that the young Kathleen Mary should adopt a stage name: one that was memorable, short and less Irish. He suggested the name Carol Raye and that was that. He assigned one of the experienced chorus girls to instruct Carol, to teach her how to apply stage make up and to curl her eyelashes: 'Take the child and show her how to put on her makeup' he said, as she had no idea of the craft. Carol watched in awe as the more experienced actors rehearsed their complicated routines over a couple of weeks in Manchester: it was just as well she had been so attentive because at the dress rehearsal the young leading lady, Sally Gray, injured her leg during a dance routine, when she and her partner careened into a set.

Carpenter worked all of the next day with Carol, the 16-year-old novice, so that she could appear in place of Gray that night when the show opened. With Carpenter, Carol perfected the fast dancing moves, lighting quick costume changes, satirical sketches and at least one number that recalled nostalgic songs from the past. Carol was nervous but did not disappoint. Every London critic praised the performance, with several stating that the teenager from Portchester brought to mind the actress Jessie Matthews. Carol enchanted audiences with her sweet voice, lithe presence, large brown eyes and dark brown hair, and her gift for dance. *Funny Side Up* was the first of the glamorous large-scale wartime revues, satirising the blackout and the Ministry for Information (the Ministry of Shh!), reviving popular tunes from the First World War and featuring a few risqué moments. There were impersonations of Clara Butterworth, Ethel Levey, Elsie Janis, Harry Pilcer, Gaby Deslys, Violet Lorraine and George Robey

– the musical stars of the first war. Carol was praised by critics for her charming impression of Elsie Janis.[1] As one of the stars of the show alongside Florence Desmond, Lupino appeared in various guises, including as a 'hush hush Whitehall bureaucrat'.[2] Suddenly Carol was being talked about in every newspaper as a 'future star', a 'big star', 'an outstanding success', and 'a starlet to watch'.[3]

Carol Raye, aged 17.
Courtesy of Carol Raye.

---

1   *Daily Express* 12 January 1940.
2   *Evening Gazette* 8 January 1940.
3   *Evening Gazette* 8 January 1940; *What's On* 19 January 1940, *Daily Express* 8 January 1940; *Blackpool Gazette* 8 January 1940.

CAROL RAYE

Carol Raye's rise to stardom was instant and almost effortless; she had not been pushed as a child, and she had no formal training in acting or singing. She was a particularly talented dancer, a very quick learner, and she loved comic revue. Over three years as a teenager, Carol rose from one appearance for the amateur musical theatre in Portsmouth to become a cherished starlet of the West End. She had no expectations about herself or her career when she appeared for the first time in the amateur Portsmouth Players, and hoped she would be able to teach dance for a living. Demure, girlish and fresh faced, Carol embraced musical comedy, revue, pantomime and ballet – everything that was offered. With her whimsical smile and graceful dancing, she worked with Stanley Holloway in the pantomime *Robinson Crusoe*, playing Polly Perkins to his Will Atkins in a daytime season in Manchester, scheduled to try to avoid the night time bombing raids by the Germans of 1941. By the end of the year her smiling, slightly dreamy face had appeared on the cover of *Picture Post* and *Theatre World*, in all the newspapers, and she appeared modelling a wide shouldered, sophisticated dark trouser suit in *Harper Magazine*.

It was another dancer from Adelaide, Robert Helpmann, who choreographed a role for her in the rather sentimental but hugely successful ballet routine in the revue *Fun and Games*, in which she played a dancer who tries on shoes and performs a mesmerising routine in front of an old cobbler (played by Richard Hearne); later she asks the shoe mender to repair her ballet shoes. In spite of the accolades this charming role brought her, Carol recalls 'Bobby' Helpmann urging her to dedicate herself to traditional ballet rather than 'wasting time' in what he saw as the rather inferior musical theatre. The designs for the show were made by a soldier in barracks (Gunner Billie Chappell) – like so many theatre people – he was away from London, serving his country. In fact, Freddy Carpenter was by this time Flying Officer Carpenter in the RAF, and stationed on a base outside London, so he could no longer look after Carol. But he ensured that she was in the capable hands of an agent. Carol was now the darling of the West End, and on the opening night of *Fun and Games* in London at the Princes Theatre, the audience interrupted the drum roll that preceded the National Anthem at the conclusion of the show, imploring the 18-year-old to give a speech, shouting 'Carol, Carol'.[4] It was an unprecedented break in protocol and the young actress shyly came forward, not knowing what to do. She still recalls her embarrassment at this moment, and her sense of anxiety about doing the wrong thing by the other star performers.

The critics praised Raye, with one offering due compliments to the celebrated stars of the show (Arthur Riscom, Sydney Howard, Richard Hearne and Vera Pearce), and remarking that 'the girl who got the biggest hand was Carol Raye, who jumps, or rather pirouettes, straight into star class …'.[5] It wasn't simply the London critics who wrote about Carol Raye. A column appeared in the *New York Times* reporting that 'the show was stolen … by a little dancer', claiming that 'Miss Raye is no glamour girl. She is that character so well loved by fiction writers and so seldom encountered on the actual hard-boiled stage, a nice little girl from the suburbs whose quiet charm gets its chance in the final pages and triumphs in the last paragraph. Once you have noticed her you find that she has youth, freshness and that queer something known as personality … She [danced] with an effortless grace …'.[6]

---

4   *Evening News* 23 August 1941.
5   *Sunday Chronicle* Manchester 24 August 1941.
6   W.A. Darlington, *New York Times* 31 August 1941.

Carol Raye recalls this period of her life with joy, remembering her pleasure in performing and doing what she loved which was dancing. As a young and inexperienced performer when she set out in Manchester she felt safe and protected amongst the cast, and her mother was always with her during the out of London try out seasons. She does however recognise that she was naïve. She had little thought for her future or any doubts about what she was doing. She recalled for me that when she received her first pay: 25 shillings a week the first time in 1940, it felt like a bonus and a privilege. Looking back, she says that this was because she so enjoyed the work, and had no sense of the gruelling challenges many aspiring performers endure in order to succeed. For her it had been easy. Yet the theatre culture was less forgiving of the perils of naiveté and froth. Herbert Farjeon in the *Tatler and Bystander* noted that in the 'boy and girl numbers of *Fun and Games* ... Miss Carol Raye, a newcomer, is the chief attraction'. Commenting on her fresh charm and 'delicious dancing' he worried that the promising young dancer may not be able to 'resist swarming up the ladder of fame' and that she may waste her talent, and 'even end up in a gaudy grave in Hollywood'. He hoped that she would resist the lure of simply performing 'in a vacuum', stating that 'It is out of the quality of the work you do rather than out of the applause you get for it that satisfaction ultimately lies. One would not worry about Miss Raye if she were not unusually promising. As she is, one worries a good deal'.[7]

Robert Helpmann, or Bobby, as Carol still calls him, arranged the dances for her next show, a glittering revival of the old operetta, *The Merry Widow*, in which Carol appeared in a spangly satin dance

---

7   *The Tatler and Bystander* 3 September 1941, p. 300.

dress and calf length lace-up boots performing with the chorus in a vigorous version of the can-can. In the autumn of 1943 Carol appeared in another musical comedy by Stanley Lupino called *The Love Racket* at the Victoria Palace Theatre in Westminster, alongside the tiny, bespectacled comic actor from Liverpool, Arthur Askey. Jack Hylton took Carol out of *The Merry Widow* in order for her to star in Lupino's musical. (Lupino died in 1942.) The satirical story presents a trio of impecunious Hollywood film stars along with their husbands who try to run their own film studio. The dancing was a feature of the musical comedy in which the Hollywood obsessions with money and sex are lampooned in a nonsensical plot. The critical reception was mixed and in some cases lukewarm. There was consensus however that Carol Raye's dancing was superb and that her singing voice was stronger than in her earlier musical roles.[8] One critic insisted that Carol saved the show: 'At first she seems just a pretty girl, but when she dances she becomes ethereal and lovely, and at one point one has the pleasure of seeing her reflected in four mirrors, dancer and corps de ballet in one'.[9] The comic clowning of Askey was riotous and the antics of the characters entertaining. There was absolutely no reference to the war in the script or the story. It was wilfully escapist, frothy and witty entertainment.

But the war was literally right outside. Each theatre was fitted with large flashing red air raid sirens positioned high up on the side of the proscenium. When the lights flashed the audience could leave their seats to take refuge in the nearest underground shelter. But Carol recalls that very few audience members did this, and the

---

8   *Daily Telegraph* 27 October 1943; *Daily Sketch* 27 October 1943.
9   *News Chronicle* 27 October 1943.

shows did not stop. Carol was mid-way through an intricate solo dance routine wearing a full-length flowing pale coloured backless gown in front of a set of massive mirrors when she heard a loud bang. Dust, chunks of old plaster and several heavy steel capped lights from the flies crashed to the floor. The orchestra came to a dead stop and an eerie calm followed. Carol looked around, a few seconds passed and she heard the tapping of the conductor's baton on his stand and his arms lifting before the orchestra sprang to life again. She picked up the dance steps and the show went on. It was only afterwards as she sat in her dressing room, that she thought of what might have been. The towering mirrors that lined the stage for the solo dance number had not shattered, and she had been spared. In a theatre only a block away where the bomb had exploded others were not so lucky.

Carol was used to air raids, blackouts, unlit theatre marquees, carrying a torch in case of pea soup fog around the dim streets of the West End, and removing the distributor cap from her car engine, lest a German parachuted in should gain access to a vehicle. All of these precautions were normal and the actors worked around them. Entertainment was important and Carol and her colleagues never even considered withdrawing from a show in fear of a direct hit. She didn't hesitate when she was asked to perform in benefit shows for the Manchester Air Raid Distress Fund, appearing at the Palace Theatre in Manchester with Leslie Henson, Gavin Gordon, John E. Coyle, George Neil, Leslie Lester, Stanley Holloway, George Formby, Fay Compton and Tommy Trinder.

Theatres in London closed several times during the war and during the Battle of Britain in 1940 the show in which Carol was scheduled to appear called *Learn to Love* (a musical version of *The Charm School*) was abandoned as the risks were simply too high.[10] A cartoon of the time showed Londoners going about their business on the street, with every figure shown with an unnaturally large ear – listening for doodlebugs, the bombs that hummed, then exploded without warning.

In 1944 Carol appeared in her first feature film, a farming drama, playing Molly, the extravagant young wife of a wealthy man, played by Billy Hartnell in an adaptation of *Strawberry Roan*, Arthur Street's charming story of English country life. The cast spent a month on location near Salisbury for filming. It was pleasant for Carol, who had always loved the outdoors and rural life, to be on the Salisbury plains and in the villages of Wiltshire and before long Carol was cast in *Evergreen*, a television musical for the BBC (screened in 1945). The series of the same name had been popular on radio, with Jessie Matthews playing the role of Harriet Green. Carol took this role for the television adaptation, and soon afterwards appeared in an adaptation of J B Priestley's musical *The Good Companions* but it was the feature film *Waltz Time* that took her to Broadway for the premiere screening in New York. The British film was set in the nineteenth century in Vienna when the waltz was first danced. The handsome son of a peer, Peter Graves, played a young army lieutenant who teaches the young Maria, empress of Austria, played by Carol, to waltz. The costume drama was gently comic, romantic and its focus was on dance itself, with lavishly staged ballroom scenes, a massive cast and sumptuous designs. The film reflected a kind of cultural push back against the more hectic, noisy swing and jazz music and dance of the 1940s. The plot entailed an arrest of the bewitching empress for dancing the waltz, which had been banned as a vulgar,

---

10   *Evening News* 23 August 1941.

Carol Raye and Peter Graves in the popular British film *Waltz Time*, 1945. Courtesy of Carol Raye.

immoral pastime. Maria overturns the ban, decrees the waltz to be the official court dance, removes the tax on bread and of course marries the gallant young lieutenant. The critics were generally positive, with a few quips about the plot and the froth of the film. It was a nostalgic and picturesque cinematic extravaganza that eschewed the ostentatious look and feel of contemporary American musical films in favour of a more courtly, tasteful, old fashioned charm.

Carol was flown to New York for the first screening of the film in New York City. She recalled for me the breathtaking view of the lights of Manhattan Island as the aircraft approached. At the Waldorf Astoria Hotel Carol was stunned by the opulence of the city

Carol Raye, publicity photograph for the British film
Green Fingers, 1947.

after the years of blackout and austerity in London. Her breakfast tray held a gleaming silver dish with enough butter to feed a family for a week in Britain. The premiere party at the off-Broadway cinema was unimaginably luxurious and Carol found the experience both uplifting and empowering, knowing that she was now a recognised actress in the United States of America.

Love and Television in East Africa

After the war, when Carol's father retired from the Navy, he bought a pub in rural Berkshire at Goring-on-Thames. Carol occasionally helped her parents at the pub during her breaks from the theatre.

CAROL RAYE

One Sunday lunch time a tall, good looking young man appeared in the private bar. He had long curly hair and was sporting a purple shirt, leather jerkin and corduroy trousers pinned over the knee with a large safety pin. He looked somewhat bohemian, and caught Carol's eye. Under his arm he was lovingly holding on to a small, bright-eyed terrier. Over a ginger beer the two of them got talking. The man's name was Robert Ayre-Smith, he was a final-year veterinary student, and he invited Carol to go out walking with him and his dogs.

Carol accompanied Robert to the New Year's Eve Chelsea Arts Ball that year, arriving late, after appearing in a special television broadcast. Robert was dressed as a pirate and Carol in a swishy Victorian crinoline borrowed from wardrobe at the BBC. He was exuberant and merry, jumping up on a table and singing to the assembled guests. In telling me this story Carol launched into the song he sang as though it was yesterday. Carol was smitten, and for three years the two of them met up in Cambridge where he continued his studies. He was keen to work on large agricultural projects and proposed to Carol before setting off for the United States on a Fulbright scholarship. Carol appeared in *Dear Miss Phoebe* playing the lead role. It was based on a play called *Quality Street* by JM Barrie and was a triumph at the box office. One critic wrote that 'Few actresses of today possess the attributes which make a satisfactory Barrie heroine – a kind of frisky demureness, a charm allied to wide-eyed simplicity. Carol Raye suggested just such a personality in the title role of *Dear Miss Phoebe* at the Phoenix Theatre last night – and so helped to preserve some of the quality in Barrie's *Quality Street* ...'.[11] The painter, (Sir) William Russell Flint created a delicate

---

11   Harold Conway, *The Evening Standard* 14 October 1950.

pen and ink sketch of Carol performing, and also painted a scene in oils, capturing Carol's sylph-like form and the rich costume designs of the production in crimson satins, soft pink silks, and the vivid colours of the Napoleonic soldiers' uniforms. The painting appeared at the Royal Academy in the summer exhibition when Carol's show closed in London.

In 1951 Carol packed the wedding outfit she had made, a matching silk jacket and skirt, and sailed on the Queen Mary to New York, travelling on by train to Baton Rouge, Louisiana to meet her fiancé. Carol and Robert were married in a cavernous, empty Presbyterian church, with only Robert's professor and his secretary as witnesses. They spent a few days exploring the area in an old car. Someone lent them an old fishing shack for their honeymoon in the Bayous. There were no curtains, and when Carol, exhausted after her trip, sat down on the bed it collapsed. They didn't have much money, as Robert was living on a student grant, so Carol taught children elocution in a local school in Baton Rouge, worked as a nanny and as a maid, and then in a department store selling swimwear. It was a far cry from the luxuries of the Waldorf Astoria and the glamour of the West End.

At 28 Carol Raye was now Mrs Robert Ayre-Smith and overnight relinquished her place in the national spotlight, giving away her status as the new Jessie Matthews, and her future as a kind of Gertrude Lawrence. She disappeared and began a new life in which her husband's work took them as far away from the West End as possible. Talking about this with me Carol has no regrets: 'That's what you do when you love someone', she says, smiling.

In 1954 Robert joined the Kenya Colonial Service in order to work on large agricultural projects. Sitting up in her hospital bed after giving birth to Sally in London, Carol recalls her teary remonstrations with Robert, and her fears of taking a new-born baby to Kenya during the Mau Mau Emergency. Robert reassured her and she set about all the preparations. Sailing for Nairobi with a baby on a soon to be retired ship with no laundry facilities, Carol washed nappies in the cabin sink and hung them to dry on the decks. On the night they arrived she awoke in fright to hear the beat of drums and pounding steps close by the house in which they were staying. Disoriented and exhausted, she wondered what she had come to and hoped that they wouldn't be caught up in any Mau Mau violence.

During the ten-year stint in Kenya, much of it spent 'up country' on experimental farms, Carol devoted herself to motherhood, giving birth to three children and looking after them. But she didn't withdraw from work altogether, performing in several amateur plays and appearing in a leading role in a film called *No Rain at Timburi* (1954). Having appeared in the new medium of television in the UK during its infancy, Carol began to think about working on the other side of the camera. With the knowledge that television was about to start up in Kenya, Carol spent a summer break back home in the UK, completing the BBC producers intensive course, learning the rudiments of television production, alongside producers from countries all over the Commonwealth. It was Carol Raye who made the first announcement on television in Kenya. Recalling it many years later in Australia she said 'I was the Bruce Gyngell of television in Kenya'.[12] Carol produced five live to air programs a week for the fledgling national broadcaster in Kenya. Her production work included children's drama, a magazine program with interviews, an Indian dance program, and a Swahili women's program.[13]

---

12 Interview with Brendan Horgan, *Screensound*, 28 September 2000.
13 *The Sun* 13 November 1964.

Making *Mavis*

On a sunny autumn afternoon in 1964, Carol and her family arrived in Australia on the *Oriana*, sailing into Sydney and marvelling at the sparkling beauty of the harbour. Robert had joined CSIRO and the family set up their new home in Beecroft to the north of the city. Carol knew she wanted to produce television and had the requisite skills after her three years with Kenya Broadcasting Corporation; she wasted no time introducing herself to people in the emerging television industry in Sydney. In a meeting with Charles Moses at the ABC she was told that her ideas for programs and her production experience may well appeal to the commercial stations but that at the ABC they either trained their own producers up from cadets or imported experienced producers from the UK. She set off to meet James Oswin at Channel 7 in Epping. By the end of March, Carol was appointed as 'Live Programme Consultant' at the station. Her brief was to devise a new late-night show to compete with Graham Kennedy's hugely successful *In Melbourne Tonight*. Carol had in mind a program that mirrored the topical satirical sketch show *That was the Week That Was*, which she had seen on a visit to London. The British hit television show featured David Frost, Millicent Martin and Bernard Levin. Carol noticed immediately that there was nothing of its kind on television in Australia, although there was an appetite for variety, comedy and revue. Carol wanted to make topical journalistic satire in the Australian context, going well beyond revue, and she knew she needed a David Frost type character. Frost was the tall, elegant straight man of the UK show. She also needed a funny man and a woman.

When Carol first explained her idea for the show to Jimmy Oswin, he was sceptical: 'I don't think Australians are ready to laugh at themselves', he said. 'It's too BBC', he objected. But Carol talked him around and was given 1200 pounds to make a pilot. At the time, she did not know anyone in Australia, and didn't realise that writers for television might be difficult to find. Michael Plant, an Australian journalist who had been working in Los Angeles came on board and helped Carol find writers, and later co-produced the show with Carol, also writing many sketches. Ken Shadie, a mild mannered man who worked in the engineering department at the station appeared one day with a script, his hands shaking, and went on to contribute material, and later became their main staff writer. A young man from Melbourne by the name of David Sale wrote some brilliant lyrics based on the news of the day, and also produced the show after the sudden death of Michael Plant. The actors also contributed to the writing and devising of sketch material. Looking back, Carol says she marvelled at the number of talented people who worked on *Mavis* in that first year.

Carol was also fortunate to have Tommy Tycho on hand, the Hungarian-born pianist and musical director, who had spent his war years in a concentration camp, and was making his career in Australia. Tycho could write music to order in an instant from a scrap of a lyric on a piece of paper during the afternoon before recording the show. He improvised for the cast, and he tirelessly arranged and devised orchestral music for the show. Don Burroughs was amongst the musicians Tycho engaged at Channel 7. In Gordon Chater, the English comic actor, Carol found her funny man and a great friend. Then, on a chance visit to the Neutral Bay Music Hall, Carol found her straight man. As soon as Barry Creyton began to speak, Carol knew she had found her David Frost. The 24-year-old Creyton was tall, slim, dark-haired and well spoken. Carol was delighted when

Barry agreed to join the show and found him to be a modest, kind and talented man with whom she connected. She marvelled at his ability to perform, and to write both lyrics and music. Her efforts to find a female to sing, dance and perform in the satirical sketches that would form the bedrock of the program, proved more difficult. Judi Farr and June Salter were already committed and time was running out to make the pilot. Noeline Brown, who had appeared with Creyton in the music hall sketches, had planned to go to London like so many other Australian performers at that time. It was then that Chater who had seen Carol's work in London, convinced her to appear in the show, at least for the pilot, so that they could show management what they had in mind.

The name of the show came out of a conversation with one of the writers who mentioned that in Melbourne the actors would sometimes refer to a bad actress as a 'Mavis Bramston'. At the time, overseas non-entities were frequently brought to Australia to appear in lead roles on stage and the joke was a reference to these kinds of actresses. When Carol and the others heard this story, they leapt on it for the name of the show. In the publicity, there was much made of the fact than an overseas actress would feature.

Carol, Barry and Gordon appeared in the pilot, with Ruth Cracknell as the first guest on the new program. Chater opened the first episode with an announcement. He explained that the team had been expecting an English actress called Mavis Bramston to feature on the show, but when her audition tape arrived it was a bit of a surprise. 'We will show you', he said, as the cameras shifted to Noeline Brown playing Mavis, walking down the stairs singing in a horribly off-key voice 'I could have danced all night'. When the 'tape' was finished, Barry Creyton explained 'As you can see, we decided to

Carol Raye on the set of *The Mavis Bramston Show*, 1964.
Courtesy of Seven Studios.

go ahead without Mavis Bramston. Welcome.' The three performers launched into the tune that became synonymous with the popular show. It was called 'Togetherness' and was written by Creyton.

In her office at the studio on what they called 'mahogany row', where the executives sat, Carol could hear the gales of laughter as Oswin showed the pilot to the others. Carol was still dealing with the informality she found in Australia. She couldn't get used to the fact that everyone used first names. Even Rupert Henderson, the small and rather wizened CEO of the Fairfax empire who owned Channel 7, had insisted that she call him Rupert, rather than Mr Henderson, as she would have done at home in the UK. Rupert was delighted with the pilot and the first six episodes, but gave Carol an ultimatum. She wanted to produce the show not to be in it, and she made an appointment to explain her wishes to him. In his broad Australian accent, he made the situation plain: 'Well Carol, you've gotta' make up your mind: either you stay on camera or you don't have a job'. Nonplussed, Carol stood looking at the man, bemused at his boyish but tyrannical stance. In an attempt to placate her, he said 'Give me a kiss' and when he came closer, he embraced her in a fatherly manner, as if to say 'No hard feelings'. As she was leaving he said 'You're a difficult woman, but you're not a bitch'. Carol retreated, astounded at his comment and disappointed with his decision. She went home to Robert and said 'What shall I do?' He said 'do it, you like doing it, so do it'.

The Mavis Bramston Show was an immediate hit with audiences. Gordon Chater, Barry Creyton and Carol Raye became household names, and the show quickly achieved the highest ratings of any television program screened in Australia at the time. The *Sun* referred to *Mavis* as 'authentic, biting, saucy, swinging satire … It was all done with crisp rhyming, timing and miming, brightly written lines and lively, bouncy music – a pattern familiar to audiences of the small revues that have been holding their own on the edge of theatre-land'.

The style and forms of sketch were familiar but the satire was much more barbed than in intimate revue. Robert Menzies was the target of an acidic attack in the first show on his new defence plans and the *Voyager* disaster: 'he's begged the navy not to go out on its own after dark …'. The *Sun* critic commented:

> Carol Raye "sent up" the airlines war with a parody on a hit tune that substituted "Canberra" for "Camelot", a rather bumpy, rhythmical road. Mr Chater wound up the show with an apology to the Queen, Mr Calwell, Andrea, Sir Frank Packer "and anyone else we may not have dealt with". "Don't worry" he leered. "We will".[14]

Kessell praised the newcomer: 'Carol Raye is one of the best things ever to happen to Sydney TV …'. He praised both Chater and Raye and said 'This is adult entertainment with a capital A, the boldest breakthrough since TV began here'.[15]

One of the problems Carol and Michael Plant encountered at the beginning was in finding suitable writers: Carol naively assumed there would be a ready supply but discovered it wasn't so straightforward. There were writers willing to contribute scripts and ideas, but few were ready and skilled enough to produce the volume of appropriate sketch material needed for the hour of television each week. Thirteen writers contributed in the first series and for the first time, at Michael Plant's insistence, they were paid properly for contributing a three-minute sketch. Plant and the writer Lynn Foster, who became an editor for the scripts, read 200 scripts each week. Rehearsals were from 1 until 5 each day and all day on Tuesdays when the show was taped, beginning with hair and makeup around 9am, and finishing up around eight at night. Carol was exhausted but undaunted. She relished the acting and

---

14   Norman Kessell, *The Sun* 13 November 1964.
15   Ibid.

the camaraderie of the small team – it was a new world for her and nothing like the musical comedy work and film acting of her early career. The chemistry between Chater, Creyton and Raye seemed to her to be a miracle – something that only happens occasionally in performance and it was intoxicating. She told me it was like 'living on champagne'.

Eventually it became clear that Carol could not play all the female roles herself. June Salter joined the permanent cast and Maggie Dence became the face of Mavis, travelling around Australia to promote the show and its sponsor, Ampol. Word reached Carol that Qantas pilots were re-arranging their schedules so that they did not miss the Thursday night broadcast of the one-hour show each week. The humour was topical, sharp and satirical and marked a significant moment for Australian comedy. No subject was off limits. The Vietnam War was satirised, there were jokes about the Pill, the foibles of the Prime Minister, Robert Menzies came in for a pasting, censorship and social mores were frequent targets; even the death penalty in Victoria was the target of a sketch, with Carol singing a song about Henry Bolte, questioning the barbaric practice in a lyrical lament 'Dear Henry Bolte, does it have to be this way?' One of the sketches caused a scandal, with Carol playing a housewife ostensibly talking about flower arranging and indicating po-faced how the stalks of flowers shouldn't droop too much. It was tame stuff by today's standards but upset Fred Daly and the slightly suggestive nature of the piece led to outrage from the Catholic Archbishop Muldoon. Questions were raised in parliament about the show. Gordon Chater was accused of being a 'vulgar entertainer'. In the federal parliament, the Postmaster General, Allen Hulme, attempted to explain that some licence should be allowed for satire. Looking back Carol laughs at the fuss, remembering that in the early 1960s nobody had even said 'bum' on television.

Dozens of profile pieces, columns, interviews and behind the scenes articles filled the newspapers and magazines. Carol, who had always shown immense self-control and natural charm, excelled in the art of media management. Shown at home in pearls and an apron calmly serving dinner, with her son Mark beside her, or outside beside the swimming pool, she was always gracious and amusing in interviews and in each photograph, she is immaculately dressed in smart, tailored linen or tweed. There were no signs of strain. It is a feature of women's careers that strains are simply not allowed to show. Carol was asked countless times about how her husband felt about her working. She told one reporter in the early months of the Bramston phenomenon that 'he doesn't mind as long as it doesn't interfere with the household; he still expects me to produce clean shirts with buttons on, and in the half hour or so that I get home before him, I do a quick tidy up, see that his favourite ashtray is polished, and so on. He knows the alternative is a frustrated, fractious wife around the place as I'm just not cut out for full-time domesticity'.[16]

Chestnuts and Colour TV in Kensington

When Carol began to sense it was time to move on, she handled the media storm with judgement and flair. After more than a year co-producing and appearing in a leading role in the show, she did begin to feel the pressure and the strain. With three school-aged children and her husband frequently travelling overseas for work, arranging and supervising the building of a new house, and with her parents

---

16   *New Idea* 27 Jan 1965, p. 11.

now living in Australia, she felt that the time might be right for a break. She thought that the show had lost its way, and lost its satirical thrust, becoming lukewarm revue. In her view it required significant investment in writers in order to do what it set out to do. But the stress of standing up for herself and her views was tough. Years later Carol admitted to a reporter that her marriage had taken 'a beating' during this period.[17]

After a break Carol appeared on stage for the first time since her West End triumphs some seventeen years earlier. The play was a Phillip Street Theatre revue called *Lie Back and Enjoy It*, directed by her friend from *Mavis*, David Sale. The show included an hilarious parody of 'Hair', with one of the supporting actresses, Beryl Cheers, lying on the stage floor, rolling around and refusing to take her clothes off: 'We don't have to, we're talented', she winced. But revue was not what Carol wanted. She hoped for an opportunity to work in the 'straight' theatre or a chance to perform in a big musical, realising that at 44, the chances of work in musicals were diminishing, and that her dancing days might be over.

In spite of her reservations, two years later Carol was invited to return to *The Mavis Bramston Show*, while Channel 7 prepared a new series for her written by Anne Deveson and David Sale. Meanwhile she had appeared with Mike Walsh, Barry Crocker and Peter Whitford, in a lavish musical program, with extravagant costumes and elaborate dance numbers, called *66 and All That* for Channel 10, in *Beauty and the Beast*, the crime series *Riptide* and several other programs. With Robert's work increasingly focussed around major projects in the Caribbean, the family decided to move back to the United Kingdom.

---

17 Sonia Humphrey, the *Weekend Australian*, 30 April – 1 May 1983, p. 9.

Carol, wearing a pink chiffon dress in the revue *Lie Back and Enjoy It*,
Phillip Street Theatre, Sydney, 1969.
Courtesy of Carol Raye.

It seemed to Carol the obvious move to make given her husband's work, and her sense of home was still firmly England. Ironically the actress Googie Withers had told her when she first came to Australia: 'You'll enjoy working here so long as you don't stay for more than four years. After that, they'll think you're a local, darling, and that's fatal'. Carol was leaving Australia after five years. It is unlikely that anyone thought of Carol as a local at any stage of her long career, and certainly not in the 1960s. Her strong English accent never mellowed and her persona was very English, particularly in this period.

Back in London, and established in a house in Kensington, after a brief disastrous move into a former brothel in Mayfair, Carol wrote a regular chirpy, artsy column published in the *Sun-Herald* in Sydney, made several guest appearances on BBC television and enjoyed resuming her friendships. In the column, she articulated her love of the English countryside, the creamy flowers of chestnut trees, afternoon tea, the extraordinary facilities at the BBC with its 18 studios, hemlines and most significantly reported knowledgably on the theatre, describing Keith Michell's performance in *Heloise and Abelard*, and the ructions caused by *Oh Calcutta*. In many of these columns she referred to Australia as 'home'.

Early one morning at home in Kensington she answered the telephone and an American voice on the other end began talking to her about a new television drama set in a block of flats in inner city Sydney that had exploded on to the screens of Australians. It was *Number 96*, and Carol had seen several episodes of the program while on holiday in Australia a few months earlier. The voice on the telephone belonged to Bill Harmon who was a producer for the Channel 10 series. He invited Carol to return to Australia to join the cast for a few months. Carol hesitated, knowing that the producers of the show, Bill, and Don Cash, had a penchant for nudity and racy scenes. Harmon suggested she play a new character, Joe Hasham's Aunt, a character who would inject more humour into the story of a quiet homosexual lawyer and his difficulties, played by Don Finlayson. The portrayal of a gay man in a key role was a first for Australian television. Carol knew that David Sale was one of the creators and writers for the series and was tempted by the offer; she levelled with the producer, laughing as she said: 'Bill I'm too old to get my gear off'. He reassured her that in playing Baroness Amanda von Pappenburg, an Auntie Mame type, this would not be necessary. With great excitement, she agreed to appear in the series for a three month stint.

Number 96 and *All That*

Carol returned to Australia after three years living in England, a period in which she had missed her adopted home. She had appeared on television in colour for the first time in 1970 and enjoyed the opportunity of contributing to television plays. But she was happy to be back in Sydney, and soon the whole family followed to make their home again in Australia, including her parents, Reuben and Ethel. They set up the family home in Mosman, enrolled the youngest daughter Harriet in school and Carol began again in television, re-starting her career after an extended break for the fourth time. Carol's involvement in *Number 96* was particularly enjoyable, as she connected with many Australian writers and actors, a few of whom she had known during her Mavis days. Ken Shadie, Eleanor Whitcombe, Michael Boddy, Robert Caswell, Pat Flower, Johnny Whyte, Bob Ellis and many others wrote episodes of the long-running series, which is now considered to be important in Australian television history for breaking taboos and securing enormous audiences. The cast included many actors with whom Carol enjoyed working: Pat McDonald played Dorrie Evans, Elaine Lee appeared as Vera Collins, Ron Shand as Herbert Evans, James Elliott as Alf Sutcliffe, Elizabeth Kirkby as Luce Sutcliffe and many others. Carol discovered a great affinity with one of the other actresses, Sheila Kenelly, and they became close friends. When her stint as Amanda finished, Carol was invited to join the production house Cash Harmon, to work in casting and production. This was the job she had wanted for years, ever since she married, well before *Mavis Bramston* took off, had pursued successfully in Kenya, but had not been able to continue in Australia. She spent a lot of time working on new program ideas and discussing them with Eleanor Whitcomb. Together they talked about developing an historical drama about the life of Caroline Chisholm, and another on the convict Sarah Dane. After her short stint in production Carol relinquished her dream job in order to look after her parents who were both frail and needed care. Just as she had given up her glamorous career in the West End, to marry Robert, leaving London for Louisiana and then East Africa, Carol withdrew from the world of entertainment once more to focus on her family.

Footlights and Fame

In 1976 Carol did not work outside her home. She took a much needed break after caring for her parents, who both became seriously ill and died within months of one another. Exhausted and grieving she rested. For the first time in her life, she did not have any plans or any contracts. Her two older children, Sally and Mark, were working and had lives of their own, and Harriet was at high school. Out of the blue Carol received a call from Hayes Gordon at the Ensemble Theatre in Sydney. The actor and director, who had once been hounded for his left wing leanings during the witch hunts of the McCarthy era, had established an independent theatre company in 1958 in a boatshed at Kirriblli, and had built up a successful independent theatre. A Bostonian, Gordon, had studied Method acting in New York before moving to Australia after the war, and he also ran an acting school from their small harbour-side theatre with

Zika Nester. The theatre focussed on producing contemporary plays and Hayes wanted to direct Neil Simon's new comic suite of four short plays called *California Suite*.

For Carol, who was in mourning, and feeling flat, the invitation to appear on stage at the Ensemble was precious. She had not performed in the theatre in Australia for 11 years. It was a challenge working in the round with the audience 'almost on the stage', as she recalls it. But she thrilled to the material and the complex demands of portraying four different characters. The publicity for the show unfailingly referred to Carol's role in *Mavis Bramston* with which she is still indelibly linked. On opening night, she experienced that intense relationship with the theatre audience she had not felt for so many years, and told me that 'the waves of energy and excitement you get back from a live audience you can't get anywhere else'. The plays blend farce, satire and comedy, demanding complete transformations from one vignette to the next. Set in the Beverly Hills Hotel, one play presents a divorced couple who are attempting to work out the future of their 17-year-old, another presents a husband trying to disguise his sexual transgressions from his wife (while a young woman hides in his bed), another portrays the acidic dynamic of two couples on holidays. The fourth short play presents a play about Hollywood in which Carol played an English actress attending the Oscar ceremony with her husband, exchanging venomous barbs for much of the action before settling for an affectionate truce.

Gordon Chater and Carol's children, Mark and Harriet, were in the audience for the opening night as Carol was still trying to get used to the intimate performance space. She told a reporter at the time that she was 'quite terrified, the audience is practically on stage with you – you can see and hear all their reactions quite plainly ...

At times the dialogue is quite cutting and I distinctly heard one man say – "bitch". Other times you can feel the whole audience withdrawing – it's quite unnerving'.[18] Carol's performance in each of the plays, and her swift transformations received praise from the critics although the *National Times* reviewer Barry Lowe felt Neil Simon's play was uneven and that he may have 'burned himself out in moving from New York to sell his soul to Hollywood'.[19] Another reviewer said that it was the funniest play she had seen in a long time:

> Carol Raye is magnificent as she slips from the personality of the caustic editoress from New York, to the nervous and flitty Oscar nominee from London and to the gangly, twitty tennis player on holiday from Chicago. She changes roles as easily as her clothes ... In the scene where the editoress comes to LA to drag her daughter from the clutches of an ex-husband, a fast, witty scene, and a clever reality, for their reunion is one of interchanging, biting comments – an intellectual spar. Stanley [Walsh] unfortunately, is overshadowed by the zealous Carol.[20]

The following year Carol appeared in *The Pleasure of His Company* with Douglas Fairbanks Jr, David Langton, David Goddard, Christine Amor and Stanley Holloway, with whom she had worked in Manchester as a novice during the War. It was a box office triumph that played over the next two years all over Australia and in Hong Kong. Carol also appeared as a regular panel member on Graham Kennedy's popular *Blankety Blank*s game show with Stuart Wagstaff, Noeline Brown, Kate Fitzpatrick and Ugly Dave Gray who puffed on a cigar throughout every show. She discovered Kennedy to be a true 'creature of television' and one of 'the funniest ad-libbers in

---

18   *The Entertainer* 18 December 1976.
19   *National Times* 6–11 December 1976.
20   Penny Hemphill in *The Daily Telegraph* 11 December 1976.

the world once the camera came on'. Carol lent sophistication and glamour to the panel; she was witty, breezy and affably cooperative with Kennedy's comic regime of word play, innuendo and silly lines.

Carol Raye was once more a household name in Australia, but still had never had many opportunities to perform on stage, and never in a 'straight' play. She was now 56, and John Bell invited her to play the leading female role in a new play by David Williamson called *Travelling North*. In spite of his success as a playwright who had established himself as the most popular playwright of his generation, Williamson had been criticised for failing to write good roles for women. In *Travelling North* he wrote three strong, sympathetic roles for female characters; his male characters in the play are also engaging, realistic and compelling figures. In its 30 quick scenes, the play demonstrated a new breadth and humanity, and a new seriousness in Williamson's work, in amongst the satire and swirling comic fabric of the play. In creating Frances, a middle-aged woman who falls in love with a man who is 20 years her senior, and leaves her life in Melbourne, including her two difficult married daughters, to travel with Frank and live in a warmer climate, Williamson created a masterpiece. Through the rehearsal period Williamson made extensive changes to the script after the actors experimented with new scenes. It was a rewarding period, and the cast one of the happiest Carol had ever experienced in her career. The reviewers raved about the play itself, and lavished praise on the actors, director, designer and every element of the production. Critic after critic identified the warmth and understanding Carol brought to her leading role as Frances.[21] The *National Times* critic remarked on the way Carol

---

21   Keith Thomas in the *Australian* 25–26 August 1979; Leonard Radic in *The Age* 8 November 1979.

engaged audience sympathy right from the start.[22] The complexity of her character – a person under a brittle exterior – did not escape notice, nor the subtlety of her interpretation.[23] Harold Kippax did not hold back in his fulsome praise for the production, explaining that Carol and Frank Wilson in the role of Frank:

> bear the chief responsibility buoyantly ... Miss Raye gives us a lovable Frances without underestimating her limitations. Her scenes with her daughters (a crackling performance from Miss Hagan, and a clever one from Miss Hamilton) are, in turn, effervescent and blistering, the best-written and best-played in the comedy. For theatre lovers, mandatory.[24]

Carol was riding high after the success of the Williamson play. After *Travelling North*, she appeared in a range of plays including *The Merry Wives of Windsor* in 1980, *Hay Fever* (1981), Tom Stoppard's *Night and Day* (1982), *You Can't Take it With You* for the Sydney Theatre Company in 1982, and then as Dotty Otley in a sparkling production of *Noises Off* in 1983, directed by Michael Blakemore, alongside her old friend Barry Creyton and Stuart Wagstaff. This technically demanding comic extravaganza is a play about theatre and is exhausting to perform. Unusually, it is uproarious even in the first few moments.

In spite of her outstanding achievement in *Travelling North*, Carol was disappointed that she was not chosen to play Frances in the film adaptation. The role of Frances went to Julia Blake, with Leo McKern playing Frank. It was not just disappointment about the role – Carol accepted the decision as actors must when they are not offered a role

---

22   Michael Le Moignan, *National Times* 8 September 1979.
23   Ken Healy in the *Canberra Times* 6 October 1979; Helen Thomson in the *Australian* 9 November 1979.
24   *Sydney Morning Herald* 24 August 1979.

they want. But Carol was angry with the producer, Ben Gannon, because she had suggested to him that she would like to produce a film adaptation of the play, and that they could work together. She wanted to ask Michael Blakemore to direct. But Gannon went ahead with his own plans without a word to Carol about it until he had put all the arrangements in place, leaving her out completely. To this day she has not seen the film version of *Travelling North*.

Comedy Queen

In 1982 Carol teamed up with her old friend from *Mavis*, Barry Creyton to present a short sketch each week on the *Mike Walsh Show*. It was like the first few weeks of Bramston all over again for the two actors, who became satirists-in-residence on the show. Both of them were so busy that they never seemed to have time to rehearse but the sketches, written by Creyton, were a success. In one sketch Carol played Margaret Thatcher with stiff coiffed hair, an oversized handbag and pearls, complimenting Australians on their wonderful 'kangaroo butter' and declaring that she had just told the Prime Minister, Mr Peacock, how much 'we in Britain love your kangaroo butter; it's beyond me how you milk the kangaroos but we love your kangaroo butter'. Creyton, as interviewer, reminds her that the Prime Minister is Malcolm Fraser, whereupon 'Thatcher' tells him that she was told Peacock would be Prime Minister by the time she arrived in Australia.

> Creyton: Who leaked that?
> Thatcher: Mr Peacock ... *(looking perturbed)* 'Don't tell me they put him out to stud?
> Creyton: No, he couldn't get his popularity poll up.
> Thatcher: *(smiling agreeably)* Dennis has that trouble too.

This memorable sketch continues with Carol assaying Thatcher hilariously. Alluding to the tensions with Argentina over the Falkland Islands Creyton says: 'Mrs Thatcher, is Britain ready for war?' Thatcher says emphatically 'Oh yes, we're dying to get rid of all those old ration cards'. Creyton says 'And so all of your mighty warships are steaming towards the Falklands?' 'Yes, it is', affirms Thatcher, looking somewhat sheepish, and going on to explain that the Queen has lent them her royal yacht to carry munitions. She tells him that he might consider coming along to join the war effort: 'Lots of your kind are coming, even Vanessa Redgrave'. Creyton says: 'Vanessa Redgrave has joined the British Army?' 'No, no' says Raye as Thatcher, 'she's joined the Argentinian Army'.

* * *

Carol had risen to become a celebrated entertainer with frequent invitations to play in various stage and television productions. She preferred the rhythm and regularity of the theatre and was beginning to enjoy a slightly less pressured life, living on a small farm in the valley of Wattagen State Forest, and renovating an old farmhouse. Carol fought hard with her local progress association to prevent an open cut mine in the district, ran for the Senate and was a member of the NSW Liberal Party for some years. In 1983 at the age of 60 she sought pre-selection for the seat of Mosman in the NSW State parliament, competing with Malcolm Turnbull. Neither Raye nor Turnbull gained pre-selection but in the months she spent in seeking the endorsement of the party, she explained the work of performers and their intense discipline to many reporters, and repeatedly articulated the importance of women gaining seats in parliament.

Later Carol served on the Theatre Board of the Australia Council, the first actor to be appointed to that Board.

Carol has appeared in numerous stage productions since then and in guest roles on television. Her last role before she retired was playing the mother of the protagonist in the popular television series *Seachange*. It was a particularly rewarding experience, in part because Carol's daughter Sally produced the series. In recalling how much she enjoyed this television series, she observed that Australian comedy has broadened and deepened in the years since she first created and produced *Mavis Bramston*, and that *Seachange* was rare and refreshing in its charm, warmth, romance and affirming qualities of pathos and gentle humour. Carol Raye is often remembered for her major contribution to the landmark *Mavis Bramston Show*. She also contributed to significant and innovative theatre both on the stage and television over four decades, including *Travelling North* and *Number 96*. Raye's fine understanding of satirical comedy, and her ability to charm and entertain gently is an enduring and precious gift.

Chapter 2

BARRY HUMPHRIES: 'A BIT OF PSYCHIC NUDITY?'

Who is Barry Humphries?

(B. 1934)

I travelled to London in the northern hemisphere summer of 2010 to talk to Barry Humphries about the manuscript of a full-length biography I had written about him. We'd met twice before in Sydney and in Dublin but I had never been to his home. He had generously given me introductions to his family, and we had corresponded. We spent a full day on task, and at the end of the second day, he showed me a light-filled wardrobe of resplendent gowns worn by Edna. I had seen the magnificent Opera House Hat in the Victoria and Albert Museum in London, and had closely examined dozens of Edna's extraordinary gowns in the Performing Arts Collection in Melbourne. But when Humphries ushered me into his large special costume room at his home, and showed me the gowns himself, allowing me to examine their majestic taffeta, silk and satin textures, exquisite hand-sewn sequin details and hand-painted embossing, the magic of Edna and the power of this creator shimmered in the air around us.

During our conversations about my manuscript, Barry made it clear that he disagreed with one strand of my interpretation of him: that buried in his psyche was a sense of self-loathing that drove much of his behaviour, especially early on in his life. He wrote about this as a teenager, in his papers. Sitting beside me in his living room he said '[I] have never felt self-loathing in my entire life'. It is perhaps a paradox of personality and biography that an element of a person's psyche apparent to a biographer, and that person's explicit rejection of it can both be regarded as true. Barry did not request that I remove the comments that he rejected. Since that meeting, I have seen Humphries perform several times and he very generously invited me to Edna's farewell performance at Jupiter's Casino in 2012. We have chatted after shows and exchanged letters and emails.

On a sultry Saturday evening in May 2018, Barry opened a new show at the Civic Theatre in Newcastle. In the stalls of this exquisite Spanish-Moroccan style theatre, before the show began, I noticed Lizzie Spender seated a few rows in front of me. Lizzie is Humphries' wife of nearly thirty years. She looked nervous. *The Man behind the Mask* seeks to offer Humphries 'as himself', reminiscing about his life. When the lights went down and we saw him standing in the middle of the vast stage under a bright spotlight, smiling, with his palms outward like a preacher, he appeared dapper in a crimson velvet jacket, red socks and loafers as he addressed an adoring audience, hungry for the nostalgia promised by the evening. A couple of times during the performance it seemed to me that Humphries felt uncomfortable on the stage: the roar of laughter and applause that erupted after several clips were shown on a massive screen of Edna skewering and pontificating in her glory days, seemed to upstage the 84-year-old, who sat watching them with his back to the audience.

But this show demonstrated beyond any doubt Humphries' own maxim that 'the stage is my comfort zone' and my 'refuge'. It also highlighted the theatrical fact that it is in the characters that refuge is taken and comfort found. There were some touching stories about Louisa and Eric, Humphries' parents, and a few seconds of home video footage of Eric beaming and bare chested, running along the beach. There were a couple of candid moments, such as when Humphries described his mother as the 'mistress of the vocabulary of discouragement', and a hilarious visual montage on-screen, re-packaging images of Sir Les Patterson alongside images of Gina Rinehart, Clive Palmer, Hawkie and the Governor-General, Sir John Kerr, who sacked Gough Whitlam in 1975. Humphries kept the mood light, the stories amusing and his recollections of his creation of key characters structured the show. It is not a show that allows for genuine or sustained revelation or confession however – that would be anathema for this man – but *The Man behind the Mask* conveys the life of an outlandish comic actor. His stories of crippling stage fright, destructive drinking, an amusing admission of bullying as a child, and his delight at being designated as a 'fucking icon' by a young motor cycle rider shouting at him from across the street recently, offered a glimpse of the man behind the mask.

Humphries told a reporter on national television during the rehearsal period for his show that there would be 'no total nudity, but … a bit of psychic nudity … in the sense that I'm quite frank in this show about details of my life …'.[1] Quite frank for Humphries, but the mask he has worn since he began performing in the 1950s is still firmly in place.

Camberwell Child

As a small child Barry Humphries walked with his mother's helper, Edna, to Mrs Flint's kindergarten. He was terrified of Mrs Flint, a stern widow dressed in a huge apron and thick brown stockings. Sometimes Mrs Flint left crying children outside in her backyard and one day she tried to force Barry, who was just three years old, to stand in the corner and count to one hundred until Edna rescued him. On another occasion she grabbed him by the arm and marched him down the corridor, opened a cupboard and forced him into it, closing the door with a loud bang. Alone in the darkness he howled. He couldn't wait for the sound of Edna arriving to collect him. At last he heard the chimes of the doorbell. Mrs Flint opened the cupboard door and released him to Edna who stood smiling in the sunshine. He ran towards her and didn't look back. When he told his mother about what had happened Louisa Humphries withdrew him from Mrs Flint's kindergarten.

---

1   Humphries speaking to Leigh Sales, *7.30*, ABC, 20 November 2017.

Humphries' early experiences of school were not happy either. Barry's father, Eric, collected him every day in the family Oldsmobile and drove him home to Christowel Street in Camberwell where he ate his lunch as a solitary picnic in the back garden or while chatting to his parents inside. He took his toy submarine to school one day and a group of boys formed a circle around him demanding that he hand over his prized toy. Barry picked up a handful of gravel in case he needed it to fend off the menacing boys who quickly backed off. When they returned to the classroom, Barry's teacher pulled him up in front of the class and reprimanded him. She sent him to corner for the rest of the day as a punishment for throwing stones. Even worse, she hung a sign around his neck that read 'I am a bully'. Barry was mortified at being chastised for something he had not done. It left a scar on the small boy who was not an aggressive child, but one who felt slights keenly.

He didn't suffer this tyranny for long. The following year Barry's parents enrolled him at Camberwell Grammar School. It was a bracing bicycle ride away from home, and the daily ride gave Barry a new sense of independence and freedom. Before long, his teachers noticed his prodigious vocabulary and originality of expression. But Barry struggled with arithmetic. Eric worried about his son's inability to comprehend figures, but his attempts to help only made Barry's frustration worse. Nor did Barry take to games. A cruel Scottish sports master noticed his awkwardness in the gym, and belittled him with the nickname Granny Humphries. The boys in his class yelled out 'Come on Granny' whenever Barry reluctantly participated in the hateful sports carnivals organised regularly for the boys. But Barry's aptitude for language and his ability to sketch stood out. One teacher cautioned another about displaying Barry's extraordinary prose offerings because they made the other children's work look so poor. His school reports were excellent, and he flourished academically. One of his ambitions was to be a magician, and at his request Eric bought him sparkling cape to wear as he performed for the family. When he was six, an adult visitor to the house put the question: 'What would you like to be when you grow up?' 'Famous', the young Barry replied without hesitation.

Barry, aged 7, in fancy dress.
Courtesy of Michael Humphries.

Louisa and Eric Humphries, and their four children, were connected to their local community in many ways. They were active in the church; Barry taught Sunday school for a short while as a teenager. Every week Louisa and Eric played tennis at the Camberwell club, and Barry looked forward to the afternoon tea break, when one of the ladies would slice a vast cake for the players, who would sit idly in the shade with their cups of tea, chatting. Ever curious about the adult world, Barry listened to the grown-ups' conversations intently. Louisa had an eye for human foibles and her sharp observations always amused the children. She could be very direct and sometimes sarcastic, preferring to tell the truth than spare a person's feelings. Louisa perhaps did not appreciate how hurtful her barbs could be, and she could never have predicted that the overheard snippets of ordinary conversation would be indelibly imprinted on her son's imagination.

As he grew older Barry spent more and more time on his own reading, mystifying his parents who were not readers themselves. Barry became introspective, cheeky and argumentative. He felt his parents were overly critical of him, and he began to be angry and defensive. He found his mother mysterious and distant, and as he approached adolescence he and his father were often embattled. When Barry was confronted by a group of local toughs, Eric bought him some boxing gloves so he could learn to defend himself. Although Barry felt ashamed of his fears and physical weakness, and anxious about what his parents thought of him, he had no interest in learning to box. But he longed to please his parents, and began to feel that in some inexplicable way he didn't belong to his family. Louisa repeatedly and hurtfully expressed her own sense of alienation from her son. 'Your father and I don't know where you came from', she would say. Barry felt unworthy of his parents: that he did not and could not measure up. At times he suffered from debilitating shame and resultant narcissistic rage. His feelings were exacerbated by his parents' ever-growing worry about what people would think of him.

At Melbourne Grammar, Barry loathed the crushing regime of school sport. He was so awkward when he attempted to run that the cruellest boarders jeered at him derisively, referring to him as 'Queenie Humphries'. Barry refused to cooperate; on sports days he would appear for the roll call, and then slip out the gates unnoticed into the throng of St Kilda Road, and head into town to browse in Mrs Bird's second-hand bookshop at the top of Bourke Street. When his truancy was discovered he was caned viciously by one of the prefects. In time Barry found a way to survive Melbourne Grammar – through provocation. When he was called to the headmaster's office and reprimanded for failing to cut his hair to regulation length, he stared coolly and said: 'There's one man in the chapel that has hair that is longer than mine. His name is Jesus'. Barry's comment was not punished, and before long everyone had heard of his audacious retort. He hated the compulsory attendance at school football matches. Old boys, parents, teachers and students gathered to support their teams. Forced to walk to the MCG on icy winter afternoons Barry found an ingenious way of expressing his view of the proceedings. On more than one occasion he positioned himself in a chair with his back to the football field, facing the spectators. Slowly he drew out of his specially made Gladstone bag a set of large knitting needles and a ball of wool, and would sit for the duration of the match calmly knitting a cardigan. Many of the boys found his behaviour disconcerting and strange, but at last everyone knew who he was.

Barry Humphries arriving at a Melbourne Grammar function with a friend, 1971.
Herald and Weekly Times.
Courtesy of Barry Humphries Collection,
Australian Performing Arts Collection, Arts Centre, Melbourne.

Barry worried about what would become of him, and he feared that he was terrible disappointment to his father. Just before he left school the new headmaster turned to him and said: 'I hope you're not turning pansy'. It was impossible for Barry to answer him. He knew that Eric and Louisa were extremely anxious about his future, but his self-doubt was not something he could ever discuss with anyone. Instead he poured his energies into aesthetic interests and buried his doubts. His feelings of uncertainty faded into nothing in his exhilarating moments of performance, on and off the stage. The more extravagant his performance the safer he felt.

Prankster

At Melbourne University Barry was wraith-like, with unfashionably long hair and large, dark overcoats and long scarves. He always looked mysterious, as if he was escaping from something. He wore rust-coloured woollen gloves, with elongated fingers like a long prongs hanging off them, and entertained readers in the library by dashing through the front doors clad in a billowing opera cloak and Cavalier's hat with a peacock plume in it. He mimed admiring a painting or a bunch of flowers, or mischievously piled up towers of books to the ceiling. One day Humphries stood in front of a portrait of the Queen in the small women's lounge of the union building, and gravely announced his intention to execute a painting. He pulled out an axe and chopped up the portrait of the monarch. In a revue called *Call Me Madman!* Humphries caused a riot in the university theatre as he parodied the greed and racism of Australians. In a sketch called 'The Indian Famine' he appeared in a wig and a floor length evening gown, playing the wife of a missionary. Sitting at a table on stage laden with a pyramid of raw and oozing meat, vegetables, slimy raw fish, creamy pastries and cauliflower heads, as alarming famine statistics were read out, he shrieked in a falsetto voice: 'I don't care … don't be boring … I've got plenty of food, lots of food and they've got nothing, wogs, nigs, yids'. After flinging food at the audience a mass of angry students stormed the stage in retaliation, as 'God save the Queen' blared out over a gramophone at various speeds over and over again. As the strains of the anthem rang out, and food was hurled around the auditorium Barry took refuge in the dressing room.

In 1955, Peter O'Shaughnessy cast Humphries as Holofernes, the pedantic schoolmaster in *Love's Labour's Lost*. In this and in his role as Thomas in the Moliere play, Humphries seemed to find his voice. It was apparent to the director that Humphries excelled at portraying grotesque and monstrous characters, and that he seemed to grasp instinctively the way in which timidity can so easily become 'monstrous arrogance'.[2] The transformation was a blueprint for the later development of his signature character, Mrs Everage. Humphries' Edna Everage drew on the traits of the Moliere character, becoming pompous, domineering, and full of false, self-devised notions of her own authority. Mrs Norm Everage, the shy housewife from Moonee Ponds would evolve into a monstrous caricature of a celebrity. In these early roles Humphries relished the potency of the actor's mask, and the way it offered him escape and freedom from himself.

Both on and off the stage, Humphries affected eccentric ways. He frequently adopted a strange persona on the street, in the pub or on the tram. The more outrageous the act the more satisfaction Humphries gained. With a heavily disguised friend on a suburban train, dressed in a garish outfit with large rings on every finger, Humphries smoked a foul-smelling Turkish cigarette, and read a large German newspaper, while the friend hobbled to a seat with a plaster cast on his leg, a neck brace and dark glasses. Every passenger fixed his eyes on the ostentatious 'foreigner' and the 'cripple'. When the train drew into a station Barry gave the 'blind', 'crippled' man a brutal kick, snatched at

---

2   Peter O'Shaughnessy, 'How Edna Everage took to the Stage', the *Age* 26 January 1985, p. 9.

his glasses and tore his neighbour's Braille reading sheet in half, before escaping out the door and onto the platform. It was an outrageous stunt that left the other passengers gasping in horror.

More than once Barry surreptitiously placed a bottle of chilled champagne and a cooked platter of chicken in the bottom of a garbage bin near the tram stop in Swanston Street at rush hour. When a crowd of people gathered he would appear dressed as a tramp and scavenge the planted food and drink from the bin, sit down in the gutter, and have his meal. Anxious onlookers were amazed to see what he had found in the rubbish. Some would curiously look inside the bin. Others feigned oblivion. No one ever said anything.

Even worse than this stunt was Humphries' other tramp impersonation; he would stoop on the pavement, pulling a spoon from his pocket and crouch down to eat the spilled contents of a jar of Heinz Russian Salad, a concoction of coarsely chopped carrots, peas and potatoes floating in a greying soup of mayonnaise. Smeared over the pavement it resembled greasy vomit. In these strange street spectacles Humphries secured the desired response from his audience of onlookers. People were visibly disgusted, disturbed and confused. He would always tell a friend about his planned prank in advance, so that someone would see the act, someone would be able to report on his performance, someone would remember the horror on the faces of the onlookers.

Bun Fighting and the Bard

Humphries delighted in entertaining and annoying his fellow cast members on the long, dusty bus rides of a Victorian country tour of *Twelfth Night* directed by Ray Lawler. In the play, Humphries appeared as a strange, spidery looking Orsino in ridiculous tights, who made the children laugh. Humphries put on a falsetto voice for the cast members in the bus, in cruel but hilarious parody of the predictable words of thanks given in every town by ladies of the CWA or Arts Society over tea. These 'bun fights' were held in dreary church halls with everyone in their finest clothes, and tables of food weighed down with lamingtons and sausage rolls. Humphries' relentless mocking, high-pitched mimicry of the speeches nearly drove the other cast members mad. These impromptu bus performances in which he ridiculed the well-intentioned women revealed the way his satirical impulse was often directed at those who admired and appreciated him. It marked the beginning of a talent for barbed parody and a penchant for a tormenting humour that Humphries cultivated and honed over the next five decades, in which teasing of his adoring audience became a hallmark.

With the Olympic Games to be staged in Melbourne the following year in 1956, the organisers were fixated on the problem of housing the influx of visitors, and the fact that the athletes' village at Ivanhoe was not yet finished. In parody of the Australian, and specifically Melburnian tendency to pronounce 'average' as 'everage', Barry called his plain and timid character Mrs Norm Everage or Edna, after the kind lady who had looked after him as a small child. In a sketch for a revue, Edna Everage offered her home in Humouresque Street, Moonee Ponds, to a visiting athlete, and asked the most preposterous questions about the visitors. In the sketch the government official listed the nationalities of the potential guests and Edna responded with bigoted comments about all of them. The sketch was called 'The Olympic Hostess' and Noel Ferrier played Mr Hopechest, the official interviewing Mrs Everage. Barry had suggested that Zoe Caldwell play Edna, but Lawler insisted that Barry do it himself.

SEVEN BIG AUSTRALIANS

Mrs Norm Everage in her travelling abroad outfit, appearing live on television, 1959.
Courtesy of Barry Humphries Collection,
Australian Performing Arts Collection, Arts Centre, Melbourne.

The character invented to pass the time on the bus on the *Twelfth Night* country tour of Victoria, made her debut in Ray Lawler's Christmas revue on 19 December 1955. 'Excuse I', said Edna timidly, as she entered. Although Humphries used phrases he'd heard his mother's helpers use, she became a 'composite' portrait of various women whose speech habits had imprinted in his brain. With his new character, Barry offered the audience a view of suburban Australia, anticipating the great international event of the Olympic Games. Humphries seemed to summon a whole new world to the stage, and create a comedy of ordinariness that had never been represented before.

He borrowed a yellow felt hat belonging to his mother and wore a twin set underneath a light beige coat, the kind of garment women wore into the city on the tram to cover their bare arms. The six-foot tall, spindly legged Humphries spoke to the audience in their own vernacular about their own homes. It was an important moment for Australian theatre, but the audience was slightly stunned, and the sketch was regarded as only moderately successful.

A Nice Night's Entertainment

When Humphries' first full stage show, *A Nice Night's Entertainment*, opened on a gusty winter evening in Melbourne, 30 July 1962, Edna strode the platform-like stage in a green pill-box hat with a net à la Jacqueline Kennedy, and a crimson coat, gloves, pearls and butterfly style glasses with diamante details. Edna threw off her dowdy look of the early Melbourne shows for a more gaudy, but fashionable outfit. She told the audience all about her visit to the old country and reassured them that they had nothing to fear in overseas fashions:

'I visited all the big cities, and though I was from Australia, quite a few heads turned, I can tell you!'

It was Edna's first homecoming and Humphries was physically ill with anxiety. He worried about whether the skits were sharp enough, whether the sketches were varied enough, whether there was sufficient music, if the show was too long, whether his ad libs would go down well with the audience, and whether there was a clear theme to unite the seven sketches. For the first time Edna cast judgement on all things Australian, as one who knows, because she has been OVERSEAS. Edna appeared without face makeup except for a dash of lipstick.

Barry Humphries in Toronto, 1963.
(Photographer unknown) Courtesy of Barry Humphries Collection,
Australian Performing Arts Collection, Arts Centre, Melbourne.

The back cover of the programme offered a black and white close up photograph of a benign-looking young man in coat and tie. Barry, who was looking straight at the camera with a faint smile on his lips, appeared wide eyed, innocent and almost whimsical in this photograph. He included in the programme a quote by John Betjeman who called Sandy 'a sort of verbal and Australian Charlie Chaplin', a figure who is decent, honest, kind hearted but deeply conventional'. Betjeman immediately recognised that Barry's inspiration was derived from his childhood in Melbourne, and Barry knew that theatre-goers would be impressed by a quote from the esteemed English poet.

For ten years Humphries worked in the UK. He wrote a popular comic strip that was published in *Private Eye*, with the illustrations provided by Nick Garland and appeared in two controversial films about a gormless Australian in London called Bazza McKenzie, based on the comic strip. He fought and overcame his dangerous addiction to alcohol and spent months recovering in a Melbourne hospital with his family desperately fearing that he might die. During his years living in London, Humphries performed Edna whenever he could but did not get much traction. A brief television interview in the UK changed Humphries' fortunes almost overnight, and propelled him back onto the British stage. Although he had appeared in several sketch comedy shows Edna had never succeeded in Britain. She was now a movie star however, and a dame, thanks to the extraordinary appearance of the Prime Minister, Gough Whitlam (in the second Bazza McKenzie film), who elevated Mrs Everage to damehood.

Humphries' appearance as Edna on Russell Hearty's popular chat show in 1975 changed everything. Edna wore an orange and black wool coat purchased from Selfridges, and white knee-high, lace-up boots. Trundling on to the set clutching her handbag she greeted the host 'Hello Simon', as she nodded 'How do you do?' to the studio audience. Edna apologised for getting Hearty's name wrong and said 'Haven't you done well? You started from nothing and look at you'. She was outlandish, ridiculous and funny, apologising that Barry Humphries was unable to come on to the show due to jet lag, and because of 'a vasectomy on diner's card'. Years later Humphries told Melvyn Bragg that it was the first time that Humphries *felt* funny as Edna in the UK.[3] It was twenty years since he had first played Edna in Melbourne, a shy and genteel housewife. Humphries was already well known in Australia, and over the next ten years Edna would become a household name in Britain.

Shortly after his appearance on Russell Hearty's program, Michael White approached Humphries with a proposal for a new stage show. Humphries was ready to launch himself in the West End again. The orange and black hound's-tooth coat went into mothballs. It was the last time Humphries bought Edna's costumes off the rack. As the racing season approached, Barry asked his wardrobe designer, Jane Hamilton, to arrange for a special hat to be made for Dame Edna.[4] Lorraine McKee created the hat that would launch Edna's image around the world. This headpiece featured a massive model of the Sydney Opera House, the building that had recently replaced the boomerang as the icon for Australia. The upper side of the brim was made of blue and purple satin with turquoise netting. White lace wave caps simulated the waters of Sydney Harbour, complete with

---

3   Humphries interview with Melvyn Bragg, *The South Bank Show*, 19 November 1989, London Weekend Television.
4   The Opera House hat is now held in the Victoria and Albert Museum, London.

six canvas yachts and a shark's head baring diamante-studded teeth. The hat measured 120 centimetres in width and 41 centimetres in height. A sumptuous model of the shell-like buildings in stiffened white satin draped in beige rayon twill resulted in a crowd stopping racing carnival hat, completing Edna's otherwise demure outfit, a floral dress and white gloves at Royal Ascot.

In the past Edna had often failed to attract attention, once throwing herself into the path of Sir Robert Menzies outside the Savoy in London, only to be ignored. But her appearance in her new hat was a triumph. Edna appeared in the grounds of Windsor Great Park sporting her magnificent hat at the famous summer racing carnival, attracting massive publicity. Her appearance that day at Royal Ascot turned out to be one of the most spectacular appearances of Humphries' career as Dame Edna. The image of Edna peeping cheekily out from underneath the *broderie anglaise* underside of the brim, with its rich purple tinsel braid around the edge was quirky, kitsch and whimsical. Photographs of Edna at Ascot splashed across newspapers in the UK and Australia. In fact Edna received more coverage than the Queen and her entourage on that auspicious day.

Arise Dame Edna

Edna Everage provides a mask for Humphries to satirise all that is wicked, ignorant, small minded and hypocritical in people of all sorts. She is also a device that affords comic licence to an audience to laugh at the obscene and the grotesque views she espouses, and for a few hours to escape propriety. Occasionally Humphries' satire takes on the less forgiving, cruel and venomous satirical characteristics associated with Juvenalian satire. Like the Roman satirists, Humphries is a master of invective and uses denunciation, mockery, distortion, exaggeration, sarcasm and wit in order to arouse contempt, fear and mirth in his audience. But in the end, there has always been the forgiving ritual of the gladdie waving and prizes, serenades and accolades for the 'victims' who become part of Edna's star cast. That gentleness and celebratory joy of Humphries' performances makes Humphries primarily a Horatian satirist, his comedy offering the audience a form of optimism.

Humphries first appeared in his own television program in 1980. It was a one-off chat show entitled *An Audience with Dame Edna*. In this first *Audience* Humphries offered everything that television variety shows had created since the early days of television. The show presented a sumptuous spectacle, in front of a studio audience, to recreate the atmosphere of a live event. Without an audience Humphries could not perform. But Humphries also offered a parody of the values of light entertainment as it is called in Britain. In doing so he began to create a whole new genre – the parodic chat show, in which he went on to subvert the formula of this genre and its variety origins. Chat is held up as the ideal but monologue is what actually occurred in Edna's first parody of the genre. The celebrity 'guests' in the audience, rather than being the focus of the chat, are simply the targets for Edna's jokes.

Humphries began to 'let' Edna construct herself as a megastar, crafting her own legend, and Humphries' sheer talent willed it into existence. Incredibly Edna's rise to stardom is all fiction, assertion and aggrandizement – a fitting 'simulacrum' of celebrity culture in real life. And the British audience thrilled to Edna's game. The show offered a carnival of reversals and unmaskings. Just as Humphries' stage shows celebrated the ordinary, the crass and the banal responses of handpicked members of the audience, in order to transform them into 'stars' of her show, Edna celebrated the ordinary viewer in this television extravaganza. In answering each question posed by the celebrity, Edna re-focussed the attention back onto herself, reversed the roles, and put each celebrity firmly back in his or her place.[5] Barely three minutes into the show Edna lampooned the station and kept up a steady barrage of insults against the obsession with ratings, station identification, the rivalry between ITV and BBC, as well as a whole lexicon of magazine jargon, media speak and political spin.

Edna presented herself as a busy but generous television personality in her galloping opening monologue: 'the bottom line, to use a little phrase I've picked up in question time … There are going to be some bombshells … I won't be doing all the talking tonight, 99% of it – I think there should be a little margin for you'. With a long and rambling answer to the very first question Edna told her own story, a parody of the recent activities of certain stars. 'I'm doing a book called *The Compassionate Camera of Edna Everage*, she reported, 'a moving book of documents and statements'. Then after Shirley Williams' question about whether she would consider entering politics and raising the tone of public life she was off, talking about the Prime Minister Mrs Thatcher: 'You've got the Iron Lady in charge in this country – I'm more of an aluminium lady or formica lady … I see people modelling themselves on me. Because people follow me so scrupulously I have to keep detached from the political life of Britain. I'm a bit like Margaret Thatcher in that respect, but I could be called in an emergency – a sort of Kissinger figure'.

Humphries did not drop the mask in the forty-five-minute broadcast. In spite of the hilarity aroused by some of Edna's

---

5   Roy and HG developed a similar kind of television show in the 1990s in Australia with their own slant on the world of sports celebrities.

'mini-celebrity' guests, she never let the audience forget who was in charge. In fact Humphries has never dropped the mask of Edna on television, or in the theatre. Even when Kim Basinger unexpectedly began to caress Edna's knee in a rather erotic manner during an interview for an American network some years later Humphries stayed in character, smiling and gently reminding Ms Basinger to desist or 'I might forget myself'. On television Edna constantly drew attention to the details of the actual performance and its artifice. She hailed the cameramen loudly on camera, instructed audience members to sit back if they were blocking others, and complained about the station and its relentless attempt to build the ratings.

Michael Parkinson gave Humphries a spot on his show just before he opened his new stage show, *An Evening's Intercourse with the Widely Liked Barry Humphries* at the Theatre Royal in Drury Lane in 1982. Les Patterson presented an adoring 'Ode to Parky' to celebrate the release of a book on the celebrated television interviewer. Taking full advantage of the opportunity offered by Parkinson, Barry also appeared as himself, as Sir Les and as Dame Edna. It was the first of only two occasions in his entire career that he appeared as all three characters on one television show, and it was a momentous occasion. As himself, Humphries explained to viewers that for a long time 'Australia was a very peculiar and remote place to the British public, and I perhaps flatter myself that I may have been instrumental in towing it, if not as close as the Isle of Wight, almost as close ...'. He declared his ambition to show people that Australia 'is a funny place'. Humphries' appearance on Parkinson marked the beginning of his immense popularity on television, and he drew on the experience, parodying the popular host's seemingly effortless stream of urbane conversation with celebrity guests, on Edna's next *Audience*.

* * *

By the 1990s, Humphries had a huge audience in the UK, and was less anxious about his image in Australia than he had been before. The *Dame Edna Experience* television extravaganza and the stage tour that followed in 1989 brought Humphries popularity, recognition and wealth. His achievement had been Herculean. Humphries, true to type, opted for 'more', and decided to try out his television act in the United States. Barry would never forget the humiliation and disappointment of his poor showing in New York back in 1977 and the one-word review that sank the show in the New York Times: 'Abysmal'. The vision of his wife Diane or sometimes a stage manager running down the lane beside Theatre Four to see if anyone was heading towards the theatre to see the show, is etched in his memory.[6]

After twenty years working in television Humphries longed to return to the stage and to the pleasure of performing in a one-man show in the West End that would echo the heady days of New Labour in Britain: he called his next show *New Edna*. In Britain, the Labour Party had won an election in a landslide, and was busily shaking things up. They cut a swathe through the House of Lords by removing dozens of hereditary peers. He was disappointed by the reception, and smarted from the reaction by critics. Charges of snobbery Humphries could handle, and he could swallow accusations of being conservative. He was used to those labels. But to be castigated for a 'ruthlessness' towards Australia and its people, cut to the quick, and seemed to him, to demonstrate a failure of understanding. Humphries' art is satire, and Australian life his primary subject. His goals as an

---

6   Barry Humphries, 2004, *My Life As Me*, Melbourne: Penguin, p. 308.

entertainer throughout his career have been to make people laugh, to bring them joy, and to understand Australia. Sometimes satire is ruthless. Humphries' art springs from an interest in people and social life. Many Australian critics had decided that Humphries himself was monstrous some years earlier, and were sticking to their script. Humphries had tried everything to distance his own image from that of his characters. His own highly crafted persona was one of his ways of ensuring that he would not be confused with Edna or Les. But this also added a complication: Humphries refused to allow any outsiders to see the man behind the masks. It was not just a case of ensuring his privacy, or maintaining an artist's mystique. Rather it reflected an anxiety about being acceptable to others as himself, an anxiety that had plagued him since he was a boy. He was wounded by the insults and worried about what to do next.

Humphries in Canberra.
Courtesy of Barry Humphries.

The Great White Way

Once more Humphries turned to the United States in a bid to enchant a fresh audience. None of the enduring Australian hostility towards Humphries mattered to Americans. In the USA nobody knew or cared about the way Humphries tried out his act on his tours in Australia before returning to London, or any of his clever methods of re-cycling and re-inventing material. He knew he did not have to re-make Edna for the audiences of the USA. The decision was clear: there was no better time for Barry to head to the United States. This time he would try his luck in San Francisco.

In Australia the Sydney Gay Mardi Gras had become the social event of the year. It was a spectacle and an experience of celebration for thousands of Sydney-siders and visitors from all over the world, especially from the West Coast of the USA. The popular film *Priscilla Queen of the Desert* captured a change in the status of drag, and its new topicality for mainstream audiences. In Australia and in the US drag had become glamorous and exciting. It was not just about dressing up however. By the mid-1990s the power of performance in drag had never been so politically potent. Humphries' act had never been political in the sense of offering a precise agenda for social change, but he had made a joke of gender categories for a long time. Like the satire of his countrymen, the novelists Christina Stead and David Foster, Barry's satire ridiculed social mores, public figures and human behaviour in a multitude of ways, with no precise program for reform. Since his earliest experiments with Dadaist art, Humphries has been an anarchist and his satire is amoral and subversive.

When Humphries arrived in San Francisco in 1998, the Sisters of Perpetual Indulgence were preparing to celebrate their twentieth birthday. The cultural and political stage was therefore well and truly set and the audience primed for the arrival of the Dame. Popular theatre and street theatre had brought new audiences to the theatres of the Bay Area and beyond. Although Americans had no real tradition of the pantomime dame, this no longer seemed to matter: they 'got' her as a latter day matron of music hall and saw in her a glorious parody of entertainers like Liberace, Dolly Parton, Elton John and Joan Collins. Edna was in good company.

On 7 October 1998 *Dame Edna: The Royal Tour* opened at the Theatre on the Square in Post Street, downtown San Francisco. The stately theatre with its decorated wood panels, restored tiles and gold frescos was built in 1924, and offered a relatively intimate theatre space. The show began with a wiggling gladiolus stem thrusting out from behind the closed curtain and some jaunty film clips showing Edna in the arms of Nureyev in a waltz, flirting with Charlton Heston and volunteering to powder Richard Gere's bottom. The chat and audience byplay was interwoven with songs from Billy Philadelphia seated at a white grand piano. One of the songs offered a centrepiece to the show and celebrated Edna's son Kenny, who was as yet unmarried. Edna called the song a 'Ditty of Denial'. It was bound to go down well with the folk of the Bay Area. The chorus presented a rousing hymn of praise to the gay men in the audience, without ever stating anything quite so obvious. Humphries was cultivating this group as never before: 'I never thought that I would see so many Friends of Kenny', Edna sang.

The energy, costumes, rhinestone-studded glasses, sly wit and audience interaction received full praise. Houses filled, the Bay Area embraced Edna, and *The Royal Tour* was extended until mid-January. Humphries was delighted and hugely relieved at the positive reviews and full houses for Edna at Theatre on the Square. When he received an invitation to play on Broadway, at the Booth Theatre for an open season, he felt a sense of vindication for his act and its reception in the US. *The Royal Tour* had even been awarded the San Francisco critics' award for the Bay Area. He knew Broadway would not be easy but the success on the West Coast filled him with confidence, and signalled great possibilities for the Big Apple. Nevertheless he felt extremely nervous. He had persevered with American audiences on various occasions over the last twenty-two years, but still had to crack it on Broadway or his success in California would not count for all that much. Broadway as every entertainer understands, is the key to the vast American theatre scene. Humphries was very nervous about playing Broadway again. As Barry and Lizzie moved their possessions into a penthouse apartment on the upper east side of Manhattan, with views across to the elegant Queensboro Bridge and Roosevelt Island, Barry tried to put his vivid memories of *Housewife Superstar* and Theatre Four in 1977 out of his mind. He hoped that the current *New York Times* theatre critic would be kinder than Richard Eder had been. But he knew from bitter experience that the *Times* has an incomparable hold on theatre in the city, and that anything was possible.

Humphries' designer, Stephen Adnitt, had accompanied him for the opening of the show to ensure that nothing was amiss with the costumes. As always Ian Davidson, who Humphries relied on for jokes, local references and last-minute changes to the routine, was also present. In addition Humphries had brought Andrew Ross, his trusted pianist, from Sydney for the show, rather than relying on someone he did not know for this very important Broadway season. Humphries was able to breathe a small sigh of relief when he read a profile by Frank DeCaro in the *New York Times* a fortnight before opening night. The journalist began his long and deferential article with a glorious description of Edna's 'day wear', a sequined frock with a model of the façade of Radio City Music Hall in appliqué on one shoulder and an image of Broadway embroidered on the other, her glasses decorated with a lady holding a torch 'at one temple and a row of spikes at the other, the glasses make air-kissing an extreme sport', he noted. Both Edna and Barry were quoted exhaustively, with the act summed up brilliantly and breathlessly, in Humphries' words as 'a character actor dressed up as an Australian housewife who thinks she's a mixture of Barbra Streisand and Jocelyn Wildenstein, with a little bit of Susan Sontag and Martha Stewart thrown in'.[7]

It was six years since the Hollywood executive had vociferously questioned Humphries' English television producer, Claudia Rosencrantz, about whether or not Barry was gay, and attempted to persuade her that Barry should appear in a sequence as himself with his wife, before any shots of Edna were shown, in the lead up to *Dame Edna's Hollywood*. Humphries had not forgotten the suggestion, and made sure that he referred to his family in his press interviews. DeCaro wrote 'Although he is gay-friendly and a bit of a dandy, Mr Humphries is not a drag queen', and followed with details of Humphries' wife, explaining that he has four children.[8] Humphries breathed a sigh of relief. In the publicity blitz that preceded the show, Barry had it both ways. Many of the profile pieces included a statement about him as an actor who is married with children, like the one in the *New York Times*. And yet Barry also rejoiced in the glamour of drag and all its associations. Another critic articulated the showbiz truth:

---

7   *New York Times* 3 October 1999.
8   Ibid.

'The performer has discovered there is gold in drag, particularly in England, where this exotic creature has flourished for more than two decades'.[9] Barry did his utmost to ensure that his image would appeal to as many groups as possible, and the early signs were very positive.

Dame Edna: The Royal Tour opened on 17 October at the Booth Theatre in West 45th Street. With seating for almost 800, modest by Broadway standards, the theatre was built in 1913 as the smaller and less ornate of a pair of playhouses. Both houses boast sgraffito decoration on their exterior walls, the only buildings in New York City where this kind of work can still be seen. The Booth is an elegant theatre with classical decor, pale blue ceilings and gracious chandeliers; it was the perfect size for an Edna extravaganza.

Edna's purple 'cotton candy' hair, her glittering pink shift dress, diamond-studded eyewear and massive rock rings on every finger, impressed and wowed the audience, including the critics. There was scarcely a negative comment in the New York reviews. The show was described as 'mighty entertainment'.[10] With audiences gleefully enjoying Edna's withering attacks on celebrities, Edna cast herself as cult queen of them all. Critics raved about Edna's 'outrageous, funny, bitchy and uninhibited' barbs.[11] In a risky quip Edna shrieked 'I'm so happy to be back in New York. I feel so at home here. Besides, just like Hillary Clinton, it gives me a chance to rediscover my Jewish roots ... it explains a lot about my taste in beautiful jewellery...'. Edna went into overdrive, crowing about how she had mentored Germaine Greer many years ago. 'When the "great feminist" was a child, she would come to my house and watch my husband scrubbing the floor.

---

9   Associated Press drama critic Michael Kuchwara, *AP Online* 17 October 1999.
10 Ibid.
11 *New York Daily News* 17 October 1999.

That's when she saw that traditional roles played by the sexes down through the years could be rethought', she reported. Humphries gave the performance everything he had and did not hold back with the jokes. Edna talked about acid reflux and joked about the Attorney General Janet Reno. Nothing and nobody was sacred. She skewered and she barked. She pranced, stomped and mugged, her astonishing mouth twisting downwards in her signature expression of distaste and disdain. She told reporters that she had advised Hillary Clinton, Margaret Thatcher and most recently, Nicole Kidman: 'she was a drama student of mine ... I was the first person she took her clothes off for. Now she does it for everyone', Edna chirped. Even the Queen herself, reported Edna, 'with all the worries she's had with her family, looks to me for advice'.

There were some risky moments. One night, Edna questioned a couple about their baby-sitter for the evening. During the exchange Edna gleaned that the child minder was an immigrant 'without papers', or 'undocumented' as Americans call them. Edna took the bull by the horns and roared: 'One of the great things about democracy is that you can have a slave class without calling it that'. The audience gasped and then broke into squalls of laughter. It was a close call; Philip Olander reported that the audience 'almost turned'.[12] The audience reaction, as always was integral to the momentum of the show. As Edna often scoffs to her possums, they pay to see her in a show, but then as various members tip toe on to the stage, they 'are the show'. In the glossy pages of the *New York* magazine with a cover story on Dame Edna the question was put: 'Can a rude, clueless, provincial Australian woman who's actually a man conquer

---

12   Philip Olander, 'Edna in America: The Shtick's the Thing', *Meanjin*, 2002 vol. 61, no. 4, p. 181.

Broadway and win a place in the American cultural pantheon?' The answer: 'Barry Humphries' Dame Edna is on the verge'.[13]

Edna was hailed on Broadway as 'the world's most celebrated drag act'. Edna's style was captured in succinct phrases by the award-winning drama critic Jack Kroll, who called her 'the patron saint of the politically incorrect', 'an insult comic who made Don Rickles sound like a Hallmark card'.[14] This kind of comment was more than Humphries could have hoped for. Rickles is a celebrated American comedian, who has made insult an art form over the past fifty years. The *New York Post* declared *The Royal Tour* to be 'by far the funniest and cleverest show in town'.[15] *Newsday* ran a short piece urging readers to go to the show: 'You'll have the time of your life', wrote the rather breathless, folksy reporter, because 'such hilarity hasn't reigned since "Hellzapoppin"'.[16] John Lahr observed that the show was 'generous and gallant', and that Humphries 'is almost single-handedly bringing the vaudeville tradition into the twenty-first century'.[17] The *Wall Street Journal* critic sounded one of only a few negative notes. She said that 'the whole campy endeavour feels a bit shopworn'.[18] And *Newsday*'s theatre critic stated that the act was a 'cross-cultural acquired taste'.

It seemed as if Humphries had outdone Joan Rivers, outshone David Letterman and trumped Jackie Mason. He had read the audience and although he did not change Edna's style, he dropped references to Moonee Ponds and worked in tricks and gags that were

---

13 *New York Magazine* review quoted by Andrew Rule, *Sunday Age* 19 December 1999.
14 *Newsweek* 18 January 1999.
15 *New York Post*, 18 October 1999.
16 *Newsday* 21 October 1999.
17 John Lahr, *New Yorker* 1 November 1999, p. 120.
18 *Wall Street Journal*, 20 October 1999.

familiar to his New York audience. He had 'dragged up' just enough. His local references were perfect. In Australia during Paul Keating's term of office as Prime Minister, Edna dropped the 'Dame', having discovered that she was Catholic and therefore in her twisted logic, naturally sympathetic to the Australian Republican Movement. In New York, Edna 'discovered' her Jewish personal history, and that she was distantly related to the US Secretary of State, Madeleine Albright, who had been brought up as a Roman Catholic but in 1997 learned of her Jewish heritage.

The sweetest victory for Humphries was waking up to the *New York Times* review of *The Royal Tour*, written by the newspaper's chief theatre critic Ben Brantley, who recognised Dame Edna's attack on the monstrous behaviour of celebrities, and praised Humphries as a 'great instinctive physical comic'.[19] Brantley identified exactly what it is about Edna that enraptures an audience. It is not so much the content of the jokes, but the 'overwhelming presence of the narcissistic creature making them', he said. 'The Dame lifts an audience' with her in her 'reality warping, rhapsody' he continued.[20] Brantley understood the power of Edna over a live audience, and Humphries' monumental stage presence. At last Humphries had found the universal in his comic repertoire. He had successfully translated his comedy by making it accessible for a whole new audience. His instinct for holding an audience in the palm of his hand had now enraptured thousands of New Yorkers. No longer tied to jokes about Australia, his appearance at the Booth Theatre was more liberating than any show he had ever launched. Humphries demonstrated his essential power as a performer, his understanding of the dupe, his wizardry in

---

19   *New York Times* 18 October 1999.
20   Ibid.

improvisation and his mastery of aggressive sport with his audience. At 65 Humphries had charmed a live audience on Broadway. He was ecstatic.

Humphries' success was reported in the British and Australian press. To Barry's delight the newspapers ran news of the standing ovations the show received in its first week playing on Broadway. It was music to his ears. *The Royal Tour* commanded huge audiences, and the show ran on for another month, then another, and ultimately for ten months. It captured the imagination of the town and impressed the Broadway cognoscenti. If Edna was born again as a Broadway star, Humphries was too. He was overjoyed with his success on the Great White Way. Suddenly he had a new career, a planned tour around the United States and thousands of new fans. In the first year of the new millennium he had achieved his heart's desire.

During the tour Barry fielded numerous phone calls regarding his invitation to appear as Dame Edna on stage at the closing ceremony of the Olympic Games in Sydney on 1 October 2000. He had met with the director of ceremonies, Ric Birch, several times to discuss a possible appearance. With an audience of millions across the globe, the ceremony would be an extravaganza for Edna beyond anything she had achieved before. Birch wanted Edna to close the Games with a speech and a song. Robyn Archer stated her public support for Edna to 'strut the stage' at the Australia Stadium in Homebush Bay. Archer, who was director of the Adelaide Arts Festival, told a reporter that 'I can't think of a more endearing drag queen farewelling the world from this most important event'.[21] But the Board wavered and Edna did not appear.

---

21   *Australian* 10 March 2000.

Humphries went one better, with a stunning appearance at the Queen's Jubilee Concert at Buckingham Palace in June 2002. Twelve thousand Britons assembled in the Palace grounds, with more than a million filling The Mall and London's parks, to enjoy a pop concert to celebrate the monarch's fifty year reign. Some 200 million viewers throughout Great Britain and the Commonwealth watched the 'party at the palace' on television. Edna joined Lenny Henry, Elton John, Eric Clapton, Paul McCartney, Tom Jones, the Beach Boys, Shirley Bassey and others to entertain the massive crowds. Brian May played *God Save the Queen* from the roof of the palace. Sir Les also enjoyed a cameo role: he appeared on screen, in a drunken and futile attempt to gatecrash the party. But Dame Edna outdid every other celebrity, when she introduced the Queen with the words: 'The Jubilee girl is here possums'. The laughter of thousands rang out across London. Edna looked up at the Royal box during the concert and assured the Queen that she need not worry about the damage to the grass in her prized palace gardens. 'I'm sure it's a write off, Ma'am', Edna said, once more sending the massive crowds into gales of laughter. Edna Everage had dared to make a joke about the Queen, and she got away with it.

Humphries continued his extravagant stage tours and has appeared in recent years with the Sydney Chamber Orchestra and with Meow Meow in a special tribute to the music of Weimar. He was awarded a CBE by the Queen in 2007, the James Joyce Award in 2009, and several years later he mounted an extravagant farewell tour for Edna under the magnificent title *Eat, Pray, Laugh!* in which he performed a high energy, three-hour show in character as Dame Edna, Sir Les and Sandy Stone for thousands of theatre-goers across Australia. He directed the Cabaret Festival in Adelaide in 2015, and still scorns any suggestion of retiring, but he no longer appears in the full-scale shows that have filled his career. His recent 'Beyond the Mask' tour marks a significant change in his style and approach to comic performance – completely different from the riotous shows that relied so heavily on physical strength, stamina, movement, character and complex monologue. In Humphries' autobiography *More Please*, he confesses that for his entire life he has always wanted more – more of everything. In his senior years this appears to be true but no longer possible. Farewell Edna. Thank you Barry.

Chapter 3

NOELINE BROWN: 'I'M NOT AFRAID OF THE AUDIENCE'

(B. 1938)

From the slowing train, I noticed Noeline patiently waiting for me on the platform at Mittagong, hands in her pockets, braced against the icy wind. She stood ramrod straight, elegant in large sunglasses and tailored trousers, looking ahead. It was a bitter August day when I visited the actress at her home in the Southern Highlands. The daffodils were peeping through and the apple blossom in Noeline's large, steep garden a welcoming sight. Brown is a no-nonsense funny lady, a sharp witted and easy person to be around. Her stylish house overlooks the rugged escarpment and coastal plain high above Shellharbour. I spent two days talking to Noeline at home and learned about her life as a comic actor and lover of people. Her generous spirit spills over into every conversation. She is honest, practical and straight talking. There is no nonsense and no pretence with Noeline. Talking about a man she loved when she was barely 20 years old, she told me she has corresponded with him ever since: 'Once you've loved someone you always love them', she said. Her house is built for entertaining and Noeline has lots of friends. Love of people is evident in her anecdotes and in her manner. Brown is a comic performer who is not like others; there is no anger, malice or shielding of uncomfortable truths in this accidental queen of comedy.

'I was Born Happy'

Where Noeline Brown grew up, in the inner Sydney suburb of Stanmore, the people worked hard and voted Labor. It was in many ways a 'working man's paradise'. Noeline's father Leo worked for the travelling post office for some fifty years, almost his whole working life. His team of postal workers travelled by train all over New South Wales delivering the mail. Leo and his colleagues stood up in the carriage to sort the mail for each town, carefully placing the mail into timber pigeon holes that lined the walls of each carriage. When the train arrived at the station he would heave the sack of letters onto the platform and hoist it up on a large hook, ready for the local postal worker to collect and distribute. He jumped back on the train and continued his work for the next town. The men took their own food in their tiffin cans for their long journey and slept on the mail sacks on the floor of the carriage at night in summer and winter. They were away from home for days on end. Leo was a union man and fought for better conditions and overtime pay. Some of the meetings were held in the living room at Noeline's house. These were the long Menzies years and Leo felt strongly that Menzies hated the 'working man'. The pay for working overtime on those arduous days away from home made a difference to his family, to Dyra and the three children: young Leo, Noeline and Peter. Eventually the travelling postal workers won the right to a bed and a meal each night away on those railway trips. But the overtime pay and the small comforts they won for the workers could never fully compensate Leo Brown for the long absences from his home in Stanmore, and the time he missed spending with his family. He would appear at the back door on a Friday night, exhausted, and sometimes the children were so engrossed in their uproarious games, they barely noticed him standing there watching them like a stranger.

Noeline's mother, Dyra also worked hard at home, sewing all the children's clothes, cooking and cleaning. Noeline remembers going with her mother out to Liverpool on a journey to collect fresh fruit and vegetables from a farm during the time of rationing through the war, and for several years afterwards. Mrs Brown had one helper, a washerwoman called Mrs Sheay who appeared twice a week. Noeline watched in horror when she noticed for the first time the skin on this woman's arms: seared and white from the lye that she used for her constant washing. During the war Noeline's Dad arranged for a woman lodger to keep Dyra company while he was away; he warned the children that if the Japanese invaded Australia, to cough a lot, because the enemy soldiers would be terrified of contracting Tuberculosis. Leo went off to the army for two years but his knee was injured in an accident and he was discharged. Noeline knew that her parents had experienced their own hardships. Leo's mother Isabella had left the family farm in the Hunter at the age of 14, and travelled around on her own, working on farms and in pubs in order to send money back to her family. Later in life Isabella lived alone in what Noeline thought was a glamorous apartment in Earlwood, with handsome architectural details, stylish furniture, magazines and a busy night life. It was Isabella who the young Noeline particularly admired, with her independent life as a single woman, her extraordinary energy, fashionable outfits and interesting friends.

Noeline Brown recalls her childhood with joy and nostalgia. 'I was born happy', she says: 'my childhood was idyllic'. She still dreams of lying in bed in her childhood bedroom at the house called 'Roslyn' in Stanmore. Her parents were contented individuals, loving, gentle and hard-working people. The neighbours nicknamed Noeline 'Smiley' because she had a wide, broad smile for everyone she met. As a young girl, she was round faced with long, straight blonde hair pulled straight up from her forehead in a ribbon. Even setbacks did not seem to affect her for long. At the age of five Noeline was sent away to the 'coast hospital' at Bunnerong, where people were often sent to die. Suffering from Scarlet Fever she was kept there for several weeks and recalls the shock of being given an enema by a scary nurse. Dyra and Isabella made the long trek to the hospital to visit her by train, tram and bus, with the boys, one of whom was a babe in arms. When they prepared to leave, she sobbed. But five minutes later she was bossing other children around in the ward. With her brothers and other neighbourhood children, Noeline roamed as far as Cronulla, defying their mother's warnings about never going to the lonely sandhills of Wanda, which became the site of a notorious murder. They walked from Stanmore to Central Station and took the train to Como and hired a boat on the Georges River, absent from home for hours and re-appearing by dark after a day of adventure. Dyra was indulgent with the children, rarely expressing anger. She had lost her own mother when she was four and never had a secure, family like the one she created for her own children. She made all their own sweets, toffees and cakes and in spite of the war there was no shortage of food.

Noeline was not a natural performer; in fact she was shy, but from an early age she was drawn to theatrical activity, organising entertainment for the neighbours in her back yard, with seats hauled from inside, one penny admission and comical interludes in which she featured. Noeline delegated the financials to her two brothers while she took care of the entertainment. Looking back, she says 'It was the first and only time she had creative control' in her whole career. She loved taking the bus with her brothers and the gang of neighbourhood children to the department store, Grace Bros, on Broadway to see plays and Tivoli-style productions presented especially for young people. Noeline loved to sing, but not in front of strangers. Hoping to steer her to the genteel art of piano, Noeline's mother offered to get one for her daughter. 'I'd rather have a banjo', said the young and forthright Noeline, who ended up with neither instrument. At ten years of age Noeline wrote a play that was selected at her primary school for production: she also cast herself in a supporting role, and was incensed when the leading actress arrived at school in a prissy new dress with her hair curled Shirley Temple style, even though her character was supposed to be poor and dirty. Noeline would not have the performance wrecked and took to the little girl's face with heavy smears of black boot polish.

Noeline Brown in 1946, aged 8, ready to dance.
Courtesy of Noeline Brown

When Dyra fell ill, Noeline's happy childhood changed. Her mother's face became drawn and she seemed to droop visibly with lethargy. No-one knew the cause.

Later Noeline learned that it was her grandfather who came to live with the family and was still recovering from Tuberculosis that exposed the family to the deadly disease. At the movies one day with her brothers, Noeline listened wide eyed to a public service film about how to recognise the symptoms of TB. Noeline rushed home to her father and declared that she now knew what ailed her mother. Leo was furious at the mention of the disease and swore at her in a way he never had before or since. He warned her not to speak of such things. Dyra was sent away for treatment, a major operation, and then Leo nursed her back to health for a full year in the main bedroom, which was given over to her for her convalescence. He gave up his job to take care of his wife who eventually made a full recovery.

'There's Magic Going On'

The trauma of her mother's illness and the stigma of the disease affected Noeline over the next year. Some neighbours refused to come near the family for fear of infection, and the prospect of losing her mother propelled Noeline into adulthood. Although Leo did not burden the children with extra responsibilities, the strain on the family was heavy. The delights of the theatre became even more important to her. At the age of twelve Noeline saw a touring production of *As You Like It* at the old Princess Theatre in Pitt Street, a steeply raked jewel box of a theatre. She recalls the production as mesmerising. After that Noeline and her friend Carol would sit together after school reading the plays of Shakespeare aloud to each other in Noeline's bedroom. Noeline's little brother, Peter, crouched down outside the door and whispered to his mother 'There's magic going on in there'. At school, they wrote a review of the production they had seen at the Princess Theatre, and Noeline was fulsome in her praise. At Fort Street Girls High Noeline found the teachers old fashioned and remote. She had always loved English, art and history but there was no opportunity for art, even less for drama and Noeline felt crushed by the 'Victorian era dragons' who ran the freezing cold school with iron fists. Noeline appeared in her French class one day wearing a shower cap to protect her head from the spit that drenched pupils in the class as the teacher barked at the girls. It was her defence against tyranny, and it made the other girls laugh. The following year Noeline transferred to Stanmore Home Science School and remembers feeling much more comfortable as a 'big fish in a small pond'. She passed the Intermediate Certificate in all seven subjects and received a reference from the Head Mistress, recommending her for employment in any field and congratulating her for her work as school captain. Noeline left school when she was 15 like so many girls at that time in spite of her academic strengths.

In her first job at the Marrickville Library, Noeline was fortunate to meet a young woman in charge who encouraged her to read and to act. Frances Charteris put her to work reading Hemingway, Steinbeck, Salinger and Nabokov. In the evenings Noeline and her boyfriend Ron marvelled at the intimate revue at the Phillip Street Theatre, admiring Bud Tingwell, Ruth Cracknell, Lyle O'Hara and others. Back at the library the following morning, Noeline would re-enact the sketches for her colleagues. Frances Charteris suggested that Noeline join a theatre group, and the Library even set up an amateur group of its own, called 'The Marrick Players'.

In 1956, as Australia was preparing to host the Olympic Games, Noeline was presented with a sash and a title at a local Council meeting. As Miss Marrickville Olympics, it was Noeline's job to raise money for local competitors in the Games. Noeline was slim, elegant and blonde, with a broad, friendly face. Her good looks and obliging personality led to a series of roles in local theatre that she deplored because of the scanty outfits required. A friend invited her to come along to the New Theatre where she saw Frank Hardy performing in his own play about a mining crisis, *Black Diamonds*. Impressed with the play, Noeline joined the New Theatre immediately and began rehearsing for a satirical revue called *Fission Chips*, in which the cast attempted to create a vision of a world after nuclear annihilation, with Noeline shivering in a skimpy and shabby rabbit-skin bikini on stage at the Waterside Workers Federation Hall. Noeline cooperated but found it confronting, especially as so many of the old men in the cast and crew kept their eyes fixed on her in her scanties. Noeline was not prudish: in fact she admits to an unusual sexual precocity as a young teenager, but she resented the focus on flesh in the productions. Fortunately, it did not last, and within a short time, Noeline was performing with Frank Hardy in a production of Douglas Stewart's *Fire on the Snow*: Brown narrated and Hardy played Oates.

Unlike many other actors, Brown did not have a mentor, guide or teacher in her early days. She did not attend any classes to learn acting, singing, dance or movement. Instead she learned on her own on the job, through observation and practice. When Norman McVicker cast her as Mary Morgan in *The Sleeping Prince* her fortunes began to change. McVicker was a working class, openly gay, outlandish and enthusiastic director, who she remembers 'could put an "s" in "banana"'; he worked for Qantas by day and spent his evenings in the amateur theatre. Immediately he saw Noeline's potential and in his own authoritarian, somewhat hectoring way, propelled her along. He was not encouraging, however: McVicker told the 20-year-old Noeline in no uncertain terms that she would never make it as an actor during a rehearsal when she ignored his directions. Noeline made a decision at that point to focus, to succeed and to prove McVicker wrong. In spite of his comment, Noeline valued his advice and support for her, and he valued her contribution to the production. But the director had no truck with Brown's boy-friends, and once berated her 'lack of commitment' to the theatre. When Vivien Leigh appeared with John Merivale and the Old Vic Company in Sydney in *Lady of the Camellias*, Noeline missed a rehearsal in order to see the celebrated actress perform the role, directed by Robert Helpmann at the Theatre Royal. McVicker was furious and to this day Noeline recalls his tirade. But she also recalls the vision of Leigh performing, the way that she seemed to 'own the stage, and move like a dream, in those splendid costumes': for Noeline it was worth the fallout.

Noeline had first met McVicker when she auditioned for his amateur theatre group at the Pocket Playhouse in Sydenham. She appeared in that first production of *The Sleeping Prince*, at the tiny theatre in Terry Street that had once been a Rechabite Hall, wearing a dress made by her mother in the lead role of Mary Morgan. The play takes place in London in 1911, at the time of the coronation of George V. On opening night Noeline was wretched with nerves, vomiting and shaking. The reviews were extremely encouraging, with Brown singled out for high praise. In an extraordinary turn of events, during Vivien Leigh's Sydney visit, Leigh saw Noeline perform the role that had been written for the visiting star by Terrence Rattigan.

McVicker answered the telephone at the Pocket Theatre one day and when the caller said her name 'Vivien Leigh', he replied 'And I'm the King of England'.[1]

Leigh arranged to come and see a performance of *The Sleeping Prince*. Arriving at nightfall for the special Sunday evening performance in a black limousine, Leigh swept into the theatre in a mink jacket, elegant black Dior dress and toque, with a cascade of pearls. In Sydney, Leigh was appearing in three separate productions at the Theatre Royal in Castlereagh Street. Opposite Noeline in the role played by Lawrence Olivier was Edward Lansdowne. Leigh sat next to a jittery McVicker for the performance. She spoke reassuringly to him but the actors were nervous. Noeline recalls that props were dropped, entrances were mistimed and lines forgotten. At the end of the performance, McVicker invited Leigh and Merivale on to the stage and presented them with a large box of white orchids and a painting by the abstract artist Tom Gleghorn, who lived near the theatre. Leigh signed Noeline's program but did not add any message of encouragement to the young actress. In the photograph of Leigh and Merivale on the stage, Leigh looks somewhat dour and is standing in front of Brown, obscuring her whole body, except for Brown's feet. Leigh wrote to McVicker thanking him for 'the perfectly charming evening', expressing her 'admiration for the courage, initiative and enthusiasm with which you run your theatre'.[2]

After the production, Noeline was introduced to people as 'Noeline Brown, actress', rather than 'Bob's girlfriend'. It was a turning point for her as an actor and as a woman. Noeline's boy-friend, the lanky and wild haired Bob Hughes, arranged a luncheon party for Vivien

---

1 Geoffrey Ostling, 1993, 'The Pocket Playhouse 1957–1973', *Heritage*, no. 6, p. 1.
2 Ibid.

Leigh and John Merivale at Hughes' family home in Rose Bay. In spite of the thronging crowd of guests, Noeline managed a few words with the glamorous, diamond-studded visitor, but recalls only one emotion: jealousy. When Leigh made a beeline after lunch for Hughes, asking if he would show her his paintings in his studio, Noeline fumed. For the young Noeline, the siren actress was a dangerous woman, whose reputation as femme fatale was legendary. The star of *Gone with the Wind* and *A Streetcar Named Desire*, looked spectacular in blue Capri pants and an oversized straw hat with a light chiffon scarf tied fetchingly under her chin. When Noeline talked to me about this day so many years ago, she laughed as she recalled that her anxiety was ridiculously misplaced, fired by her feverish imagination as a woman some 25 years younger than Leigh, brimming with the fantasies of tabloid journalists and women's magazines. The middle-aged Leigh (she was 48 at the time), who suffered from mental illness, died just four years after the Sydney visit, due to a recurrence of Tuberculosis. Remembering her on stage at the curtain call of her first show in Sydney, Noeline still recalls a sense of her shining presence, almost divine grace and compelling acting.

Brown appeared at the Pocket Playhouse in the American musical comedy *My Sister Eileen*. Although Noeline wanted to play the sister with all the smart lines (based on the writer of the work, Ruth McKenney), she enjoyed the production and learned her first hard lesson: that frequently actors are not cast in the role they want, and must make the best job of the role assigned by the director. At the Pocket, Noeline enjoyed performing for children and mixing with them before the show began so that they would not be too frightened to come up on the stage during the performances.

Noeline making up for *Bell, Book and Candle* at the Pocket Playhouse, Sydenham, Sydney, 1963.
Courtesy of Noeline Brown.

What's New? Phillip Street, Music Hall and *Mavis Bramston*

In 1962 Noeline seized an opportunity to audition for the Phillip Street Theatre in the city, and was offered a role in *What's New?* staged at the new premises in Elizabeth Street alongside a cast of revue artists: Earle Cross, Maggie Dence, Colin Gorman, Reg Gorman, Arlene Dorgan and several others, all of them under 25 years of age. It was the all-important break she needed, and gave her a taste of professional, popular intimate revue theatre, allowing her to give up her library job. Noeline told the local newspaper at the time that she had no aspirations for dramatic acting 'I did entertain such ambitions, but I do really feel more at home in comedy; and, let's face it, I've just got that sort of face!'[3]

In this production Noeline met the tall, dark eyed Barry Creyton, and soon joined him in *The Face at the Window* at the Neutral Bay Music Hall, marking the beginning of what was to be a life-long friendship and professional partnership. It was at the Music Hall that Noeline learned to ad lib and to control her nerves. The continuous work with children, the constant rehearsal of new material and the opportunity to perform melodrama gave her confidence as a performer. Noeline spent long evenings at Vadim's, the late-night haunt of actors, writers and artists. The small restaurant in Challis Avenue, Potts Point was named after the owner, an eccentric Russian who served Sydney rock oysters, borscht, beef stroganoff, steak and red wine in coffee cups. Vadim didn't have a liquor licence and was always anticipating police raids, hiding the wine bottles under the tables. It was at Vadim's that Noeline had first met the golden-haired, loquacious Bob Hughes, and the theatre critic Harry Kippax, who would be found at his own table on the upper level of the restaurant every night eating steak diane and drinking red wine. Gradually Noeline befriended Kippax and occasionally he asked her to join his table. Kippax wrote theatre reviews under the pseudonym 'Brek' and was a difficult critic to please. Noeline didn't hesitate to express her dissatisfaction with the conservative government of Robert Menzies, arousing disdain and sometimes fulminations from Kippax who called the Labor Party 'a pack of commos', and castigated Noeline for her views, as though she was a foolish child.

---

3   The *Guardian* 5 July 1962, p. 3.

When Noeline first met Bob Hughes she found him witty, intelligent and handsome. He spoke in an accent that was cultivated, had been educated at St Ignatius, Riverview, and seemed to know every artist in Sydney. On that first evening Noeline explained that she lived at home with her parents in Stanmore. His face crumpled in bewilderment. He exclaimed: 'Good heavens, why?' When they met up with Kippax the talk often turned to art as all three of them shared an interest in painting and sculpture. Noeline took art classes at East Sydney Tech, and Bob Hughes was a keen student of art who loved to draw portraits of people. Even at Vadim's amid the smoke from Noeline's acrid Sobranies, and the noise, Hughes sketched the patrons, producing a cartoonish likeness of Noeline with a shock of hair, a frown and an enviable cleavage.

Bob and Noeline were inseparable and mixed with a group of artists that included Colin Lanceley, John Olsen, Robert Klippel, John Coburn and Albert Tucker. Tucker referred to Noeline as Nefertiti, impressed with her noble and distinctive profile. One night Noeline and Bob slept on the pavement outside the Macquarie Galleries in order to gain admission to an exhibition of paintings by Ian Fairweather who lived on Bribie Island, off the coast of Queensland. It was a gesture of generosity by the two youngsters who managed to purchase a painting for Kippax. Bob, whose full name was Robert Studley Forrest Hughes, was the youngest child in his family, seemed to Noeline to have endured a lonely childhood. He lived in a studio above the garage at his mother's house in Rose Bay and frequently visited Noeline at home in Stanmore. Talking loudly on the phone to one of his student friends, in the hallway one day, Noeline and her mother heard him swearing. The word 'Fuck' shattered the quiet of the house and Dyra was appalled, urging her daughter to chastise her boyfriend. It was the language the students used with one another but never in the presence of their parents. He would not have dared utter the word in his mother's presence. Bob's mother Margaret gave Noeline the distinct impression that she found her a little 'common' when she visited: and the young actress was surprised to find Bob's mother wearing a tea gown in the afternoons. A chance remark Margaret made about a splendid silver-plated samovar that Noeline gave Bob amongst other gifts for his birthday, cut her to the quick. She said disdainfully that Noeline would probably like to buy lots of things rather than 'one good thing'. It did not diminish the affection between the young lovers: the intensity and playful joy of their relationship shines out from one photograph they took of their faces up close, with Noeline's long frizzy blonde hair cascading over Bob's brow, both of them eager and smiling into the camera. When he left Sydney for London in 1964, Noeline set about planning her own trip to England and missed him with an intensity she had never felt before.

Fortunately, Noeline's performing career became very busy. During the day, she appeared with Barry Creyton in *Beauty and the Beast* for children at the Neutral Bay Music Hall, and in the evening they performed in various musical revues at the same venue. Noeline's sparkling eyes, strong facial features, bright smile and energy on stage delighted the children in the day time and the adults at night. The two performers became close friends and worked well together, sharing a sense of humour and dry wit. Together they wrote and recorded the first comedy spoken word LP ever produced by Festival Records in Australia called *The Front and Flipside of Barry Creyton and Noeline Brown* which was a popular success in spite of being banned on radio because of some of the mildly suggestive material it offered.

They spent a lot of time together on and off the stage, and made a handsome couple: they were both baritones and spoke with resonant authority. Barry was good looking in a classical manner, slim, tall with glossy dark hair and strong, even facial features. Noeline charmed audiences and friends with her blonde, sultry beauty and deep voice; it wasn't long before there was speculation in the press that they were romantically involved. The ruse suited Noeline, because she missed Bob, and always had a partner for social events.

It was at the Neutral Bay Music Hall that a newly arrived English producer for Channel 7, Carol Raye, spotted Barry Creyton, who she invited to perform in a pilot for a new television show that became *The Mavis Bramston Show*. At a party with Creyton, and some of the others who were to be in the show, Noeline found herself saying yes when someone suggested she play the eponymous Mavis. With minimal television experience Brown managed to sing and dance in her portrayal of the gormless English actress called Mavis. Her rendition of the popular song 'I could have danced all night', with orchestral accompaniment was hilarious and is now iconic, and so began Noeline's extraordinary career in comedy on television.

Brown left *Mavis* after the first few episodes in order to seek work as an actor in London, like so many of her contemporaries, and in hopes of meeting up again with Bob Hughes. Although she found work on the BBC as a reporter on *This Week in Britain*, she never felt comfortable as a news reporter, and found it difficult to get the roles she wanted on stage and television. But this didn't put her off her adventure in England: Noeline lived with the Australian artist Colin Lancely and his wife Kay, and met others who would drop in and exchange homesick stories about Australia. John Olsen and Colin Lancely painted a comical work together for her entitled 'London

Sufferers'. Brown missed Australia and when she heard about the popularity of *The Mavis Bramston Show*, she began to think that the opportunities for her were far more promising in Australia; she even turned down an audition for the film *Georgy Girl*, fearing it was a 'sordid, dirty story totally devoid of laughs'.[4] Charlotte Rampling played the lead and the film was a box office sensation. Shortly afterwards, when the producer of *The Mavis Bramston Show* invited Noeline to return to Sydney to appear once more on the show, she took the next flight home at her own expense.

Noeline Brown never went back to the UK for work, and made her name as a comic actor on stage and on television in Australia. Back in *The Mavis Bramston Show*, Brown found her feet immediately and relished being part of the weekly satirical program, alongside Gordon Chater, Barry Creyton and June Salter. June, Barry and Noeline would meet at the Hotel Australia for a beer before rehearsals on taping day, such was their relaxed approach to television acting. Brown became a household name and was swamped with fan mail and media attention. She excelled in revue, sketch and musical comedy, but over the months, the quality of the writing in the sketches deteriorated, and the roles for women became clichéd. Noeline recalls her disgust at being given a 'point number' about a pet cemetery. Clearly the topical and biting satire of the early shows had disappeared. She complained about it and began to look out for other opportunities.

A year later when the producers began to feature English artists in spite of the original joke of the show, Noeline decided to leave, joining the cast of the situation comedy about a working-class family called *My Name's McGooley, What's Yours?* The script was written by

---

4 Noeline Brown, 2005, *Noeline: Longterm Memoir*, Sydney: Allen & Unwin, p. 101.

one of Brown's favourite writers, Ralph Peterson, who had performed in the wireless drama of her childhood *Yes, What?* There was no audition required and it was a hit comedy in which Brown played Wally Stiller's sister Rosemary (called 'Possum'). Wally was played by John Meillon and Gordon Chater played the magnificent McGooley. When Noeline appeared in the show, she would put on a wig as a disguise to go outside her house, and still people in the street would shout out 'Hello Possum'. So infectious was the term 'possum', that Barry Humphries borrowed the quintessentially Australian salutation later on when greeting audiences as Dame Edna: 'Hello Possums', Edna chirped as she sashayed onto the stage. *My Name's McGooley* ran to 115 episodes over three years. Spike Milligan made a special appearance in one episode during a visit to Australia, playing a pest inspector who checked her out in case of a white ant infestation.

In addition to *Mavis*, Brown appeared in the television series *Jonah* that portrayed the life of a colonial trader, the television play *The Right Thing* by Raymond Bowers in 1963, the ABC's television play adaptation of *The Recruiting Officer* in 1965 with John Meillon, and in other television drama, as well as on the popular talk shows, *Beauty and the Beast* and *Would You Believe*. The latter quiz show focused on Australian history of the colonial period and Noeline revelled in it, alongside Jacki Weaver, Cyril Pearl, Len Evans, Michael Baume and her old friend from the New Theatre, the author, playwright and actor Frank Hardy. After the recording one night at the 729 Club in St Leonards (named for the three local television stations nearby), Noeline was approached by an ASIO agent who seemed to be looking to recruit her to keep tabs on the author Frank Hardy who they suspected of spying for the Soviet Union. Noeline was shocked, and she declined to be of service to the security operatives.

Noeline has always been a staunch Australian Labor Party supporter, participating in campaigns in various electorates. With great pride she recalled for me sitting next to Gough Whitlam for the opening of the Whitlam election campaign, and the thrill of being in the audience for the recording of the *It's Time* campaign advertisement in October 1972, performed at the Capitol Theatre by Alison McCallum; the video of the *It's Time* live recording is now a prized record of this historic event (see YouTube). At the time though, Noeline's appearance in the advertisement sitting next to Whitlam, ensured that Noeline was black-banned by the Packer network. Noeline continued to work in the theatre, appearing in Buzo's *Rooted* (1972) and Williamson's *Don's Party*. She enjoyed the Buzo play because of its meaty chunks of dialogue. With Williamson the theatre was compelling, in spite of Noeline's reservations about his success in writing the women's roles. Cast against type, Noeline played the dowdy Jenny, with Martin Harris as Don, the teacher and would-be writer. The notices were excellent, with a Melbourne reviewer remarking that 'I have seen no actress on the Melbourne stage – apart from Miriam Karlin when she is here – who can fire a one-line gag from the hip quite as accurately as Noeline Brown. And that is much how she is cast in David Williamson's *Don's Party* at the Russell Street Theatre: once again she presents what is in fact a lean and alluring face as a hatchet job'.[5] Remembering the privations of a long tour of the play, she urges other actors never to go on long tours with a large cast. In the 1973–4 tour of *Don's Party* a couple of the actresses were arrested for shoplifting, one actor went AWOL, and two of the other actors came to blows out of the sheer torture of close

---

5   Gerald Mayhead, *Melbourne Herald*, 2 May 1973.

quarters in shabby accommodation, and the lack of home-cooked food. In spite of all of this, the production delighted audiences throughout the regions, with a reviewer in Albury commenting on the uproarious laughter in the theatre. Noeline's performance was singled out for praise: 'Timing was the highlight of the show, and of the girls, Noeline Brown was outstanding. Her off-beat quips delivered in gorgeous gravelly contralto gave one the impression that she had more than her share of laugh lines'.[6]

Even with the privations of touring, Noeline welcomed the role: it was rare for her to play a character like Jenny, the somewhat downtrodden and exhausted suburban wife of the leading man, Don. Brown frequently played strong, sexy, streetwise women on television and began to tire of such roles. She was outspoken about this at the time and deliberately sought out more variation in the theatre as a result. After appearing in several episodes of *Number 96* Brown was determined to return to the stage. She told a reporter that the program had sent her back to the stage … 'Four episodes of that last year – playing not only a tart but Ronnie Shand's love interest – turned me right off. I did it for the money. What other reason would you have for appearing in *Number 96*? It looks like the sort of show we should have been doing ten years ago. The only thing I can say in its favour is that it has made the faces of actors familiar to Australian audiences'.[7]

Noeline's quick wit, ability to play verbal games, animated face and earthy manner meant that she excelled in talk and game shows. One of the first was the talk show *Beauty and the Beast* with the first 'beast' Eric Baume, adapted from the popular radio show 'Leave it

---

6   No byline, 'Don's Party Mirrors Our Foibles', *Border Mail*, August 1973.
7   *Listener in TV*, 12–18 May 1973, p. 2.

to the Girls'. Baume behaved in a beastly manner to his four female panellists who answered letters from viewers. Noeline took the advisory role on the show with a grain of salt, but she answered the questions truthfully in her audition, shocking the director who questioned her about her views of abortion. Unlike Ena Harwood and Pat Firman who took the sessions so seriously that they spent the afternoons in tears, Noeline laughed off the nonsense, certain that the questions were simply inventions for the program.

Noeline worked with John Meillon in both comic and dramatic roles. He was more experienced than her and she observed him closely on camera when she began to work on television, recognising his idiosyncratic approach to performance. In *The Weird Mob* he was extraordinary in comic mode; she vividly recalls an episode in which his bricklayer character attempted to eat a pavlova that exploded in his hand. In the dramatic television play *The Fourth Wish* he was superb as the grieving father of a dying child. Noeline learned from watching him how to keep her own performance contained yet dynamic, and free of tricks and shortcuts.

Naked Vicars

Brown's appearance in *Don's Party* marked the beginning of a long period working on the stage. She appeared in *Cowardy Custard* (1974), *Three Men on a Horse* (1974), *Hotel Paradiso* (1974) and *The Naked Vicar Show* (1976). Gary Reilly and Tony Sattler (known as RS Productions) wrote the scripts for *The Naked Vicar Show*, which was performed by Noeline Brown, Ross Higgins and Kev Goldsby for a live audience in the ABC Forbes Street Studio, and broadcast on Sundays. The halcyon days of radio and live audiences of an earlier era revived with this popular sketch show, which was precisely the reason they had written it. They had noticed that radio comedy was dying. Channel 7 later adapted the show for television, with Noeline playing in a regular sketch with Julie McGregor: in the sketch two women meet at the tea trolley in a factory and Narelle (played by Julie) tells an extravagant, story about her adventures the night before. Noeline's character, Lois, listens to her improbable tales and fanciful commentary about social club evenings, known as 'Tia Maria and chop tasting' parties, and when Narelle eventually asks Lois about her husband Kevin, who she learns has 'fallen into young Lyle's piranha tank', the gormless Narelle says: 'Oh that's bad Lois'. Regardless of their conversation, Lois replies 'You're not wrong, Narelle'. The droll expression became a familiar expression amongst ordinary Australians in conversation, and is sometimes still heard today.

Noeline radiated charm in *The Naked Vicar Show*, with her shining blonde hair cut in a neat page-boy style, and resplendent in spectacular full length gowns: these were jersey halter-neck dresses that draped decorously around her waist and hips. Noeline recalls this year as one of the happiest of her life. At the beginning of each show she would sit between the two men, all of them sitting on high stools, offering up parodies of the news, with Kev and Ross dressed in gleaming white safari suits. The material was hilarious, surprising, unconventional and diverse. They presented parodies of television itself, especially the pompous British documentaries that filled the Australian television schedule. Australian television was also lampooned. Noeline assayed Grace Sullivan in a sharp parody of the long running popular television series *The Sullivans*. Seated at the table in a floral dress she says: 'For what we are about to receive may Hector Crawford be truly thankful'. The Prime Minister and his wife were the satirical targets of a particularly amusing sketch showing the two of them in bed, with Noeline as Tammy, splattering large gobs of cold cream on her face and all over Malcolm's papers, as she goads him into imitating Gough Whitlam for her, then braying and snorting like a horse as she laughs uncontrollably. Noeline is exquisite in this sketch, in her pink frilly nightgown and swirly brown wig. The format and the style foreshadowed *Full Frontal* and *The Gillies Report*. There were parodies of Joh Bjelke-Petersen who announces he has changed the name of Brisbane: 'Henceforth it will be known as Jo-rusalem'.

One of Noeline's favourite segments lampooned gardening advice programs; it was called 'Getting Rooted'. The political satire was minimal and muted but in one sharp parody of John Singleton the advertising king was introduced as Mr Singleton, of Vulgar Incorporated, and Singleton referred to the Deputy Prime Minister, Doug Anthony, as 'Mal Fraser's barrel girl'. Sometimes Noeline played men and the two men played women: the opportunity and actual play that the sketch material required was challenging but enjoyable. The three actors were tight knit and happy to be working together and the comedy was irreverent, daring and whimsical. In 1978 Noeline Brown won a Logie Award for the most popular NSW-based female personality on television.

The scriptwriters worked around the clock to create new material for the show and everyone seemed to appreciate the talents of everyone else: there was a sense of genuine respect between the writers and actors that provided solidarity and trust. During the stage run Tony Sattler invited Noeline to lunch and so began an intense relationship of the kind she had not experienced since her early 20's with Bob Hughes. Tony moved into Noeline's terrace house in Pyrmont and on a bright winter's day in 1976 they drove in their Mini Moke to St Mary's Waverley to be married, Noeline resplendent in a cream silk full length dress with panels of Japanese turquoise silk set into the bodice and Tony in a suit and smart white shirt. Somehow, they managed to keep the cameras and reporters away that day.

Noeline took a long break from work after the wedding while Tony worked. It suited them both after the gruelling schedule they endured during *The Naked Vicar Show*. Noeline gave up smoking and hoped to become pregnant. She missed working and the months passed with no sign of conception. For both Noeline and Tony it was a time of sadness. Summoning all her courage, Noeline said to Tony that she would understand if he left her in order to marry someone who could give him children. He stayed with her and life returned to normal for the couple who both immersed themselves in their work.

Graham Kennedy and *Blankety Blanks*

Noeline and a group of other actors eagerly reported to a motel in Artarmon for a mystery residential audition for Channel Ten just before Christmas in 1976. No-one knew exactly what was required and who they would be working with as they played games on camera and chatted with one another. After a day or two of group auditions it was clear that the auditions were for a game show. One morning silence descended on the group as Graham Kennedy walked into the room to audition the gathered singers and actors, as host of the proposed new show. The wild-eyed King of Comedy had decided to make a comeback on television with a game show called *Blankety Blanks*. Kennedy was both a larrikin favourite of television audiences and infamous: he had been banned from live television after uttering the word 'FAAAARK' (he referred to this utterance as his crow call) on his own variety program, *The Graham Kennedy Show* in 1975.[8] Because of that incident Kennedy was required to pre-record his shows. He needed a cast of celebrities as a panel to appear regularly on the show. The format was based on an American game show called *The Match Game* but was modified so that the panel members offered lines to the host. A contestant was given a part of a line and the panel members had to fill in the blanks. If the contestant's answer matched the answers supplied by the panel the contestant won a prize. Kennedy selected actors who he could rely on to play the game with wit, gusto and genial bonhomie.

For Kennedy, it was important to have panel members he liked as people, and could rely on in the gruelling blocks of recordings necessary to produce five nights of light entertainment a week. He selected Noeline who became a regular on the show, along with Ugly Dave Gray, Stuart Wagstaff, Noel Ferrier and Carol Raye. It was important not to have another comedian so that Kennedy could perform in his cheeky, irreverent manner without fear of clashing or being upstaged. The mix of banter, wit, short, suggestive quips and innuendo found an immense audience. Double entendre featured strongly, with the comic repartee becoming the focus of the show and the game itself at times incidental. An imaginary character called Dick enlivened the dialogue that relied on the quick inventiveness of the participants. Personality was everything, along with the chemistry between the 'King' and the panel. Noeline seemed to come into her own in this odd, rather rambling game and became a particular favourite of the host who would frequently walk up and kiss her on

---

8   Alan McKee, *Australian Television: A Genealogy of Great Moments*, South Melbourne: Oxford University Press, p. 26.

camera. The show was recorded in front of a studio audience and surprised everyone with its popularity and unprecedented ratings, running to some 500 episodes. It brought Kennedy a Gold Logie, and put Noeline in front of a national television audience once more.

Applause

Noeline's distinctive low, sultry voice is not unlike some of the great actresses of Hollywood such as Katharine Hepburn and Tallulah Bankhead. Overcoming her anxiety about the inflexibility of her voice however, is one of Brown's most significant achievements. Invited to audition for the stage musical, *Applause*, Brown found herself in a crisis of self-sabotage. She appeared at the audition in old clothes, wind battered, having driven to the venue in her Mini Moke with the roof down, to find every other Sydney actor ready and primed to audition for the iconic lead role. Brown proceeded to tell the director that she couldn't possibly perform this role. Later, when he and the musical director began to try to talk her into it, and allowed her to choose the male lead (she suggested Alan Dale) she relaxed, and made the decision to take intensive singing lessons with Peter Casey, in preparation for the role. Playing in *Applause* was important for Brown who sang with a 27-piece orchestra, creating the role of Margo Channing, an actor who is jealous of an up and coming rival. *Applause* starred Lauren Bacall on Broadway in 1970. It was based on the hugely successful film *All about Eve* (1950), with Bette Davis playing Channing. Playing the lead in a musical of this kind represented a major challenge and opportunity for Noeline. She had never starred in a full-scale musical, and understood that the role was iconic, but she felt that she could relate to the imaginary Channing character as a woman of her own age, with a similar level of experience in the 'business'. The difference was that Brown felt she was less ambitious than her stage character. Playing Margo Channing was difficult, and Brown recalls that the set, particularly in the opening scene was unattractive and awkward to negotiate. The costumes seemed ill suited to her shape and there were horrific sound problems on the opening night. But once the cast 'settled in, it was a joy' recalls Brown, and she found that she could sing and carry off the role of lead in a full-scale musical.

Brown returned to the stage after her appearance in *Applause*, playing in *The Shifting Heart* (1984), *Barmaids* (1993) and *Emerald City* (1995). Cast once more as a 'tough dame' in *The Shifting Heart* she did not disappoint. The national theatre critic Michael Morton-Evans on the *Australian* praised her: 'The Bex-swallowing Leila Pratt is deliciously portrayed by Noeline Brown, rough as guts, a salt of the earth type ... soft as marshmallow except when it comes to her husband's binges and then as sharp as a buzz-saw'.[9] Brown's instinct for the right 'role' took some years to develop. In the early years she often took roles, like many actors, because she had to in order to work. Later if she had doubts about whether she was right for the role, she did not hesitate to decline. In recent years Noeline has played various comic and dramatic roles. Many actresses experience a diminution of roles in their middle years and struggle to keep their careers alive. Noeline was nearing her 50th birthday when she appeared in *Double Act*. It is the role of which she is most proud. The play was written by Barry Creyton especially for himself and Noeline. The sustained allusions to Noel Coward provide a comic sub-text in this play about two unusual people whose marriage has ended. It is a difficult

---

9   Michael Morton-Evans, *The Australian* 24 July 1984, p. 10.

two-hander however, because the two characters are frequently addressing an invisible person, the comedy demands complete and frequent solo concentration as well as some creative stage business. For example, the play opens five years after the couple's divorce, as they meet at a restaurant; Alexandra's bra strap breaks and her ex-husband assists her with fixing it. Noeline recalls having to work at this because it is not farce and requires a kind of dual choreography of movement to make it work, as husband number two approaches during the manoeuvre. The play explores what actually happened in the marriage, and Creyton drew on colourful, sometimes cutting expressions he had heard Brown use over the years in the script. It was not an easy rehearsal period in spite of the long friendship between Creyton and Brown, and Brown recalls the guiding hand of Sandra Bates as vital throughout. Brown recalls her feeling of exhilaration as she waited to make her entrance in the wings of the Ensemble Theatre in Sydney, as the rousing 'March of the Gladiators' music set the mood of combat between the characters. Even at the morning matinee, Brown felt a joyous surge of energy, as she and Creyton took their positions. It was enormously gratifying for her as a performer, playing opposite her long-term friend and performing partner in a role that stretched her, and brought the two of them so much attention. On opening night, the founder of the Ensemble Theatre, Hayes Gordon, appeared full of praise which for the actors was unexpected and moving.

The premiere production of *Double Act* was an immense success and Creyton's play went on to be produced all over the world and translated into many languages. Creyton and Brown also appeared in *Glorious* by Peter Quilter in 2007, once again in premiere at the Ensemble Theatre in Sydney. This play portrays the singer Florence

Foster Jenkins. Brown once again took singing lessons in order to play the out of tune singer. John Cargher advised her not to take the role, warning that she would ruin her voice. But Brown succeeded in singing soprano in this extraordinary play. In 2009 Brown and Creyton performed in a two-hander called *Duets* in which they played four characters each. Most recently Brown appeared in a stage adaptation of the 1980s television series, *Mother and Son*, with Darren Gilshenan as the stay at home son, and Rob Carlton in the role of the other son.

For Noeline comedy is something she has grasped since her youthful forays, and she observed other performers closely: Barry Creyton, John Meillon and Graham Kennedy. Noeline told me: 'I know how to deliver a funny line'. I understand it. I've played characters who are over the top. But it's not me being over the top. Flacco says he is frightened of the audience. I'm not afraid of the audience. I give in to them. I don't hide behind anything. I like a great character. I'm not a comedian'.

Brown has worked with her husband Tony Sattler in their own production company for many years, continues to appear on stage and twice ran for state parliament as an ALP candidate in her southern highlands electorate. She has published two books and is a committed historian of her paternal family and their convict past. Brown competed in *Dancing with the Stars* in 2006, and in 2008 she was appointed as the first Ambassador for Ageing in Australia. She received the Equity Life Time Achievement Award in 2017. As she nears her 80th birthday, this Australian queen of comedy walks briskly, and is unsparing in her comic teasing and witty retorts in conversation. Her baritone voice is unchanged with age, and her rich laughter is music to the ears.

Chapter 4

MAX GILLIES: MARVELLOUS MAX

(B. 1941)

Max Gillies has recurring dreams about getting lost back stage during a production and not being able to find his entrance again, forgetting the play he is in and his lines, wandering into the wrong theatre, finding that the set has disappeared and the audience members are inexplicably standing around yawning in the foyer.

Staring at photographs of Max as a young man, I see a strongly built man with Celtic good looks, blue eyes, glossy black hair, a perfect oval-shaped face and a gift for clowning. When I look at him in performance I see someone who is physically nimble on stage and exuberant in his comic caricatures. In character, he seems to find both a joy and wholeness that is not apparent off stage. Max is an intense and cerebral actor, an intellectual with a nervous edge. He is chronically self-critical and tells me more than once that he is always the slowest cast member to learn lines or a bit of choreography. Max is watchful and wary, and in his presence, you sense a brooding personality, a solitary figure for whom playing, the genuine playfulness of theatre is pure, and is the source of his inspired performances.

A lifelong believer in texts, Max is committed to the idea of learning to make theatre through making theatre rather than through classes that divide up the craft into its constituents: moving, speaking, singing, dancing. He has always revelled in the ideal of the performer-writer relationship, recognising its precariousness. Max is an artful observer and gifted mimic. But mimicry is just one of his talents. He keeps filing cabinets full of scripts worked up with Bob Ellis, Patrick Cook, Frank Moorhouse and others, that might one day find a production. His battles with television executives or 'program prevention officers', as he likes to call them, are many and varied.

It was a cold, July morning when I first met Max Gillies, the day after John Clarke's memorial service in July 2017. We sat opposite each other on plush, teal blue banquettes at the European restaurant in Spring Street, Melbourne, one of John's favourite haunts. Since then we've met on other days in other cafes around Melbourne. Once the street theatre and megaphones of a lively Stop Adani demonstration threatened to kill off our discussion. Loud drums beat over the sound of trams, hordes of angry citizens chanted and others performed on the wide pavement of Collins Street. Max talked on over the din, his focus and intelligent commentary unwavering, generous and undeterred by the heat and noise of the demo on that warm summer day in 2017.

Argonaut

The blue-eyed boy is five and in Grade 1 at Caulfield State School 773, so it must be 1946. The towering grey concertina doors are open and the children from each class sit cross-legged in a massive circle on the floor in preparation for a visitor. The children are quiet, some of them wriggling as the stranger begins to tell them about Jesus. Max listens intently as the grey-haired lady describes what happens at night to children: 'You are lifted up by Jesus and taken to heaven, she says, and in the morning before you wake, Jesus returns you to your bed'. Max is affronted: what a pernicious notion – *ipso facto* impossible either to prove or disprove. He'd waited long enough to be able to go to school, now he was here he didn't want his head to be filled with poppycock. At home he recounts the incident to his mother, Doris. He reasons it out for her: 'It might give nightmares to the kids', he says knowing his mother will understand. He asks her for a letter to excuse him from attending Religious Instruction in future. (He's shaping up to be a regular little Richard Dawkins.) The school perfectly mirrored the sectarian divide of the society of Melbourne and of the whole nation. Religious Instruction was contracted out to a variety of Protestant sects.

Max did not go back to RI and from then on, the weekly class time would largely be spent in the library with a handful of kids the system could not accommodate, mainly Jews and Catholics, all left to their own devices. The exile gave him a freedom he began to treasure. He lost himself in stories, reading all manner of books and as he grew older, would occasionally send a contribution to the Children's Session on ABC radio.

Max was a devotee of the program, a seeker after the Golden Fleece badge, as a dedicated Argonaut, hanging on the words of the Argo broadcasting crew, Ida Elizabeth Osbourne and AD Hope (known to the children as Antony Inkwell), as he discussed the children's own work with them and poetry of all kinds. Max was enchanted by the tales of Ruth Park's *Muddleheaded Wombat* and looked forward to Jeffrey Smart's segment. Smart was known as Phidias, and he talked about painting for the avid listeners. Unlike so many adults in Max's life 'they did not talk down to children', Max recalls with admiration. For him it was a deeply engaging world of the intellect and the imagination in which Hope, Smart and Osbourne developed children's interests and understanding as individuals, especially when they sent in their own contributions to be read out on the air (with their own ship name proudly affixed). The presenters taught the children to think independently, and how to appreciate the arts and the natural world. The blue and purple certificates sent back to the children yielded book prizes. For

Max, as he looks back, it was like 'a university for the young', invented by a young journalist called Nina Murdoch in the 1930s, revived in 1941 and popular for thirty years. There was another element that engaged Max as a young radio listener. This was the clowning that the core cast had with the ABC's bureaucratic hierarchy – studio protocol was overseen by the 'Stewed Soup' (otherwise known as the Studio Supervisor or Stud. Sup.), and they would engineer elaborate pranks to frustrate his overbearing diktat. Max revelled in their eternal battle with officialdom, an early intimation of satiric subversion.

At home life was not easy. One of Max's earliest memories is of his father, Frank, arriving at the front door, back from his war service in Darwin and New Guinea. Max itched with the excitement of seeing the parent he had barely known, having anticipated the moment for days. He saw his father's tall frame approaching through the mottled glass of the front door, and as it opened he threw his arms around Frank. His father began to fiddle with his canvas bag. A few minutes passed and Gillies senior strode through the house and hurled a small practice hand grenade into the back garden, causing a blinding flash, a deafening bang and a firestorm in the yard. In retrospect, Max believes that his father was trying misguidedly to amuse the children. But his mother was unimpressed. Clearly Frank had suffered in the war – some kind of trauma – but whatever he had endured was never explained to his son.

Over the next few years Frank did not have a regular job, and seemed to others to be 'a bit of a dreamer', Max told me. Dorrie grew increasingly frustrated and anxious. Frank was a talented carpenter, self-taught violinist and an accomplished pen and ink illustrator. Max recalls a lovingly crafted record player that his father built into a cabinet for Dorrie, with speakers hidden around the house. On

Dorrie's birthday one year, Max awoke to the sounds of Mozart's *Eine kleine Nacthmusik*: it was as if an orchestra had arrived in the living room. But the post-war strain of the relationship took its toll on the family. Max and his brother Don heard their parents arguing at night, as they tried to sleep, terrified by the ferocity of the fighting. The shouting was unbearable and sometimes Dorrie would leave the house and walk the streets to get away, usually finishing up at her parents' house two suburbs away. Once, when he was small, she took Max with her, pushing him along in a stroller as she trudged through the shadowy, deserted streets at midnight.

Max, aged 8, uncomfortable in fancy dress at school.
Courtesy Max Gillies.

When Max was eight years old, his parents separated. The night before he left, Frank sat down on the bed beside his son to account for the decision. He spoke carefully and took his time explaining to Max that none of the problems between the parents had anything to do with Max or his brother. It would be a struggle for his mother bringing up the two boys alone; at her insistence they were not to see their father, nor hear from him. Dorrie held down an office job in the public service, and after a year or two on a waiting list, secured a Housing Commission home. She had endured a hard childhood herself, and despite her talents had been forced to leave school early by her father, who favoured his sons in every way, indifferent to his daughters' intellectual and creative fulfilment. Doris had met Frank when she was 19. Shortly afterwards he was diagnosed with lymphoma and became obsessed with trying to recover and build his strength. He set himself the goal of cycling alone from Melbourne to Perth, and apparently made a full recovery. Over the years after his father's departure from their lives, Max treasured the tiny black and white photographs of Frank's lonely Nullarbor crossing, returning to the images he kept in his bedroom, and marvelling at his courage, as he wondered about how his father was doing and where he was now living.

Despite Max's early rejection of church teachings, at the age of twelve he befriended a boy called Chris at Caulfield North Central School. Chris had an eccentric fascination with church architecture. The two boys rode their bicycles in 'church crawls' across Melbourne so that Chris could sketch the Gothic towers of dozens of ornate steeples and flying buttresses. It was not just the architecture that interested Chris but the rituals of the high Anglican Church, the incense and the elaborate services. None of the ritual appealed to

Max, but he did give Sunday school another chance, only to find the music of his local 'low church' and the liturgy dull, arcane and utterly irrelevant. Instead he was moved by the causes of his uncles who were progressive activists ('Fellow Travellers' in the contemporary jargon), and both prominent trade union officials. The two uncles engaged Max's sense of social justice and respect for human rights, albeit travelling to Leningrad and Moscow and returning with idealised reports of life in the Soviet Union.

In the playground, at the age of eleven, Max and his friend Chris imitated a teacher whose pretensions had rubbed the kids up the wrong way, entertaining their classmates with powerful mimicry. Chris' entrepreneurial opportunism elevated their lunchtime performances, dubbing the venue 'The Dunnyview Auditorium'. Their primitive caricature gained further prestige when an indecorous teacher invited the boys inside to perform for the music class. The inevitable success of this event led to a demand for more. And week by week thereafter Max and his mate essayed each member of the school's teaching staff. The accruing notoriety would be Max's first experience of the power of satirical performance and the tidal pull of audience demand. What had begun as 'innocent' play had created a need for studied character development through observing behaviour and surmising psychology.

When he arrived at Melbourne Boys High two years later, Max found a haven, an escape from the problems of home and a place he could follow his own passion for learning. He wasted no time auditioning for the school plays, discovered the adrenalin rush of performing, under the guidance of a young economics teacher, Neville Drohan. Max played in Victorian melodrama and all the house plays. His enterprising teacher directed him in *See How They*

Run, a popular English farce full of vicars running around without their pants on. Max was delighted to be cast as the cockney maid Ida. He relished the comedy of the farce and found he could improvise too. One night he realised that all of the buttons on his dress were undone. Diving for cover behind the sofa on stage, he grappled with the buttons, popping his head up to say his lines from behind the sofa, delighting the audience. The next year he appeared as Dr Einstein in *Arsenic and Old Lace*, and another year he charmed the audience directing and playing in Wolf Mankowitz' adaptation of Gogol's *The Overcoat*. By this time Max seemed to know how to work the audience, recalling with a laugh that 'they couldn't get me off the stage'. He was delighted to win the drama prize, one of the four school prizes he was awarded in his final year (for debating, editing and art). Mr Drohan became his patron, urging him to push himself as a performer and to pursue all of his artistic interests.

Discoveries

Apart from the pleasures of acting at school, Max adored the cinema, cycling for miles to see Charlie Chaplin and Danny Kaye with whom he was besotted. One afternoon, after a hilarious afternoon watching Chaplin's *Modern Times* as the audience was leaving the cinema Max thought he spotted his father ahead of him leaving by a side-exit. Frank's hair was now greyish white and he could only see the back of his head, but he recognised his dad. Max rushed to the back of the theatre, chasing his father out the side exit and down the lane, eventually catching up with him. Frank took Max on the tram back to his house in St Kilda for the afternoon. This was the only time he had seen his father after Frank left the family home, and it would the last time he ever saw him. Frank died when Max was 21. He'd always nurtured the consoling idea that when he eventually left home himself he'd reconnect with his dad, but somehow his plans did not eventuate. Conflicting loyalties meant that he conscientiously took his mother's side. She was in constant danger of eviction with rising rents, and it took years for her to secure affordable housing through the Housing Commission. Eventually Dorrie, Max and Don moved to a house in Moorabbin.

It was not until years later that Max discovered the circumstances of his father's life in the years the boys were growing up without him. Max's father found a room as a boarder in a house in St Kilda, owned by a woman from Queensland who was single-handedly bringing up four daughters. Max and Don knew nothing about him, but did know of their own mother's despair at unreliably and intermittently forwarded maintenance. Many years later Max learned about his father's other life and his involvement with this family. Frank became close to the family, crafting furniture for the house and looking after the children. Years later, one of the daughters, Paula, asked Frank to 'give her away' at her wedding to the trucking magnate Lindsay Fox in 1959.

On leaving high school Max's intention was to become an art teacher. Coincidentally in his final year he also heard that a new national acting school was to open in Sydney and auditions for the National Institute of Dramatic Arts (NIDA) were announced. Max rehearsed and practised several audition pieces, duly presenting himself before Robert Quentin at the Princess Theatre, on the largest stage of the grandest Victorian-era theatre in the country. He walked up the back stairs of the theatre into the labyrinth of the enormous auditorium and into the cavernous, black emptiness. He did not see another human being, but a distant column of cigarette smoke under the balcony line suggested that Quentin was sitting there. Eventually a languid voice signalled to him to begin, and Max launched into the first of his three pieces. Quentin murmured an indifferent acknowledgement at the end, and Max left the stage feeling the whole idea had been a mistake. Despite his by now extensive school stage experience it was now apparent to him that his presentation had been presumptuous and he clearly wasn't cut out to be a professional. Instead he would train to be a school teacher and do an Arts degree.

When he left school, Max took an office job in the city, the only male in an office of young women, a crash course in an unfamiliar culture after four years of a boys' school. His plan was to support his leaving home and enrolling at Monash, a new university due to open the following year. But at the same time his mother suffered a crisis of anxiety and depression. She would sit at their small kitchen table with her bills, finding her financial problems insurmountable. Max sat beside her in the evenings, trying to assuage her fears. He felt responsible for her and for his brother, having assumed the role of father early on in his life. He saw his mother fixating on her own office politics, complaining constantly about her co-workers who she presumed to be evil, foreign, conspiratorial Catholics.

Some of it seemed real enough for Dorrie, but sometimes Max found her paranoid descriptions of these 'enemies' excessive and strange. Dorrie worried incessantly that her boss would not approve her permanency in the public service because he was a rabid DLP ratbag and unsympathetic to Dorrie as a divorced woman. Having burnt herself out, she began to stay home from work for days at a time, using up her accrued leave quickly. Max enlisted his Aunt Pat for help as his mother drifted further into delusion and loneliness. It was not easy seeking help for mental disturbances, and the stigma of such illness was cruel in the 1950s, but eventually Dorrie agreed to see a psychiatrist.

One day Dorrie reported to Max that as she had been on her way from work to Flinders Street Station she noticed the flags were at half-mast. She recognised this as a clear sign sent from her boss to let others know that she was on her way to the train. With a chill, he registered immediately the tipping point so strikingly captured by Dostoyevsky in *Diary of a Madman* was being replicated by his mother. In the following days Dorrie sold most of her furniture and sat for days staring ahead catatonically in a darkened room in the confined space of her Moorabbin home. Max recalls the suburb as a melancholy wasteland with narrow unmade tracks of broken asphalt and vast tracks of mud, and the memory of his mother's desolation during those long, lonely days haunts him to this day.

At the office, Max received a curt phone call from a psychiatrist. Without any introduction or words of reassurance the specialist stated baldly, 'Your mother is exhibiting distinct suicidal tendencies and she'll need to be committed'. With that he ended his call and hung up. Max felt his whole body go cold. He grasped that his mother was in psychic distress but he did not understand it. Max's aunt Pat offered support: Dorrie would have to be restrained and hospitalised forcibly. 'You can't be there when they come for her', she said. Max recalls his numbness at the thought of having to abandon Dorrie to the police, but knew his aunt was right: 'If you're there, she will hate you for it and never trust you again', said his Aunt firmly. 'But I will be there', she reassured him.

Diagnosed with schizophrenia, Dorrie was administered chlorpromazine, a recently developed anti-psychotic drug, and offered 'shock treatment', and fortuitously her supervising psychiatrist explained to Max that he would only order electroconvulsive therapy if a patient consented to undergo the treatment, a choice not typically offered. She was sedated with heavy doses of the drug, giving her horrible nightmares, turning her skin yellow and making her heavy and lethargic. Over the next few years, Dorrie fought her way back from episodes of psychosis, received a pension and lived with fluctuating 'normalcy'. Eventually she returned to work at a local doctor's surgery as receptionist. Without her ongoing prescription, and at times she would refuse to take her meds, she experienced mania and several times had to be certified all over again. After a number of these episodes, Max argued that she should admit herself upon the next occurrence in order for her to gain ownership of her treatment and thus her illness. She agreed without much conviction. But in the event, upon presentation at the hospital's reception, frightened by a random act of bureaucratic insensitivity, she had to be restrained and sedated. Max can still hear her screams as she was dragged away into the ward. For Max, it was both distressing and exhausting, just one example of the arbitrary character of the systemic response to mental health. The strain of taking care of his mother for so long had meant that he had grown up quickly; he was serious beyond his years. But he yearned to leave home and start enjoying life a little more like his carefree eighteen-year-old peers.

Like many young people at the time, Max funded his Arts degree studies with a teacher's scholarship, obligating him to serve out a three-year bond. He appeared in student productions at Monash of Beckett's *Krapp's Last Tape*, *End Game* and Ionesco's *The Chairs*, and designed a set for his own production of *Volpone*, painting a large hessian curtain with a massive fox that he subsequently hung in his shared house for years. At the Secondary Teachers' College at Melbourne University, Max taught Communication Skills with Ron Danielson, a qualified speech teacher with a reputation for being the best amateur stage director in Melbourne. Max had impressed Danielson as a student actor and he had invited him to work at the college. Within two years of finishing his own degree, Max was lecturing alongside Danielson who introduced a new, one year drama and theatre studies course for trainee teachers. The take up rate was huge and the course soon became a three-year major with five lecturers, as well as two dance and music specialists. For Max, it was a halcyon period: he devised and taught courses in everything and anything that interested him – exploring his own interests in twentieth century theatre as he proceeded. He admired the model that allowed students to play in many productions rather than simply to learn in classes, and believes in this immersive way of developing capacity to this day. Max is certain that he learned about voice, movement and all the elements of performing through doing plays, rather than through classes.

Max lived and breathed theatre, going to all the productions he could find around Melbourne. At the Union Theatre on the Melbourne campus, John Sumner gathered talented graduates and seasoned professional actors, and had built up the Union Theatre Repertory Company in the late 1950s and early 1960s on an English model – doing Shaw, Feydeaux, Anouilh, Williams and other fashionable fare. Max recalls Frank Thring as Ahab in a swirling performance of *Moby Dick Rehearsed* – refusing to sway along with the rest of the company in the simulation of the ocean-rolling Pequod. Here was an actor with his own ideas and a fighting recalcitrance. Sumner's reputation was formidable but conventional. For the young Max the productions seemed dull and unimaginative. He and his theatre mates referred to Sumner as 'Skull' after his gaunt physiognomy. On the rare occasion he would deign to attend their work he would sit stony-faced and ram-rod straight, sizing up his young opposition. In Sumner's final production for the company he had founded, by now known as The Melbourne Theatre Company, he surprised Max by casting him in the central role of Ayckbourn's *Chorus of Disapproval* with a huge cast of long-time Company members (among them Julia Blake). Sumner was an old-fashioned director with a reputation for scapegoating and demoralising at least one member of the cast in every production. Max watched him terrorise a young stage manager while charming the rest of the company ostentatiously.

There were a few memorable, even inspiring seasons, productions and performances on local stages over the years: Wal Cherry guesting as artistic director for a year at UTRC, with a brilliant *Threepenny Opera*, Tennessee Williams' *Camino Real*, and Ionesco's *Rhinoceros* with a more experimental approach than normal at the UTRC. Max was transfixed by one slight and softly spoken actor called George Ogilvie who played the lead in each, extraordinary in his ability to transform utterly and making a lasting impression. Nearly a decade later the same artist transformed into a unique ensemble creator and director for the MTC in its time at the Athenaeum Theatre.

Led by Ron Danielson, Lois and John Ellis, Max helped to set up Melbourne Youth Theatre (MYT), directing a production of John Arden's *Sergeant Musgrave's Dance* and the young John Wood in Henry Livings' *Eh?* He coached Wood for his successful audition for NIDA in 1968, ten years after his own unsuccessful audition. In a MYT production, Max appeared as Barney in *Summer of the Seventeenth Doll* for the Youth Theatre, with Kerry Dwyer playing

Olive. There would be three plays by Beckett, notably Elijah Moshinski's production of *Krapp's Last Tape*. The bare, new Monash campus was heaving with young, eager, politically minded students – often the first in their family to attend university, angry and vocal about Vietnam and the long reign of conservative government in Australia. They were outspoken, anti-authoritarian and committed to exploring their creative selves.

Pram People

When Betty Burstall opened the tiny La Mama Theatre in Carlton suddenly another venue off campus became available. It was an exciting time in the small world of theatre in Melbourne. Local playwrights were activated, including Jack Hibberd and John Romeril. Everyone was reading the *Tulane Review*. The essential notion of what theatre could mean was expanding beyond the proscenium: 'living theatre', street theatre, devised theatre, theatre with the emphasis on the performer as key creator rather than as a tool of the playwright or director. The visionary young Rupert Murdoch had created *The Australian* and a platform for the first national theatre critic, Katharine Brisbane, transforming access to information about the theatre; for the first time in Australia theatre audiences could follow developments in theatre all over the nation. Through drama festivals on the campuses of the two universities Max met Graeme Blundell, a dark-haired, bushy eyebrowed devotee of the theatre, who read drama journals, carried a brief case and talked nineteen to the dozen. Graeme Blundell called the new theatre group he helped form at La Mama, the Australian Performing Group; it included Bill Garner, Peter Cummins and Kerry Dwyer, and focused on the idea of the performer as a prime creator of theatre: it toured to Perth, picking up a few more members on its way home: Tim Robertson living in the Adelaide Hills and teaching with Wal Cherry at Flinders University, a couple of circus performers and others. John Timlin took a lease on an old panel beaters workshop in Drummond Street for the troupe, sharing the two-storey building with *The New Theatre* (surviving cultural arm of the Australian Communist Party) sharing the rent and the ground-level area. The venue became known as the Pram Factory. In their spare time, the troupe worked tirelessly to strip out grime, remove junk and discard machinery to re-make the unusual performance space with its distinctive tower, as a working space for themselves.

The company's work was blokey, highly physical, irreverent, comic and rough, with a nod to university revue and street theatre elements – the kind of theatre its performers knew best. It drew on melodrama and popular theatre and revelled in the interaction of performers with the audience. Many of the actors shared a keen interest in comic performance and vaudeville while others felt that theatre should focus on exposing class politics, and that performers could be themselves on stage, rather than playing a character. All of them held to the ideals of the Left, but argued constantly and sometimes viciously about what they were and how they might apply in the theatre.[10] Overalls and hand knitted jumpers were favoured garments, there were lots of meetings and attendance was mandatory: true collectivity is an intense and demanding business and maintaining the ideals of a theatre open to and relevant to the immediate community presented a serious challenge. Artistic vision through consensus is rarely sustainable. The remarkable thing about

---

10   Tim Robertson 2001 *The Pram Factory: The Australian Performing Group Recollected*, Melbourne: Melbourne University Press, p. 50.

the APG is that it lasted for as long as it did, and that it achieved so much both artistically and socially: it was an experiment in theatre that transformed performance in Australia. When they weren't at tense, serious meetings, arguing at full volume about the tenets of their own Melbourne-style Maoism and how to prevent the writers from dominating the performers, many of the members indulged in beer, wine, marijuana, heroin and sexual adventurism. Everyone behaved excessively, factions formed and re-formed as new members from circus, high schools and universities joined the group, and others left.

Blundell secured an arts grant for the APG to hold a six-month theatre workshop, and invited Max and several others to join the workshop. One of the first projects they set out to create involved documenting their own parents' lives. A young teacher called Helen Garner (married to Bill) agreed to take charge of the writing up of the interviews. But a month later, the project agenda changed to focus on Melbourne prior to Federation at time of the Boer War – the contemporary parallel in the engagement with Vietnam was striking. Just as in the present, with young men conscripted to serve, the Boer War had stolen, brutalised and killed young Australian lads. Gold rushes in central Victoria in the nineteenth century had created a land boom transforming Melbourne into an ostentatious Victorian metropolis. The evolving APG project would reflect these forces and become a satirical pageant/play with short scenes, and music that all of the group developed together. *Marvellous Melbourne* would become the definitional event for the APG in its new home for its remaining decade.

Marvellous Melbourne, with material contributed by Hibberd and Romeril and improvised by the performers in collaboration with the others, opened in the small upstairs space to an audience of friends, family and curious locals on 11 December 1970. The production was significant in many ways because of its group-devised material, emphasis on performers driving the creative process, and because of the independent cooperative mode of the production. The process of developing *Marvellous Melbourne* served as the model for the APG for the next few years. It also showed the appeal and resonance of politically charged live theatre. Max enthusiastically embraced the collective ethos, sharing of responsibilities and anti-authoritarian stance of the members. He was one of the oldest members of the group at 30 and approached the task of working collectively with intense focus. No one member had artistic or financial control. The question of sustaining the group preoccupied Max who was elected as chair of the steering committee. Anyone who contributed to the operation was a voting member. Attendance at meetings was vital and the requirements of the collective inevitably caused friction. Jack Hibberd left in high dudgeon a few times, coaxed back by Max. Several of the women, irritated with what they saw as the male dominated structures and approaches to theatre making, set up their own collective, producing *Betty Can Jump* with just one male performer invited into the show. It was a huge success. Max and several others continued to work in their day jobs outside the APG, and pooled their income in order to support the ongoing activities of the performing group.

Max kept up with the group ethos at the same time as developing his own individual performance style. In Barry Oakley's play *The Feet of Daniel Mannix*, he played Bob Santamaria who was named Greensleaves, but readily identified by his voice, produced by Max brilliantly as he parodied the right wing Catholic anti-communist with cloak and dagger, thrilling the audiences with the seamless caricature. It was a lesson in imitation for Max that highlighted the use of the voice as an essential part of impersonation. In a revue called the *Sonia Knee and Thigh Show*, Romeril had a Pinocchio-inspired take parodying Billy McMahon and his wife Sonia, known for her audacious appearance at the White House wearing a gown that was split provocatively up to the thigh. Max played the diminutive McMahon on his knees, in a wig, mask and huge oversized ears. Vic Marsh played the PM's press secretary and every time McMahon told a lie his penis would grow – a huge sausage like appendix that draped down from Max's crotch over the stage and down the stairs. The press secretary, in an effort to disguise the embarrassing phallus, would take off an item of clothing to cover the ever-lengthening appendage. The sketch raised the roof and for Max marked his first impersonation of a prime minister.

One autumn night in 1972 Max noticed the patrician figure of the leader of the federal Labor party, Gough Whitlam, in the front row of the audience, his long legs squeezed uncomfortably against the hard wooden bench seating. A frisson of excitement passed through the performers as they registered that their work had caught the attention of this charismatic left wing leader and champion of the arts. A young writer called David Williamson, who referred to himself as a student Maoist, contributed sketch material to the *Sonia Knee and Thigh Show*, including a sketch in which actors playing building inspectors began to remove audience members from their seats and to dismantle the theatre, in a parody of the massive destruction of old buildings and working-class neighbourhoods for freeways that was rampant in Melbourne at the time. Even Gough Whitlam was dislodged from his front row position, in this sketch written by Williamson. Whitlam took it with grace but Max winced at Gough's evident discomfort.

When the Whitlam Government was elected at the end of that year and the Performing Group secured funding, Max gave up his lecturing job to work full time in the APG for a fraction of the salary he had earned over the last ten years. He had no hesitation in dedicating himself to the Group and any income he obtained from occasional work at the ABC or other acting assignments was donated to the APG. For him the theatre was a true commune. It was also a stand-in family, replete with conflict and tension.

Max appeared in a wild and anarchic production of Hibberd's *Dimboola* in 1973 directed by David Williamson. But it was the premiere production of Williamson's *Don's Party* at the Pram Factory, performed in the round, that was contentious amongst the members of the performing group, particularly the women, and attracted great interest, played for long seasons and brought Williamson to a national audience. Some of the actors also appeared in productions at La Mama around the corner in Williamson's *The Removalists*. Australian plays were now being performed regularly and attracting large, enthusiastic audiences.

The most popular show during the ten years of the Pram Factory was another group-developed comic piece called *The Hills Family Show*. It was to become Max's most successful initiative, proposed as a performer-driven vehicle to utilise the talents of a chosen group whose ideas, comic personae and improvisational flair had been evident in workshops. It was a show that encapsulated the ethos of the APG, putting performers at the centre of the creative development of the entire production and for Max came with a certain risk. Embracing the company's evolving ethos he argued that a writer be brought in at the end of the process instead of at its instigation. The show would portray a dysfunctional family of travelling performers hanging on to their old-fashioned vaudeville acts: each performer in the Group had to develop a character and learn a performance act to play in the show. Max played a Chaplinesque drunken ventriloquist, the dreamy looking, dark-eyed Tony Taylor played a tormented young crooner in a green felt tuxedo with sequins, a costume that he made himself, arguing constantly about the music, with his sister and with his wheelchair-bound grandmother who had been a bare-back rider in her day and cracked the whip from her chair. The feisty, curly haired Evelyn Krape careened around the stage on one wheel in the role and one night, after she used her potty, she tipped the contents over a member of the audience. It was only water and the member of the audience was a member of the group, a writer, who was mortified but unlikely to make a fuss. Like the Whitlam incident it revealed the license and freedom that the actors arrogated to themselves, and the dangers thereof.[11] Tony Taylor and Bill Garner presented a mind-reading act that involved the audience, developed after weeks of research at the public library on how to ensure that the codes for the mind-reading would work. The family drama surfaced gradually as the show proceeded. *The Hills Family Show* was a huge success and toured to Sydney, Adelaide and rural towns in South Australia. Arriving one lunch time in a one-horse hamlet in the Victorian Wimmera the cast could not find anywhere open to eat; the place appeared deserted. They wondered whether a single soul would come to the show. When the doors opened however in the cool of the evening, locals piled in, with hordes of children and farmers from far flung properties, all of

---

11 Margaret Williams, 'The Pram Family Show', formerly available from https://www.pramfactory.com/family.html. Accessed 1 March 2017.

them excited at the prospect of live entertainment. Max recalls the joy of this performance because of the enthusiasm of the audience and their delight in every part of the show. Improvisation flourished and Tony Taylor's character Winston (or Windy) Hills, exasperated with his wild 'grandmother', wheeled her out of the hall followed by a crowd of eager, skipping children like the pied piper, and parked her on the railway line in the vast darkness of the desert. Under the stars in the dome of the night, the performers, who were exhausted from touring, still found ways of enchanting the audience, in their crucible of encouragement and warmth.

Max is by nature a cautious and deliberative person. He is a serious minded, reflective and careful performer. When Jack Hibberd asked him to consider playing Monk O'Neill in the premiere production of *A Stretch of the Imagination* he demurred. He admired the play but felt Peter Cummins' relative seniority and capability made him a more suitable choice. More importantly he could not envisage a way of inhabiting the character and turned down the opportunity. During an APG tour with another of Jack's plays, *A Toast to Melba*, during the Adelaide Festival in 1976, Max saw a solo show by the English vaudeville performer Max Wall. It was a revelation to him. Wall's persona was ambiguous, deconstructing his own performance as he proceeded. He leant forward, bottom out, his large, bulbous head leering in to the footlights. Suddenly Max imagined a way of playing Monk O'Neill. The following year he played the role in the second APG production at the Pram Factory, touring to Sydney and Canberra, Brisbane and Perth. He used the disdainfulness and grotesque physical excess he had observed in Max Wall's abrasive performance in order to essay Monk O'Neill. It was an important production for Gillies who now knew that he could carry a full play on his own. Max reprised the role as an older man in 1990, and told me that he feels far from finished with the play and the character and would happily play O'Neill again.

Squirts

Many Australians know Max for his portrayal of politicians on television. His distinctive talent for impersonation and for inhabiting the character of these public figures, in addition to his invented characters, has a long and colourful history. It all began with a burlesque stage show. For a number of years David Williamson had been pressing Max to develop a vehicle for displaying what David thought to be his unique theatrical wares. The genesis for *Squirts* lay in discussions Max had held with John Timlin and Neil Armfield for an evening of cultural and political portraits. The title was a term common in playgrounds when Max had been in primary school but by now seemed archaic. He'd been reading the autobiographical recollections of Sir Robert Menzies, retired Prime Minister and founder of the modern Liberal Party. Max was taken by the elderly politician's condescending description of many of his Cabinet colleagues as 'squirts', one in particular, Billy McMahon, Menzies referred to as a 'contemptible little squirt'. If the word was reverberant for such a linguistic giant as Menzies, Max thought, it should suffice as a show title.

In a forlorn motel on Glen Osmond Road in Adelaide, during the icy winter of 1981, Max, Neil Armfield, Alan John and Evelyn Krape hunkered down to make final plans for the show due to open in less than a month at the newish Adelaide Festival Centre. *Squirts* had already acquired a frisson of notoriety. A cheekily provocative full-page advertisement had been taken out by Paul Iles, the company manager and stirrer, pledging to shake up the town's staid burghers with cutting edge satire. The ad promised a revue featuring two of the Pram Factory's prominent comics, with Alan John as MD and Neil Armfield directing. There was one insurmountable hurdle: they hadn't been able to agree on a final script and were at loggerheads over the content of the show.

As the days passed tempers frayed. Questions were asked of the conservative government about taxpayer subsidy of subversive political theatre. Sight unseen, the project was acquiring an incendiary reputation with parliamentary threats to reduce the Company's next annual grant by the cost of the production. If the truth had been known, the clamour might have escalated into a major arts industry scandal the like of which only Adelaide can rise to. Far from there being scurrilous content, there was virtually no content at all. Although 24 writers had submitted scripts there had been continuous disagreement among the company about the final choice. A fortnight out from production week Evelyn left the project, returning to Melbourne with her new baby. Decisions were now made quickly, but there was virtually no time left to rehearse, let alone finesse a show which had now become a cabaret for one actor and a pianist. A review of the pile of scripts yielded great riches. Apart from the APG stalwarts Max was intrigued by a number of pieces by Patrick Cook, the cartoonist of *The National Times* and *The Bulletin*. In these garrulous streams of consciousness Max discerned an original voice that was erudite and astute. And even more delightful, he found playable comic characters.

Another uniquely new voice was that of Don Watson. Don had written parody lyrics for a national song which was to open the show and was so far the only act that had been agreed on. Max had rehearsed it already as a Victorian recitalist, with Alan John as accompanist. Stephen Curtis had designed a fancy three-piece suit befitting a pompous parlour singer, finished off with a little coiffed toupee which flew off on the final note. Max was already fond of the piece, confident that if the rest of the show's material approached it for quality, they'd have a potential hit on their hands. Unfortunately, to this point it was the sole item. Then, suddenly fate intervened and snatched even that away.

The original composer of the song lived in Adelaide. His name was Henry Krips and he was Resident Conductor of the South Australian Symphony Orchestra. Krips had been alerted by a gossip columnist that the scurrilous *Squirts* crew were planning to use his music. Fearing for his own reputation, he sent word that it wasn't to be used. Krips had fled the Nazi occupation of his native Austria in the 1930s and established himself in Australia. The song in question had been his winning entry in a 1950s competition for a new national anthem for Australia. It was a cut above 'Advance Australia Fair' and Max remembered it from his school days when it held brief currency.

Desperate to ensure that there was a show ready for opening night Max tracked down the eminent musician and pleaded with him for permission to use the song. For Max, it was a fruitless but poignant encounter. Krips, an urbane and sophisticated man, seemed fearful for himself, as if he was an outsider. His urbanity seemed to Max to be paper-thin in this Lutheran outpost. Weimar cabaret in his youth was in a different universe from establishment Adelaide where clearly he had never been made to feel at home. Krips could not be persuaded to allow the use of his music, lest he be thought to endorse dissent. Over the next few days Don Watson frantically wrote new lyrics and Alan John new music.

Max Gillies.
(Photographer unknown.)
Courtesy of ABC and Arts Centre Melbourne,
Australian Performing Arts Collection.

Max worked around the clock to prepare sketches for the seventeen characters he would play, eventually working up material from Watson, Patrick Cook, David Williamson, Barry Oakley, John Romeril, Stephen Sewell and Tim Robertson. One of Don's offerings included a whimsical portrayal of Robert Menzies in billowing angel wings returning to earth to waft across the stage. Romeril supplied a deranged character intent on unmasking the Prime Minister's wife as a secret communist. Madame Kransky (the transgendered doppelganger of Frank Knopfelmacher – a well-known academic cold-war warrior) stomped across the stage in a black hessian sack and desert boots (per Stephen Curtis again) demonstrating her theory about Tammy Fraser through numerology. Robertson's piece lampooned the conservative columnist David MacNicol in a character called St John McNoodle, described in the program as a 'lag, layabout and a bore so prodigious as to maintain a totally unsatisfying interest in himself all his life'. The satire was biting and the dramaturgy challenging (requiring one actor to play six characters in the one piece). In another sketch called 'This Place Was Made for Whites', the overt racism of the mining magnate Lang Hancock came in for a pasting. The program sarcastically described the song written for the sketch as a 'sentimental ditty about the extent of the obstruction of our progress by the Aboriginal people'.

But as the opening night approached, the pressures were intense. Overwrought and exhausted during a preliminary run-through, Max heard a hideous crack as a tendon at the back of his knee snapped. Unable to move, he was paralysed with pain: the show could not go on and the opening was postponed for a week. When it finally opened Max resigned himself to playing every character in a plaster cast and on crutches. There would be no wafting through the audience as Menzies with wings, and no stomping as Madame Kransky, the cranky numerologist.

Max recalls the whole experience of the first production of *Squirts* as a fiasco – so coloured is his memory of the threats to the future of the theatre company, as well as his injury, exhaustion and stress. But it was a remarkable achievement and it was unique in Australian theatre to see an actor playing real figures such as Malcolm Fraser, Robert Menzies, John Kerr, John Singleton and Allan McGillvray, and performing ridiculous invented characters such as the transgender

Dame Toby Fitzyarra. Not only could Max carry an entire play as he had proven in *A Stretch of the Imagination*, he could mimic an array of politicians in a fast-paced revue of sixteen sketches, singing and dancing his way through the program. *Squirts* played in Melbourne and the publicity drew on the pre-season furore of Adelaide: 'Yes, folks it's *Squirts*, billed at the Adelaide Festival Centre as potentially the most offensive night out in ages'. The open-ended Melbourne run, in a sparkling new venue, the Universal Theatre, helped to consolidate the show and refine it over the next month and a half. By the time it opened in Sydney the bugs had been shaken out, the title changed to *A Night with the Right* and it became something of an overnight sensation.

Scandal seemed to follow Max though, and the sketch called 'Advance Australia', satirising 'a fantastic media man with the common touch', who 'gives us a glimpse into the world of really big bikkies', almost had the show closed down. John Singleton identified himself with the character called Thingo in Sewell's piece, which had been one of the show's highlights since its Adelaide debut. Singo set a legal team on Gillies, serving an injunction to close the show. Forced to attend a 'conference' and 'without prejudice' about the supposedly offensive material, Max was prepared in his own 'defence' for the lawyers, to argue that there was no script so the defamation could not be evidenced, much less proven. Without a recording, a live performance was an ephemeral thing. Max duly arrived at the plush Sydney legal office, to find the lawyer for the Nimrod Theatre and the lawyer for the ad man already seated in a 'conversation pit' covered in a thick shag pile carpet. Max stepped down into the pit, naively confident of his own defence. Before he could even attempt to argue that there was no script and therefore nothing defamatory, he realised that the Nimrod lawyer had supplied a script of the sketch in question to Singleton himself, and the lawyer read from it claiming that his client was hurt by its insinuations. Max's distress was compounded when he realised that the theatre management had supplied the unedited version which was nearly half as long again as the performing script. An own goal to be sure. His heart sank as the lawyers pontificated, and his back began to ache from sitting in the ludicrous and uncomfortable pit. After much argument, it was agreed that the show would continue with the act excised and the audience alerted that a section had been truncated. It took a fortnight or so before an agreed replacement script could be written, approved and rehearsed. The overwhelming response of the nightly audience was of bewilderment.

Max and Hawkie

When Bob Hawke was elected Prime Minister in 1983, Max panicked: suddenly he had a large problem. For the first time in years Australians had elected a moderate, and what's more, someone with whom Max sympathised. He couldn't imagine how to mock this effervescent man of the people. What would he satirise? How would he play someone as charismatic as this savvy, wavy-haired populist? The inspiration came via his writing partner, Don Watson, a history teacher at the time. Don had been alerted by one of his students to the similarity between Hawke and an American televangelist. They spent a couple of Sunday mornings watching *The Hour of Power*, with its fast-talking slick star in his glass cathedral. Both Max and Don were struck by the zeal and panache of the pastor who might have modelled himself on the new Australian Prime Minister, Robert James Lee Hawke. Suddenly it all made sense: Hawke's father had been a Baptist minister after all and his son revelled in the showmanship of politics. The theatricality of the man would be vital to any parody, Max realised, and could drive the impersonation.

Max wasted no time ordering a shining silvery suit, sharply cut shirts with long cuffs and sparkling, large cufflinks, in addition to an expensive wavy-haired wig. He watched *The Hour of Power* over and over again, followed by footage of Hawke addressing press club lunches in Canberra, observing his mannerisms and gestures, listening to his intonation and syntax and watching his facial expressions with intense focus, in order to play the short, bumptious union man come national leader. The new show would be called *A Night of National Reconciliation*, referring to Hawke's main theme: the prices and wages accord, and reconciliation between workers and bosses, as part of a new dawn for economic development in Australia. Don Watson wrote several scripts for this show: it was a new beginning for Max and Don in a writing partnership that had begun with *Squirts* and lasted for many years – effectively until Don switched sides, becoming the speech writer of choice for the politicians themselves.

Kinsela's Night Club gave down-at-heel Darlinghurst a new glamour at Taylor Square in the early 1980s. The art deco ex-funeral parlour, transformed into a voguish night spot for the Sydney's smart set, including its political and journalistic elite, would become the home of the final iteration of Max's revue. What had started out as *Squirts*, becoming *A Night with the Right*, would now become the toast of Sydney as *A Night of National Reconciliation*, and run for nine months. Max made up his face using a torch and a shaving mirror in a tiny room at the side of the makeshift stage at the outwardly glamorous Kinsela's.

Max Gillies as Bob Hawke, *The Gillies Report* 1985.
Courtesy of ABC TV and Arts Centre Melbourne, Australian Performing Arts Collection.

Gillies' portrayal of Hawke struck a chord with Australians in a way that no other impersonation has done before or since. Sometimes people in the street behaved towards Max as if he was Hawke, and would react to him as the headstrong, self-regarding Prime Minister. The PM himself reacted with pugilistic approbation. If this suggested ambivalence, it was appropriate given the ambiguity in Max's portrayal – equal parts critique and celebration. The reaction revealed a lot about Hawke. It was with trepidation that Max prepared for a day when he was to appear alongside his satirical target at a major event. It is not often that performers appear in the presence of those they impersonate, and it was the first and only time in Australian history that a Prime Minister has allowed it. Max was invited to address the North Melbourne Football Club grand-final breakfast in character as the PM, knowing that Hawke would be a guest of honour. Max tingled as he entered the enormous Southern Cross dining room, a sea of faces turned towards him and hundreds of outstretched hands began clasping his, as he made the long walk through the tables, passing dozens of excited, rowdy guests. It was a room brimming with testosterone and when Max finally reached the top table he was almost deafened by the shouting and the applause, as if he were the PM. Shaking hands with everyone at the high table he ran the gauntlet of the Club President, the Lord Mayor of Melbourne and finally the man himself, Robert J L Hawke. The leering Prime Minister grabbed Max's hand so vigorously his wrist throbbed and before he knew it Hawke had pulled him into a tight face-to-face, with cameras flashing all around them. Max blinked as Hawke suddenly let go of his hand and brought his fist to Max's nose, punching him in a stinging bop to his nose, as he turned to approach the podium to give his performance of the man who had just hit him.

It was a playful but not painless pre-emptive 'alpha male' warning to the actor. The relationship of satirist and subject was maintained in brittle equilibrium for the next decade, the theatre of politics and the politics of theatre inextricable in this chaotic, distinctively Australian spectacle.

Gillies was not the only performer who seemed to have a knack for mockery of the larrikin foibles of Australian men, and their awkward performances of masculinity. Barry Humphries and Paul Hogan parodied men in their own comic creations. Max mimicked real, high profile men and his parodies were unique in their sharpness and vigour. A New Zealander called John Clarke took his own approach to the task of mocking his compatriots in a composite sheep farmer character called Fred Dagg. Max first heard Clarke as his odd character on the ABC's Science Show, speculating about existential philosophy – a kind of blokey subversion of academic-speak that sparkled with wit and whimsical humour. Max encountered Clarke around the traps and noticed how encouraging John was of young performers in the fringe cabaret world. When Max first began to develop a solo revue of his own (although at the time he did not know this was what it was) he had approached John to write some material for the show. John had a gift for monologue and the two of them sat in Max's small flat in North Melbourne laughing and talking for hours without putting pen to paper. A week would pass without any sign of John or a script until they met again. Max would telephone and say 'How did you go with the writing?' By then John and Max had forgotten what they talked about and so would meet again. It happened several times, neither of them thinking to record their session as a prompt, but each enjoying the company of the other on every occasion. Eventually Max developed a show with material from some 30 writers from which to select – *Squirts* – but conspicuously nothing from John who was sheepishly apologetic about his failure to submit anything for the show.

Squirts had been an object lesson in the protean character of the theatre. The show became a hit in Sydney that would kick-start Max Gillies' television career in political satire. By the time he returned to Melbourne briefly to reprise its Sydney success, the glittering opening at Her Majesty's Theatre was a far cry from the tiny cabaret dives in which he had so often worked, with no backstage area or proper dressing room in which to execute his lightning-quick costume changes. To make up for failing to deliver Max a script for the show John Clarke now offered to make a verbal contribution, crafting a distinctive announcement to bridge two sketches and cover a costume change. The Fred Dagg voice-over became a feature of the show thereafter. Max had explained that such an interlude 'to amuse the audience while I'm offstage' would be as valuable as a script for a new sketch. John produced a gem for the interlude, writing and performing it for the show. He appeared at Max's house to record it one day, and spent hours obsessively refining the 90-second piece, perfecting and polishing. Max was gobsmacked by John's fixation with getting the detail right, but at every subsequent performance as he made his off-stage quick change, he smiled to himself at its brilliance, and marvelled at John's apparently spontaneous perfection, at the casual perfection he achieved.

Max and John became close friends and Max found John's candour about his own anxieties as a performer both endearing and revelatory. His success as Fred Dagg, he told Max, had led him to excessive behaviour and he was unsettled by its precipitate effect. Clarke seemed to Max to fear, even loathe performing because of its effect on him, preferring writing as a consequence. It would be years before Max caught a glimmer of understanding of John's complex relationship with performance, and to experience a not dissimilar confusion.

TV Land

During the late 1970s Max made many forays into television. There were characters in the series *Flash Nick from Jindivik*, with Grahame Bond, Rory O'Donoghue and Garry McDonald, the TV adaptation of Barry Oakley's *Wild Ass of a Man* and a number of episodes of the comedy playhouse *Tickled Pink*, a varied slate of comedies both broad and narrow, and in retrospect, bearing a significant risk of immersion in water. *Wild Ass* was shot in the middle of winter but required a couple of swims at the end of a pier, a midnight skinny-dip in a lake and a fully clothed fall into an ornamental pond on a university campus. Lit and shot in slow motion to appear to be at the height of summer, not only was the water icy in Port Phillip Bay, but the weather was inclement. The degree of difficulty made the notion of acting seem farcical and was compounded as he watched from the water at the end of the pier, as back on shore the counterweighted boom arm of the camera on its rig was blown down in a gale, toppling the operator and bringing a premature halt to the entire folly.

Waterman, one of the *Tickled Pink* comedies, was written by Morris Lurie who had worked in an advertising agency with Peter Carey and Barry Oakley. The television play portrayed a copywriter who retreated to the bathtub for the day when he needed inspiration. Max had to sit in a large circular bath for the entire shoot, a full five days. He was covered in protective oil but it was not easy sitting in water all day. The script was superb in Max's view, with various visitors appearing to speak to the man in the bath as the play progressed. The man's son, played by Jacki Weaver's son, Dylan, walked in to show his Dad that he has been injured and is sent off to the freezer for ice to put on his bruised face, the cleaning lady played, by Dawn Lake, mopped around him, and the local police officer strode into the bathroom to remind the naked copywriter that he had 40 parking tickets, dropping them into the bath in a plastic bag. The last one to appear was his wife, played by Maggie Dence, who deposits a bowl of some kind of inedible, health food on the side of the bath. Throughout the play the protagonist attempts to write advertising copy to sell a golf club, fearing that if he cannot come up with the goods he will lose his job. By day three of filming, everything was going well until Max realised that his scrotum was stinging and had taken on the texture of blistered cellophane. He struggled on until the pain became insistent, and the cellophane effect was more like celluloid. He complained of extreme pain, and was hauled out of the bath and ferried off to a specialist in Maquarie Street, who prescribed large quantities of oatmeal to be fed into the bath: Max doggedly continued.

As well as the comedies, there was a notable episode in Sandra Levy's realist social drama series *Spring and Fall*. In *The Last Card* Max was cast by the writer-director Michael Jenkins as an alcoholic insurance salesman. Max had formed a rapport with Jenkins on *Waterman* and other comedies, and found his actor-centred approach innovative and successful. (His distinguished CV includes many of Australia's best television drama and includes *Blue Murder, Scales of Justice*, and *Careful He Might Hear You*.) In this next drama Robyn Nevin played the wife of the alcoholic salesman, with their daughter played by Arky Whiteley. Jenkins was a risk taker. He specifically cast actors whose life experience had been touched by addiction and domestic abuse. Michael's own family had been affected by alcoholism and had written the script for this searing realist drama. Jenkins asked Max to do a first reading of the script with a video camera to record Max while he drank heavily, to see the effect on his performance. Max was cautious, believing it was crossing a line for him as an actor. But he agreed to do it because he trusted Jenkins and he was open to what the experiment might yield. Max drank an enormous number of beers, a small bottle of whiskey and assorted other drinks during the initial reading. He was out of control during the recorded reading and for three days felt emotionally devastated and physically ill after the event. Watching the video back was instructive but also disturbing. Encouraged by the experiment, Jenkins suggested shooting some of the scenes with Gillies actually affected by drink. Max agreed but insisted on filming alternate scenes sober so that there was a choice of material for the final. This process was hard on both cast and crew. When Max, in his drunken role, smashed up the kitchen, destroying all the glassware the family owned, and lay on the floor afterwards while continuity was assessed, an on-set nurse came to check on him, whispering with tears in her eyes, that she had lived with this kind of behaviour herself for 30 years. The drama is convincing, the play was a success on television and is still used by therapists as a tool to this day.

The Gillies Report

For much of the 1970s various ideas from the Carlton gangs had been rejected by the ABC, *Australia, You're Standing in It* the singular exception. Channel 9 management made serious overtures after the triumph of *Squirts* in its final Kinsela's version, but Max believed the commercial environment would be anathema to the sort of satire he had in mind. The acting head of Light Entertainment at the ABC, Michael Shrimpton, recognised that the ABC was deficient in topical, quizzical sharpness, and the new government and its newly appointed ABC board would want the cobwebs cleared. Shrimpton made a tentative approach, inviting Max to produce a pre-recorded old-fashioned revue. Max said anything less than a live weekly mauling of the national political carcass was not worth the effort. Eventually Shrimpton agreed on the proviso that all the scripts were subject to legal vetting. A pilot was made for a notional seven-part political satire for which there was no counterpart on Australian TV. The nearest anyone could imagine was *The Mavis Bramston Show* which had screened for the first time twenty years earlier, and consisted in some of its episodes of actors perched on stools reading arch allusions to the news of the day. The pilot was judged a success and a seven-week season was scheduled, for a Monday evening slot during prime time.

No sooner had the new program been scheduled than the Prime Minister unexpectedly announced a federal election to run for an unprecedented eight-week campaign, the longest within memory by far. The season of *The Gillies Report* would exactly overlap the campaign. Max couldn't believe his good fortune. But it triggered the first battle with ABC management which would typify the relationship over four seasons. There were two aspects to these battles: management's instinctive impulse to pre-emptively buckle in the face of anticipated political pressure, and its transparent neediness for deference from program makers. Shrimpton called Max to propose that the show run be delayed until the election was over – ostensibly to evade undue pressure on Max and the team. After a shouting match down the line from Sydney to Melbourne, Max prevailed and the program went ahead as planned. It may have been a Pyrrhic victory since none of the subsequent disputes ended in his favour.

The Gillies Report propelled Max into the national spotlight on television, making him a household name. Its evolution was gradual and grew out of the stage show developed over ten years in which Max drew on all of his revue, cabaret and vaudeville work at the Pram Factory. The new television show was vitally important to Max because he wanted to reassert the performance style that generated his popular work. He believed that he was both more and less than a mimic. He never sought to compete with the likes of Gerry Connolly as an impersonator or Paul Jennings for vocal mimicry, but he did believe in the full satirical potential of his vaudevillian portraits of living politicians. He wanted to create a complete theatricalised characterisation and embody a living story of a person in a way that was different from both naturalistic acting and pure impersonation. For Max the joy came from the transformation into a character.

Max's first choices of TV Director were initially vetoed by management. Both Michael Jenkins and Ted Robinson had an independent bent and both had endured run-ins with the ABC hierarchy in the past. Max was familiar with Jenkins from the *Tickled Pink* comedies and *The Last Card*, and valued his great skill as a writer and director, his respect for actors and genuinely collaborative approach: for example, he would never shoot until he felt the actor was ready, but Shrimpton was adamant that he was out of contention. Initially he had vetoed Max's other choice. Ted Robinson had directed the *Flash Nick* episodes with the anarchic Aunty Jack gang. Ted's energy and inventiveness inspired a fierce loyalty from casts and crew. He was no favourite with management either however; he had also upset them with the risqué and controversial television series *Alvin Purple*. Fortunately, Shrimpton relented and Max felt lucky to have a director with whom he knew he could work. Ted was hyper-theatrical in his approach to the art of revue, and an expert at directing the large-scale, highly choreographed musical sketch segments they hoped to include. Once Ted was appointed the work began. The content, format and style of the show was still hazy at this point and Max found Ted had little interest in conceptualising: he characteristically only became fully engaged and energised on the studio floor and in the control room. He would arrive in Melbourne for story conferences and writing workshops, and doze during the first hour. He had little interest in re-inventing the wheel. One criticism of the show would be that its format was unoriginal, but Max was happy that nevertheless its loose parameters gave ample space for the creative energies of a very talented team. As soon as the performing began however, Ted came to life, relishing the rehearsing and recording processes. Max had been keen for the title of the show to satirise a current tabloid TV news program going under the host journalist's own name. *Willesee* was an early example of celebrity branding and personality-driven current affairs journalism. In this context Max was keen to call his new show *Gillisee*. Although important to Max this would be one of many decisions that Ted showed little interest in, beyond a dampening negativity. Max particularly did not want the show named after himself unless it was to parody *Willesee* but as an on-air date raced towards them without a suitable alternative, it became *The Gillies Report*. For Max, it went against the grain to call the show after just one performer, himself, when the project was an ensemble creation. But on this he lost the battle. It was typical of a compromise by default that seemed to be endemic in the land of television.

The Gillies Report was an unprecedented success, attracting and delighting large audiences. Max's powers of mimicry and rich, politically potent satirical impersonations seized the imagination of the whole country; the hyper- theatricality of the sketches and rollicking musical production numbers struck a chord with television viewers. If there is a *piece de resistance* in *The Gillies Report*, it is the opera parody of the events of the dismissal of the Whitlam Government, entitled *Il Dismissale*. The original idea for the sketch came from one of the writers, Phil Scott. The seven-minute musical parody is the most significant satirical sketch ever produced in Australia. The idea to create a pastiche opera was ingenious, and the use of Puccini's 'Nessun Dorma' was inspired, coming years before it was used to promote the World Cup Soccer tournament. Phil Scott and Patrick Cook wrote the words, borrowing from several other tunes in addition to the Puccini favourite from *Turandot*, and John Clarke provided a hilarious introduction as well as performing in the extended sketch. In a blonde comb over wig Clarke introduced the segment as a news reader, explaining that it was 'over produced' and 'baroque' and almost as expensive as the roof spire on the Victorian Arts Centre; he informed viewers that the piece would 'gloss over the facts' and described the recent events in our history about to be portrayed in the aria as 'tawdry, dreadful and pitifully shameful'. In glorious parody of the average monolingual Australian, he stumbled over the name of Puccini and the screen show credit flashed up, denoting the 'author' as Gian-Carlo Trimbole (Robert Trimbole was a notorious crime boss figure involved in drug trafficking in New South Wales). Max played the four protagonists: Whitlam, Kerr,

Fraser and the Queen, in this extraordinary musical parody of the constitutional crisis of 1975.

The production was an elaborate masterpiece, with costumes sewn by in-house tailors and seamstresses and ingeniously crafted sets. The Melbourne Symphony Orchestra provided the music, requiring Max to record his soundtrack in the studio one night. It was a challenge for him to produce all the voices on cue, on his own in the studio, while the orchestra played in an adjoining studio. He is not a trained singer and found the experience difficult but strangely liberating. After the sound track was recorded the full ensemble cast and twenty-something extras rehearsed and then recorded the magnificent *Il Dismissale* in the course of a ten-hour day. All the regular cast members appeared in the extravaganza: Wendy Harmer, Patrick Cook, John Clarke, Geoff Kelso and Tracy Harvey. The lyrics compress all of the political characters' foibles into a series of short, witty lines that capture the essence of each one in exaggerated and hilarious parody. As it opened, the chorus, standing in front of Doric pillars and dressed in the flowing robes of ancient Greek senators sang, with Max answering every line as the tall, haughty leader of the country:

> Chorus: Gough is our nation's leader,
> Gough: Power and fame are mine.
> Chorus: We've had three years of Labor. We're in because we said 'it's Time'. Life couldn't be more sublime.
> Gough: The arts have increased funding. How do you like Blue Poles?
> Chorus: Who'll pay for that we're wondering.
> Gough: Rex said he'd ask Khemlani.

Max then transformed from Whitlam into Fraser, in a brown suit and steel-rimmed spectacles, poking his head around a pillar like a music hall villain, looking on. In a slightly nasal, cultivated accent he says in a stage whisper: 'It's time all right ... time Gough, you know, pissed off. Something must be done. I know, I'll go see the GG'.

This musical parody represents a triumph for Australian political satire. It was 22 years since the *Mavis Bramston Show* had broadcast topical satire for the first time, and Gillies and his ensemble had created a masterpiece. For some viewers, the events of 1975 were still too raw, and were no laughing matter, but for many they broke a taboo, allowing for a refreshing comic rendering of the story of a shocking political event and a parable of political hubris. It was as audacious as Barry Humphries' 'Arise Dame Edna' mockery of the cultural cringe in the presence of Gough and Margaret Whitlam, at the end of the second Barry McKenzie movie, but it was more daring, as it lampooned each figure and Australian democracy itself. If ever there was an argument for a republic in Australia, it is prosecuted in this political melodrama, *Il Dismissale*, and especially in the hilarious performance of Max as Sir John Kerr in bed with Malcolm Fraser. Frolicking as a rotund and burping Kerr in outlandish striped pants and a waistcoat, he sings '... Governor General: what sort of job is that? / Roaming around like a fool in a big top hat (burp)'. The office of Governor-General, the man and the entire system are ridiculed in this magnificent, extended performance essay.

The Gillies Report was gruelling for the writers and performers. In general, two days of the week were recording days, one in the studio and one on location, and the live segments were recorded in front of a studio audience on Saturday nights. The pressure of creating, rehearsing and recording half an hour of topical comedy for 14 weekly episodes took its toll, including on Max. It strained relationships between writers and performers, for years in some cases. And although John Clarke sometimes seemed to Max to be the locus for some of the discontent, he nevertheless kept producing immaculate sketches in which he gave quirky and hilarious performances without a hint of the background strain in them. The schedule was extremely tight, and sometimes Max and John Clarke spent hours wrangling ideas and material well into the night, then finding it difficult to summon the energy needed each Monday to start all over again with a fresh blackboard, to begin writing, rehearsing and recording another full half hour of topical satire. Over time tempers frayed, and Max worried that some of the material fell flat. A boys' locker room humour seeped in. Everyone was exhausted. Disaffection was difficult to avoid. The ensemble ideals held dear by Max were impossible to uphold in the cauldron of television. It took years for Max to recover from the stress and disappointment of this experience, and he still laments the fracturing of relationships that occurred. Max never worked again with John Clarke, who became aloof and distant.

The first series of *The Gillies Report* went to air on a Monday night, the ideal evening, but in another apparently arbitrary decision, management changed the slot without consulting Max or Ted. It felt like deliberate sabotage. In another angry phone hook-up, Shrimpton made it plain that his essential complaint was his perception that the team were getting too big for their collective boots and needed to be kept on a tight leash. On more than one occasion he screamed down the line to Max 'I don't talk to the talent!', implying that simply to have a conversation with Max was highly irregular.

Once more, Gillies confronted the ire of his key satirical target, Bob Hawke. The day before the federal election while he was sitting in a make-up chair before the show in his bald cap, Max sensed that someone important was in the studio. There were minders circulating and phones ringing. The make-up artist hovering around him seemed tense. A few minutes later the PM was ushered into the suite to prepare for his last interview before election day, to be broadcast that night. In the mirror, Max watched him stride across the floor. He greeted Max and said with a grimace: 'I caught your first show' (in which Max had performed a monologue as Hawke, before a studio audience). 'I didn't think you cracked it', Hawke continued. 'But I heard you've improved over the weeks'. Max ventured: 'I like to think we've learned a bit as we go', and the two exchanged platitudes about the importance of aiming for continuous improvement in public life. It was beginning to sound like *The Hour of Power*. Max listened in silence, elated at having got under the skin of the most powerful man in the nation.

Two years after the first two seasons of *The Gillies Report*, 14 episodes in all, a new series called *The Gillies Republic* (1986) screened on the ABC. Don Watson and Phil Scott continued to write, but John Clarke and Patrick Cook did not contribute. Max's old friend from the APG, Bill Garner, joined the team. Bob Ellis and Mungo McCallum also contributed scripts and Stephen Sewell was a major contributor. Mike Jenkins who was by this time acclaimed for his work directing *Scales of Justice* was contracted to direct. Without the benefit of an off-air pilot, or the novelty of the scheduling advantage of a concomitant election campaign, together with lacklustre promotion, its debut was relatively inauspicious. However, the program quickly hit its stride and Max firmly believes it contains his most inventive television, proud of its most audacious technical achievement and content ambition.

A Farce, a Fiddler and a Brush with Death

The success of the Gillies revue programs on television was a two-edge sword. It propelled Max into the national spotlight as a masterful comic performer, and it established his reputation for creating topical political satire. But the other side of that success meant that he was regarded by many as only capable of 'clowning', and highly theatrical impersonation. For the first time, he understood John Clarke's wretched sense of the strait jacket of a successful character and format, and longed to move on. Although he was not associated with a particular invented character as John had been, Max felt that he was now locked into the one style of performing. He suffered the corporate speaking scene uncomfortably for a few years, working with Don Watson and Guy Rundle on scripts for trade functions and corporate lunches and despairing of ever being invited to appear in a straight play or do anything other than impersonation ever again.

* * *

Other opportunities did arrive spasmodically, having nothing to do with mimicry. In the autumn of 1990, Max received an invitation to play a lead role in the touring stage version of the popular British TV farce, *'Allo 'Allo*, because the leading man, Gordon Kaye, whose character was the linchpin of the preposterous plotting, was in a coma in hospital after a freak accident. The cast of the English television show *'Allo 'Allo* had enjoyed a tradition of performing an annual variety show at the London Palladium and were scheduled to tour Australia. The farce is set in Vichy France in a restaurant run by Rene′ and features buxom waitresses, a German harridan and several dashing English fighter pilots. It is typically English low comedy with vaudeville elements, stock characters and a rollicking story. Max recognised the style and warmed to the idea of playing the Gallic chef.

Gordon Kaye was anticipated to be out of action for an indefinite period. On the second last night of the season at the Palladium a freak storm struck London. Half the cast were stranded, unable to get to the theatre. Kaye was struck by a shard from a billboard that crashed through the windscreen of his car, as he waited at a railway crossing on his drive to the theatre. With serious head injuries, he could not resume playing in the show, let alone make the tour to Australia. Max knew none of this however when he received the phone call, inviting him to play Rene′ alongside the English cast in the Australian production. They gave him one hour to consider the offer. Max rushed up to the local video shop to borrow a copy of the show and then agreed, even though he only had a week to learn the role before the show opened at the State Theatre in Sydney. The next day the director arrived from London to help Max work up his leading role. He presented as a serious and experienced Hungarian theatre director who appeared to be 'slumming it' for the higher returns of this blockbuster comedy. When Max arrived in Sydney to meet the touring cast he realised immediately that they were having second thoughts about the tour. Clearly, they were anxious that the local actor replacing Kaye would not be up to the job, and that the show would fail. For Max, it was challenging to be learning a lead role so quickly with a cast who were suspicious and insecure in their new surroundings and seemed conflicted in their attitudes to Kaye, who in the end remained comatose for four months. Max found the company's obsessional concern about the comparative status between themselves an eye-opener. It was his first encounter with a workplace culture infused with rank. One day early in the season, a senior actress took exception to the dressing room allocated to her by the local stage manager, who was innocently ignorant of a workplace protocol informed by hierarchy. It triggered an industrial incident which nearly closed the show. Whilst this sensitivity is not simply a British phenomenon, its importance seemed to outrank any other workplace concern. Fortunately for Max, the opening night was postponed for a few days when it became clear that the cast needed three full days to rehearse with the new lead, giving him precious time to work on his performance. Somehow, Max survived the opening night and everyone seemed visibly relieved. On tour in Newcastle, he breathed a sigh of relief on stage as he heard the laughter of the audience ricochet off the newly restored ceiling of the Civic Theatre, reopened for the first time since the earthquake just one year earlier. Gradually each of the cast members warmed to Max, relaxed into the tour, and seemed appreciative of his talent and Herculean achievement in joining the show at such short notice. One by one they visited him in his dressing room during the long days of the tour, to chat, sharing their concerns about the other actors. Max came to feel that the role of personnel manager had devolved to him. It was astonishing to be confessor to these myriad accounts of bullying, and narcissism. He could relax at last and enjoy their acceptance and appreciation of him in the principal role.

It was not that long afterwards that Max received a call from the Australian Opera, inviting him to replace Hayes Gordon as Tevye in *Fiddler on the Roof*, after the celebrated Method-trained actor suffered a heart attack. The show was still in rehearsal but there was very little time until opening night. Max was unfamiliar with the musical, but he knew that the production used a *Mother Courage* style carriage on a revolve as a simple, indeed elemental, set design. He watched the film version of *Fiddler*, impressed by the epic theatrical story presented in this classic twentieth century drama of displacement and suffering set in Czarist Russia. He recognised that they needed an actor as much as a singer. But Max was apprehensive about the role as he is not a trained singer, imagining himself only capable of cod musical performances of the kind that delighted television audiences in the Gillies shows; but he was honoured to be asked to work with the Australian Opera under the American director, Sammy Bayes, sent by the American proprietors to oversee the franchise offshore. Moffat Oxenbould, the Australian Opera's Artistic Director, had wanted to mount a new production of the musical, by now twenty years old, intending to invite Elijah Moshinsky back home to direct. Max thought this an inspired idea, but it was not to be. The New York agents would only authorise a re-staging of the US original. Max and Elijah had worked together in their days at Melbourne Youth Theatre on a memorable production of *Krapp's Last Tape*. So unfamiliar was Max with musical theatre that he had not even seen a full-scale musical production since he was a child, when his mother took him to see Evie Hayes in *Annie Get Your Gun*. It was apparent to Max as soon as he arrived for rehearsals at the Opera House that the American visitor was struggling with the labour relations system in Australia. The opera company rehearsed under tightly controlled union rules with strictly maintained three-hour calls. The American was shocked when the cast walked off the job during rehearsals irrespective of what Bayes might have wanted or where they were up to in the rehearsal schedule. For Max, it was a gruelling battle to learn the role but he enjoyed the unfamiliar challenge of working with the orchestra and the assistant director, Stuart Maunder, who would explain a move or a step with a sidelong glance and a nod. The direction was practical and programmatic, with no time to explore the potential of the character and no discussion. But Max flourished and the show was a success. Two years later in 1992 the opera company remounted the production. Max was riding high.

Throughout his career Max has never lost his sense of the ideal of the actor as tabula rasa in the Alec Guinness mould, someone who could transform so fully. His childhood heroes: Guinness, Danny Kaye and Charlie Chaplin have never lost their appeal no matter what the industry threw at him. He particularly enjoyed comic acting but could now hold his head up as a musical theatre star. Over the next five years he immersed himself once more in stage drama, appearing in *A Stretch of the Imagination* and in the stellar cast of *The Sisters Rosensweig* alongside Ron Challinor, Judi Farr, Rachel Griffiths, Gerald Lepkowski, Genevieve Picot, Tony Sheldon and Jacki Weaver.

* * *

Max's interest in satirical revue never waned in spite of the effects of pigeonholing that it had brought about. By 1992 Ted Robinson was back in Melbourne and in charge of the Light Entertainment department at the ABC. Although he was unenthusiastic, he nevertheless agreed to Max's next idea for television, a playhouse season of separate, self-contained character comedies. Simultaneously Robinson was preoccupied with directing a new musical variety show with surreal elements, centring around the musical group The Doug Anthony All Stars, filmed in front of a live studio audience.

Robinson insisted on directing Max's new project in spite of his reservations about the concept and his absorption with the Dougs. There were technical challenges and a large cast required for each half hour but the stories were strong. Robinson also insisted on some short unrelated sketch material to accompany the dramas, totally at odds with Max's concept. Despite his misgivings Max acquiesced and *Gillies and Company* was born. Worried about the direction the project was taking, he found himself chain smoking with anxiety and frustrated with the sclerotic production process. Robinson was distracted, coping with two productions simultaneously, and a separate but not unrelated personal crisis. As ever, he showed little patience with planning, story development and the minutiae of preparation, convinced that his best work happens on the floor in the heat of the moment. Whilst Max certainly understood the power of spontaneity he placed high priority on meticulous and methodical preparation. Lex Marinos was brought in by Robinson to co-direct. Whilst for Max it was good to have a friend to help cope with the chaos, it was too late to resolve the fundamental problems. The performances were disappointing for Max and he despaired of the show. Every day he considered walking away but was unwilling to abandon the cast and crew. Desperately unhappy with the situation, Max travelled to Sydney to speak to the head of ABC television, Paddy Conroy, hoping that the impending failure could be forestalled. It was a futile quest.

The stress and disappointment of *Gillies and Company* (1992) had a terrible effect on Max. Arriving at a South Melbourne studio to shoot a training video for Telecom one day Max felt unwell. He was to play a harassed and angry manager but the night before had found himself unable to walk straight along his hallway at home. He was feverish and sweating as he arrived at the studio to shoot his scene. When the shoot began he found he could not produce any vocal volume, let alone evince the agitation and anger required. The director sent him to lie down. He woke up five hours later feeling strange and ill. The next day the young woman who was doing Max's make-up said 'I thought you looked as though you'd had a stroke'. After tests the doctor confirmed that he had indeed suffered a minor stroke.

Rehearsing for his role as Christmas Present in the musical *Scrooge* not long afterwards, Max struggled with some of the choreography requested by a visiting English director, and crippled with a stabbing pain in his chest as the season commenced. He experienced spasms across his torso as he walked from his car across Little Bourke Street to the stage door of the Princess Theatre. The pain would always miraculously lift after the end of Act One. Max put it down to nerves because in Act 2 he was on stage for the most intensive period of the show, and did not experience the pain during that period of exertion. When Max consulted a specialist, he learned that all his arteries were blocked. He was hospitalised immediately for treatment. Max recalls recovering from his quadruple bypass, and remembering the joy he felt when he received a letter from John Clarke. It was touching after what had seemed like years of estrangement to receive John's comforting, cheerful and kind letter.

***

Max continued to mimic politicians in various shows, playing Graham Richardson as a nightclub MC character, John Howard as a Sandy Stone figure whining nasally in his armchair, Amanda Vanstone reclining on a grand piano in a floral frock and Kevin Rudd as a sanctimonious preacher. He impersonated Julia Gillard,

Tony Abbott and a clownish Barnaby Joyce. Max was almost 70, and in spite of excellent prosthetics he realised that each politician was much younger than him and it was time to stop.

Max Gillies is known by many as a master mimic and expert impersonator of politicians. Yet in his long career he has appeared in numerous dramatic roles in a wide range of plays, including those by Shakespeare and Beckett, a variety of Australian plays, as well as in leading roles in musical theatre. His work as an impersonator of politicians is exceptional and led him to national prominence on television. In 2015 he performed a one man show in which he explained to the audience how he developed some of his key political impersonations. This show was aptly titled *Once were Leaders*, and lamented the paucity of leadership in contemporary politics.

Max continues to appear in dramatic and comic roles in a wide range of works, to enjoy opera and to work with younger actors at the Victorian College of the Arts. His satirical impersonations are just one part of his repertoire and his contribution to political comedy in Australia is magical and marvellous.

Chapter 5

JOHN CLARKE:
BAT ON

(1948–2017)

It was a blustery spring morning in Melbourne as I set out to meet John Clarke. John had given me the address of his Fitzroy office, but when the taxi pulled up I felt a wave of panic. There was nothing nearby that looked remotely office-like, only a picture framing business, and a café. I scanned each of the street numbers above the old timber doorframes, and sure enough it was the café number that corresponded to the one John had given me. I walked in and looked around the bright room, which was humming with mid-morning chatter and the whooshing sound of the coffee machine. A man in a navy blue jumper, deep in conversation with the barista, turned around as I approached. It was John. He greeted me warmly, shaking my hand and giving me that unmistakeable boyish smile. Once we'd ordered coffee he led me through the back of the cafe, past the kitchen, and then up a steep and narrow wooden staircase to the two small rooms that made up his office. One room had shelves crammed with books and movie discs, and the other was plain and unadorned, with white walls and simple furniture.

For the next four hours we sat in this peaceful room, its small windows offering glimpses of Fitzroy rooftops and grey skies, and John entertained me with tales, sometimes hilarious, sometimes heartbreaking, of his life as an actor and writer. After that day we had many more such conversations, and every time, whether I spoke to him in person or over the phone (which was more usual), I invariably felt better than I did beforehand – lighter, more optimistic. It was not just his sharp wit and funny stories that lifted the mood: John was a generous and accomplished conversationalist, who was honest, sensitive and clear about things. He was a helpful person too, always ready to offer assistance. And he was that rarest of artist: outgoing, warm, kind and wise.

Boy

As a little boy John Clarke lived with his parents and younger sister Anna, in Palmerston North in New Zealand. He spent hours riding his prized black and silver Raleigh bicycle out along the country roads, sometimes with his friends and sometimes alone: no one worried about where he was, as long as he was back at the house by 4.30 in the afternoon. He was just eight years old when he took to cycling, and thrilled to the sound of the tyres freewheeling along the tree-lined lanes and streaking out through the farms of the Manawatu. John's mother, Neva, dark haired, green-eyed, slim and practical, was a genial person who loved a chat. A keen reader and writer, she encouraged her children to observe people and imagine what they were thinking and doing. Neva was interested in the theatre and music, too, and took them to concerts and plays. At the Opera House they saw performers as diverse as Joyce Grenfell 'who was very funny', and John Gielgud, 'who was very serious', John said. John also saw a South African revue called 'Wait a minum' and thought it was exceptionally funny.

Throughout John's childhood Neva was sometimes ill with complaints that were not easily explained to a small boy, but he was aware that his mother was preoccupied and sad. His father Ted, the branch manager of a rapidly expanding national retail company, was out at the office much of the time. Ted was always busy and showed little interest in Neva's world of books, stories, and manuscripts. And he was hard on John, frequently called him 'dumb', stupid, or a 'no-hoper'. He drank whiskey, and when he was at home, John knew to avoid him. It was no use telling him any of their achievements. If they tried, he simply left the room.

It was clear to the young John that the marriage was in trouble. He says that 'there are photographs from this period in which we look like a dust bowl family who have just lost everything in a tornado'.[1] But that desperation was not visible to anybody. To the outside world Ted was a dapper, convivial self-made man. He wore expensive suits and finely woven shirts, never revealed the hardships of his childhood, and strode out as though he were an English gentleman. His mask never cracked: he had an instinct for performance, and he would entertain visitors with stories and witty conversation. Ted took long business trips overseas and without him at home the place was calm and happy. John spent hours talking to his mother, reading his American Classics Illustrated comics and playing with his friends.

It was 1958 when John became aware that his mother was writing short stories, and meeting with other writing women in the district. In the days before television, when magazines were supreme, the women talked about fiction, and sent off short stories to editors around the country. Neva's circle included several women who went on to become successful writers: the novelist Alice Glenday, and prolific children's writer, Joy Cowley. Cowley particularly impressed John when she told him about how her husband liked to turn somersaults on the front lawn.[2]

---

1   John Clarke, obituary for Neva. Online: https://mrjohnclarke.com/tinkering/page/2, accessed 5 February 2019.
2   Obituary for Neva.

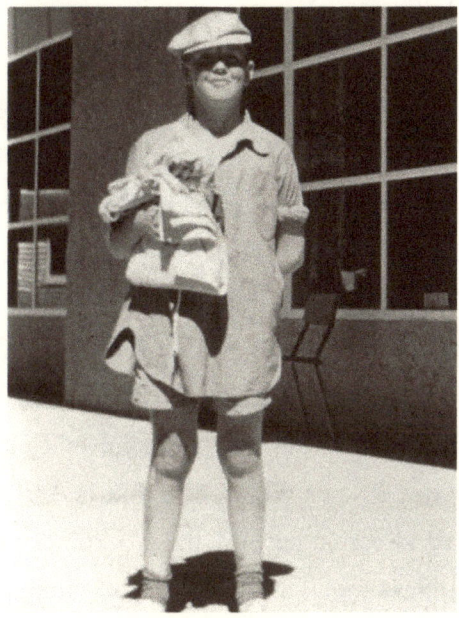

John Clarke, aged 10 at YMCA camp.
Courtesy of John Clarke.

When John was twelve, Ted was promoted to a senior position in the company's head office, and the family moved to Wellington. The steep streets spelled the end of his cycling days. Neva was happy with the move and her health transformed. She began singing lessons with George Scott Morrison, joined a radio drama group as well as various amateur theatre troupes around Wellington. She started writing seriously, and very soon she was earning an income from her short stories and reviews. From then on the sound of her typing provided a constant soundtrack to their lives. When John came in from school Neva would call out to him across the room, her fingers dancing across the keyboard: 'Hello, boy who needs a haircut. How was school and why don't you put the kettle on?'[3]

---

3   Obituary for Neva.

Often, when John arrived home from school, there would be small groups of writers gathered around their kitchen table. One afternoon, while his mother was chatting in another room, John struck up a conversation with one of his mother's writer guests, an Englishman. Over tea and sandwiches the man told John about his life. He had worked as a teacher in Malaya until, after falling ill, he'd been diagnosed with an inoperable brain tumour and given a year to live. During that year, he'd set about writing a novel. The novel was published to some acclaim, and by some miracle the man didn't die, and so he'd kept on writing. 'I was telling Mum all of this,' John told me, 'and she said: "Yes, he's quite a well-known writer; his name is Anthony Burgess"'.

The New Zealand comic novelist Barry Crump was a favourite of John's as a child. Neva took John with her to Crump's house where he was delighted to meet the creator of the 'blokey country yarns'. Crump's work is famous for capturing the distinctive way men spoke to one another in New Zealand. His comic stories, in particular the novel, *Hang on a Minute Mate*, made a big impression on Clarke, who listened enthusiastically to the author reading them aloud on the radio.

Young John was less enamoured of his mother's attempts to conscript him into plays at short notice. Once the boy who was playing Bob Cratchit's son in a production of *A Christmas Carol* broke his nose playing rugby, and John was dragooned into playing the role. He was pressed into service back-stage as well. During one memorable performance John stood off stage and handed props to Colin Watson (later a well-known sculptor in New York), who, John recalls, slammed the door of the set so hard it 'heaved and rattled and the notion that we were in Moscow, which was already in some trouble, was briefly abandoned altogether'.[4]

---

4   Obituary for Neva.

Ted took no interest in the amateur theatricals and seemed to his son a remote, if sometimes funny and sharp-witted man. He didn't read books but he spoke with a gentle musical rhythm in his voice, and would often greet the children in the morning with a few lines from Kipling's *Rubaiyat*, his lilting voice coming to rest on the magical 'noose of light'. He recited Shelley's 'To a Skylark', enchanting the listener and catching the tune of the words. Ted could sing and reel off numbers from musical hall comedies he had seen years ago. His memory was extraordinary. John frequently observed glimpses of another side of his father: with outsiders, he was charming, and was a natural performer, a born story-teller. Every so often the two of them listened to the Goons on the radio: his father would look up at him with an expression of pure joy on his face, before he convulsed with laughter. Looking back, John sees a man who felt repressed and threatened at home, and who seemed unable to engage emotionally with his own son except in these moments of comic release.

Letters from Auden

During his first few years at high school, at the prestigious and conservative Scots College, John conformed to the then dominant sporting culture without complaint. He didn't even contemplate resisting this aspect of school life. 'You did sport', he recalls with a matter-of-factness that underlines the intensity of the unspoken cultural rule. Easily distracted in the classroom, he wasn't a natural scholar, either. And he was rebellious: living with a broken model of authority in his family every day brought out his defiant, independent spirit, and he refused to accept the brutish authority of the school. He made it clear to his teachers that he rejected most of what the school stood for. When he was 14 the headmaster said to him: 'Don't think you can carry on like this – because we're going to break your spirit'. John thought to himself, 'good luck, you have no chance'; having battled that attempt at home with his father he was suspicious of authority and immune to its charades. By the end of his school days he was intractable, a 'refusenik' who was expelled because of his 'attitude'. John says now that Scots College was 'an educational Dunkirk', in that 'survival was an excellent result'. He refused to go back to the school, although they continued to invite him over many years.

There were a few activities Clarke did enjoy during his school days, however: he was a champion diver and gymnast, and he took to writing. His English teacher, Bill Hoyland, would leave the boys with a quote from Horace and let them write an essay on whatever the quotation inspired in them. This kind of activity appealed to the young Clarke, who recalls writing furiously on Horace's statement, 'They change the sky, not their mind, who cross the sea', never dreaming at the time how potent the words would be in his early adult life.

At 14 Clarke discovered a cartoon in a history textbook. It was the famous David Low cartoon of Hitler and Stalin meeting, and he marvelled at Low's unique manner of portraying evil. John was struck by its boldness and clarity, the terrible context and dead Poland, the perfectly mannered stances of the two liars, and by the fact that Low had used their own words to do it. Years later Clarke would perfect in sketch comedy what he had seen in Low's cartoons: telling a shocking political truth through humour, using the precise words of those in power to skewer them.

Clarke's fledgling interest in literature was encouraged by Hoyland. One day Hoyland came upon Clarke reading a book of

Auden's letters. Hoyland said 'If you want to read that sort of thing I have boxes of them'. Hoyland explained that some years ago, he had been on a walking tour of Iceland with Auden, McNeice, and a party of schoolboys, and afterwards they had kept in touch. Clarke took Hoyland up on his offer and read Auden's 'chatty' letters to Hoyland. He recalled that Auden's handwriting was 'small, upright, swift, assured and fluent, in a blue fountain pen, with no corrections'. He said 'I had no knowledge of Auden, of course'. The letters revealed a lot about Hoyland, the Quaker school chaplain, who gave talks on philosophical questions and ethics that lodged firmly in Clarke's mind. He was Socratic – if you asked him a question he'd ask you one back. He was completely different from all the other teachers with his liberal religious Quaker background, his friendship with Auden and his tales of travel to China and other far flung places.

John could not envisage a future for himself in any of the professions others around him seemed to be planning: 'there were about nine jobs in New Zealand and none of them appealed to me', he told me. Clarke had spent some of his summers working on shearing gangs as a rousie and sometimes as a presser, his ears tuned to the colourful slang of all the men he encountered in the sheds. He started to think about the hilarious sheep farmers he met and imitated their speech to amuse his friends, sometimes giving short impromptu performances of these men. Still undecided about his future, he enrolled in Arts/Law at Victoria University where he gravitated to theatrical revue, and worked back stage in 1968 because he had heard there was free beer. The big star that year was the playwright Roger Hall who took John aside and urged him to get on stage for the next revue. John first appeared on stage at Victoria University's Memorial Theatre in 1969 in a show called *At last the '69 Extravaganza*. In his program bio,

Clarke is quoted as saying, 'I have a diploma in false smiling'. When I asked him about this he told me that it was not his own line, and that other students wrote the program notes. It struck me that John Clarke's joyful smile could never be false.

Each revue performance was different and apart from a borrowed raincoat there were no costumes. The only scripts were scrawled on the program, and some were worked out on the day of the performance after an hour or two in the pub. In an attempt to look casual as he didn't really know if he could write or perform, John presented his sketch ideas to the others at the last minute. This meant the others didn't interfere. Most of all he wanted an audience response, and a direct connection to that audience. He had no patience for the quaint traditions of the theatre, the obedience to them he observed in others, and railed against pretentious attempts to direct him. Right from the beginning he seemed to have an instinct for emulating the distinct rhythm, cadence and lexicon of New Zealand English, and a firm grasp of comic timing.

A year later he began writing and performing regularly (with John Banas, Ginette McDonald and Paul Holmes) in a semi-professional popular late night sketch show at the Downstage Theatre. Roger Hall, who had noted Clarke's ability to devise comedy (he even used the words 'comic genius'), then invited him to contribute to a new revue called *One in Five*. The title referred to a recently announced finding that one in five New Zealanders suffered from mental health disorders. It was a ground-breaking revue, with Clarke's 'frightening realism' in a sketch portraying a one-way telephone conversation to his mate "Trev" singled out by reviewers as a highlight. Neva came to see the show and was struck by the convincing timing he demonstrated in the telephone sketch, making what was a monologue feel like a sketch with three characters. The revue signalled a shift in New Zealand comedy from standard university-style revue and formal theatre to something more authentic that spoke the language of the ordinary New Zealand citizen. This was one of John's aims: 'I was trying to land it in the New Zealander's ear', he told me, and he remembers the pleasure of performing his own material, even if it didn't always work.

Clarke enjoyed working with the other revue members: Dave Smith, Helene Wong, Cathy Downes and Roger Hall himself. Clarke remembers the satire they created as 'socially radical … We were the loud generation that nobody had heard from so far. We weren't disrespectful though … I mean, I genuinely did think the country was run by a cartel of fools, and not enough was changing, not quickly enough and not in the right ways … I was pretty annoyed about a lot of things … New Zealand was pretending to be a non-racist country for example … and there was racism everywhere. It was about to be cast into purgatory internationally for its sporting links with white supremacist South Africa, this comfortable allegedly multi-racial society'. But in spite of his own views, then and now, Clarke's satire – funny, witty, experimental, and disrespectful – is restrained and careful rather than strident.

There was no way of making a living in revue, and Clarke was not interested in acting as such. In fact, the whole idea of theatre with its so-called 'serious plays', seemed absurd to him. He studiously avoided the Drama Society at university because he did not relate to that kind of performing, and yet he relished writing and performing topical revue where he felt he could play himself. On stage you could mock your own society: it was liberating. Nowhere else seemed to offer that opportunity. So it was in revue that Clarke began to invent his own form.

For nearly a year John worked in broadcasting as a film assessor. With three others including his friend from revue, Cathy Downes, he sat in a small theatrette and watched films that had been submitted to the NZBC for purchase. They squealed with delight when the television movie of *Beyond the Fringe* (first broadcast in Britain in 1964) turned up for assessment, playing it over and over again. It was as if they had a private audience with the makers of the most audacious comedians they had ever encountered. Clarke was a confirmed fan of the comic foursome Peter Cook, Dudley Moore, Alan Bennett and Jonathan Miller and knew some of their sketches off by heart. He had an LP record as a teenager, their voices were delightfully familiar to him, and Bennett's radical television sketch comedy show *On the Margin* (1966) made a strong impression. In some of his later monologues Clarke remembers the way he 'squeezed out' words in his Leeds accent and whether he was talking about meeting Virginia Woolf or TE Lawrence, he delivered his comic lines with 'complete fealty to his own particularity'. Clarke would also become a satirist who draws on the specific sounds, rhythms and conversational quirks of his own particular milieu.

The small team of film assessors made recommendations which were sometimes ignored. For example they recommended *Monty Python's Flying Circus* but a 'timorous management' baulked at what they perceived as 'controversial' material and as a result this comic sketch show, so popular elsewhere, was not seen in New Zealand for many years. For John the work was dull at times and the salaries were low. But there was a major reward that meant everything to him: John and the others relished what they saw coming to them from the UK.

Like his father, John was entranced by anti-establishment humour; he marvelled at the sharpness of Peter Cook and Dudley

Moore, the early work of Alan Bennett and gladly watched hours of British drama. Clarke also experienced first-hand a broadcasting culture in which audience was the lowest priority: 'Nobody had any relationship with the audience. They did not know or care about the audience,' he said indignantly. At night he was back on the stage, performing sketch comedy, where there was a direct and immediate connection with an audience, and where he could speak as one of them.

Clarke sensed he had a lot to learn about the craft, and recognised the limited opportunities in Wellington. Neva and Ted had both re-partnered and seemed to have new lives of their own: there was no family home anymore. John decided to travel to Europe with his friend Michael McDonald, although he had no real desire to see anything in particular. The goal was simply to be away, and not to be in New Zealand.

Looking back, Clarke says his family was one that didn't really work. His parents were interesting, but, preoccupied with fighting each other: they 'didn't do much parenting'. Although the couple were bitterly unhappy for many years, they stayed married. Neva wanted to keep the household intact until Anna finished school and left home. Even then, Ted refused to agree to a divorce, so in 1971, Neva initiated a court case in which their young adult children, John and Anna, were forced to testify. John vividly recalls the battering he endured at the hands of his father's barrister who attempted to argue that the problems in the marriage were caused not by Ted but by John who, he maintained, was extremely difficult. He had studied just enough law to know that he did not have to answer the questions, and at one point turned to the judge who confirmed this. A chill filled the court room as Ted Clarke buried his head while his oldest child attempted to refute this preposterous fiction and the attack by the barrister seeking to confuse cause and effect. But he did not speak up for his son.

Clarke was philosophical when he spoke to me about his childhood and adolescence: it was a 'strange, unique, unhappy, dark place'. Despite the tensions in his home, John's personality is gently optimistic. He came to understand both of his parents as a mature man later on, and to cease blaming them for his sometimes hellish home-life. He tells me that he has come to the conclusion that some things about them can be explained by the war.

It was the war that brought Clarke's parents together, and possibly helped drive them apart. John's mother Neva confided in her adult son about her experiences of early romance and the struggles of her adolescence. Because of the Depression she left school, learned typing and shorthand and worked as a secretary in Whakatane, where she formed a strong attachment to a man, Geoffrey, who was a champion swimmer. They both loved dancing. Geoffrey joined the air force when war broke out, and was shot down and killed over Benghazi, Libya in 1942. Neva joined up shortly after learning of her boyfriend's death, and was sent to Italy where she worked for the commanding officer of the NZ army in the port town of Senigallia. Neva survived a sexual assault, and was surrounded by men who had been wounded in some of the most brutal campaigns of the war. One of them was Ted Clarke, who had been injured during action in his anti-tank regiment. He came from Wellington and was of northern Irish heritage like her. Like Neva Ted left school during the Great Depression and was taken on by McKenzie's retailers where he excelled as a manager. He had fought in Palestine, Syria and Turkey, and had already experienced the battles of Sidi Rezegh, Minqar Qai'm, Ruweisat Ridge, El Alamein, the campaigns in

Libya and Tunisia, and in Italy, the Sangro River, Monte Cassino and Trieste. During the desert campaigns he slipped into a pocket, a slim volume of poetry he had bought in Cairo. He read it in the field, memorising the verse, and singing it to himself in prayer-like incantations. Neva found this quick witted, honey-voiced young man and his love of poetry enchanting. Back in New Zealand, two years after the hostilities finished, Neva and Ted celebrated their wedding in the garden of Neva's parents' house in Sievwright Lane, Gisborne.

In today's parlance, Neva and Ted were both most likely affected by post-traumatic stress disorder, so it's not surprising that they didn't do much parenting. But it would be many years before Clarke fully understood his parents, and pieced together their experiences and their suffering before and during the War: as a young adult he felt that once the family had officially ceased to exist, he needed to go somewhere else for a while.

Ginette, Two Barrys, Clive, Bruce and Fred

In London, John and his friend Michael set themselves up in a flat in Kensington with several others. Michael, with all the enthusiasm of an eager romantic, adored London and planned excursions to Italy and France. John worked as a van driver and would leave his van parked outside the British Museum in the loading bay or outside the National Gallery in Trafalgar Square, with the back door open for the whole afternoon while he wandered around inside. The freedom of looking around on his own was intoxicating. A year later both Anna, and Michael's younger sister, Ginette, arrived from New Zealand, like so many other young adults who made the pilgrimage to the old world in the early 1970s. Ginette quickly plugged into the theatre scene, and suggested that John audition for the young Australian director Bruce Beresford, who, she'd heard, was making a film in which a lot of young men were required. Ginette was disappointed that there were very few roles for young women in the film. John was reluctant. He had never auditioned for anything (and still hasn't: 'I wouldn't know what to do' he said) and was enjoying his freedom and his afternoons in the pub. Ginette insisted, and telephoned the producer to make an appointment for him. John complied, and went to the audition.

When he read from the script for *The Adventures of Barry McKenzie* he roared with laughter, and was awestruck by the talent of the three men who were the driving forces behind the film: Bruce Beresford, Barry Humphries and Nick Garland. Garland, a New Zealander, had drawn the cartoons for the Barry McKenzie comic strip, on which the film they were making was based. During the filming period Beresford and Humphries shepherded Clarke along, and Don McAlpine let him look through the film camera, explaining technical details about how he planned to shoot, and where the edge of the frame was. John spent hours talking to Barry Humphries about what Humphries read as a young man. He had loved Beckett in particular, he told him – in particular the novel *Watt*. The audacity of this gangly, long-haired, young Australian and his vivid humour struck Clarke immediately, and was to have a huge influence on Clarke's evolution as a performer. Humphries performed for a world audience, and while they parodied the Australian cultural cringe, he and Beresford asserted their equality with everything and anything British at every opportunity.

During the filming, industrial unrest caused power cuts all over England, and many productions stopped altogether. However, the *McKenzie* producers simply hired a generator and kept filming.

Nothing phased Beresford and Humphries: 'There was no pre-emptive buckle because of some sense that you come from nowhere', Clarke recalls. John felt that he could be himself with these men; better still he could be himself in the film, appearing in the pub scenes singing and drinking with Bazza McKenzie who was played by the tall, thin, long-legged and gentle Barry Crocker. Being permitted to play himself was the key to Clarke's performance style and his future as a satirist: not only did it offer him a strangely comforting armour, but it provided the perfect satirical weapon and a mode of directly addressing the audience.

With the two Barrys, Spike Milligan, Peter Cook, Dennis Price, Dick Bentley and a large cast of young expatriate extras who enthusiastically played the drinking partners, filming was often interrupted by anarchic behaviour. But the cast and crew enjoyed themselves and the party atmosphere continued across the dingy, garbage-strewn streets of Earl's Court. During filming, BBC television presenter Joan Bakewell interviewed Barry Humphries for a program called *Film '72*. Dressed as Mrs Edna Everage, Humphries slipped easily into the interview. When Bakewell asked him why the film was being shot in England, Humphries, referring to the constant strikes and blackouts then bedevilling the nation, replied without blinking, 'The film is actually set in Calcutta but now London looks so like Calcutta, and of course it's so much cheaper'. Clarke overheard Humphries' remark and gasped. It was 'marketing Dada', he thought to himself, savouring the brazen sharpness of Humphries' retort.

After the film shoot had finished, Clarke met another young Australian called Clive James, and he too made an impression. He was 'big in his thinking', John recalls. James had a voice that sounded like 'cicadas' and looked to the young New Zealander as if 'he had just got out of the surf', but it emerged that he had actually lived in the UK for several years and had studied at Cambridge. In a spirited conversation James informed Clarke that he was a book and film reviewer for the *Observer*, but that so far none of the reviews had been published: 'They come back at me faster than a golf ball off a concrete wall', said Clive with a broad smile, but 'one day, one of their film reviewers or book reviewers is going to have the 'flu', and they're going to know they've got two beautifully written film reviews and two brilliant book reviews sitting in their in-tray. And they're going to run them'. James's confident assertion that he would succeed in breaking into the reviewing scene uninvited astounded Clarke. His bravado and defiant will to succeed were breathtaking. And that image of the golf ball delights Clarke every time he thinks of this first encounter.

The experience of working with Humphries, Cook and Beresford emboldened Clarke in the long run, but he was shy and lacked confidence. One night in a pub in Gloucester Road, Michael introduced John to a young woman who he had met in Italy. She was dark-haired and exotic looking, and they had a loud argument that continued for some time. The young woman's name was Helen. She was from Melbourne and had studied art history, painting and printmaking. John was struck by her intelligence and open-heartedness: 'She was practical and completely honest. I was living in a fantasy world without a clue about what I was doing. God, I met her at the right time, a glorious fluke,' John told me. After another few months in London, John and Helen returned to her hometown, where Clarke worked as a labourer while Helen studied for a teaching qualification. Helen's parents (Charles and Jean) were like her: open, friendly, no-nonsense people who welcomed him, and her father made him laugh.

In the spring of 1973, back in Wellington, Clarke got in touch with some of his friends from the revue days who were now working in theatre and broadcasting. He and Tom Scott, the cartoonist, published the first and only issue of a magazine called *Horse* based on *Private Eye* in the UK. Ted Clarke, who had never hidden his anxiety about John's future, was impressed with Helen, and made no secret of his surprise that such an accomplished young woman would partner with his 'no-hoper' son. They pledged their wedding vows in the choir stalls of the old St Paul's Cathedral, embraced by its warm and richly coloured native timbers. Together they had penned the vows 'so that nothing annoyed us too much', and received special permission to marry in the deconsecrated Gothic revival church. By the end of the year Clarke had made his first television appearance as Fred Dagg.

John Clarke as Fred Dagg.
Courtesy of John Clarke.

Dagg also claimed to be running for parliament. He was always surrounded by sheep, and generally wore a black singlet, baggy shorts and gumboots along with a cotton sun hat that his sister had given John for the role. Ted Clarke found the character embarrassing and crude, and bristled when anyone complimented him on his son, or mentioned the character Fred Dagg. He was sceptical about the whole theatrical enterprise, and would repeatedly question John about how on earth he would make a living, aghast that anyone would pay him for performing this 'long-haired lout'.

With his endearingly dishevelled sheep farmer, Clarke pioneered a new dramatic form for television, and the character became an integral element of the current affairs program. Fred Dagg was an instant and hugely popular character in New Zealand and was the subject of a *Country Calendar* television "documentary" at the end of 1974 in which the whole genre of the popular program was gently parodied. Dagg is first filmed in the shower, where he is shown carefully washing his gumboots. Then the action moves to the breakfast table, where Dagg sits, his dark wavy hair cascading out from under his hat, alongside his 'approximately' six adult sons, all called Trevor. Like their father, the Trevors are all dressed in black singlets and flapping shorts, and their cigarettes burn away as they demolish brick size loaves of bread and whole bottles of milk in one sitting. 'We do have some troubles with the boys having the same name, but generally the place runs very well', says Fred calmly, the camera following him about the farm ('the high bits and the low bits'), while he discourses on the ruinous economics of sheep farming, sitting on a tractor that only runs backwards. The 'documentary' captures his excursion into town, now sporting a jacket and tie with his shorts and gum boots, where he attempts to put a cheque into a parking meter, and has trouble crossing the road.

The commentary is hilarious, filled with the slapstick moments: Dagg constantly falls out of vehicles and plunges over verandah rails, while the Trevs wrap the sheep in their fleeces and fasten them with rivets, rather than clipping the wool. The rural idyll is a benignly mad place – nothing much happens, but nobody gets hurt.

That same year John did a sitcom called *Buck House* with John Banas and Cathy Downes. The following year he began to do regular radio pieces as Fred Dagg, and released a record album consisting of these monologues, and a hit single called 'We Don't Know How Lucky We Are', gently mocking the much repeated refrain of kiwis after they return from overseas trips. Also in 1975, without registering as a candidate, Fred Dagg started his own political party and stood for parliament in the general election. He ran his campaign in his television appearance and seven actual voters crossed out the names of their real candidates and wrote 'Fred Dagg' across their ballot papers. Citing an unprecedented 700% swing to his party, Fred called upon the new government to resign by the following Friday. It was the first time Clarke engaged in an ingenious mixing of make believe and real political activity that was later to become his stock in trade.

A stage tour of Fred Dagg brought the character to audiences all over the country and Clarke also made some cabaret appearances in character with a group of musicians who, he says, made the touring bearable. That same year (1976) he appeared in a variety special on NZBC called *A Bit of a Dagg*, and over the next few years also featured in a number of books including the whimsically titled, *The Thoughts of Chairman Fred*, *Daggshead Revisited* and *The Fred Dagg Careers Advisory Bureau*. In fact the character continued to appear in print until 1998.

Fred Dagg also charmed Australian audiences on radio, when he was discovered by hosts Robyn Williams and Bob Hudson, who regularly played Dagg's songs and interviews on their show. This indication that Fred Dagg might work outside New Zealand, did not register with John immediately. Both Barry McKenzie and Fred Dagg were children of the British satire boom of the 1960s and their creators were influenced by the leading figure of that boom, Peter Cook. They were both explicitly theatrical and nostalgic creations who spoke in the exaggerated but recognisable idiom of Australians and New Zealanders. Fred Dagg was an instant success and because of the more gentle nature of his satire, was never subject to the controversies that plagued Bazza McKenzie. The two fictional archetypes reflected the different styles of humour in Australia and New Zealand and of their creators Barry Humphries and John Clarke. Whereas Humphries' character was confronting and crude at times, Dagg was hard to dislike. Both figures offered an exuberant embodiment of cultural 'new nationalism' in the two countries, spoke in the vernacular of their countrymen, and heralded a new direction for satire.

The sheep farmer turned pollie, Fred Dagg, opened the door of popular entertainment for John Clarke when he and Helen moved back to Melbourne in 1977. For several years Clarke wrote and performed a sketch every day of the week for ABC Radio. It suited Clarke to work at home and to stay away from the gruelling schedules of television for a while, especially as he was new to Australia. Ultra-sensitive about his status as a newcomer and as an outsider, Clarke was only too aware that he needed to listen and observe the culture before trying anything too daring.

Fred Dagg's appearance in a series of Qantas advertisements on television and in other programs in 1975–6 meant that audiences saw him on television frequently. Qantas approached Clarke and told him that Fred Dagg was the most recognised figure in New

Zealand. Initially he was reluctant to appear in the Qantas ads, and made a point of talking to Air New Zealand, explaining that he would rather promote their airline. But they weren't interested. Clarke struck a deal with the Australian carrier that allowed him to write the scripts for the advertisements, to make a new ad as soon as he 'got sick of watching the last one' and to perform the entire ad without uttering the word 'Qantastic'. This first series of ads brought Clarke to Australia for filming, and gave him a chance to have a look around. In one of these ads, Dagg sits in his aircraft seat with a tray of schooners on his lap, beside a life-size koala, wearing his signature black singlet and floppy sun hat. The series of ads was hugely successful with the market share held by Qantas increasing by a staggering 50 per cent in the wake of the Dagg ad campaign. They gave Clarke a welcome financial boost and with them he learned about making a one man show.

Dutch Interiors and Dingoes

If there were models for Clarke as a writer at this time they were the American actor and columnist Robert Benchley, who said he was 'not quite a writer and not quite an actor', and the Irish humourist Flann O'Brien / Myles na Gopaleen (Brian O'Nolan). Both O'Brien and Benchley worked through an invented character, as Clarke did with Fred Dagg. Clarke, who thought of himself as a writer first and foremost, appreciated O'Brien's sense of maintaining his authentic stance as an 'enemy of cant and pretension'. After a few years, Clarke started writing imaginary interviews with Australian politicians. One of the first was an interview with Joh Bjelke-Petersen, the loquacious and divisive Premier of Queensland who, as Clarke said, 'did idiotic things'. Bjelke-Petersen, who referred to press conferences as 'feeding the chooks', veiled his chicanery and contempt for the citizenry with disdainful humour for two decades, until he was eventually tried (but not convicted) for perjury over evidence he gave in a judicial inquiry that linked his government with organised crime. Clarke wrote his imaginary interview with Bjelke-Petersen using the standard interview question often put to comedians, 'When did you first know that you were funny?' The assumption driving the 'interview' was that 'Bjelke-Petersen was a professional idiot. He knew what he was doing'. It was a subtle but potent satirical point.

The interview was published in the *Times on Sunday*.[5] That day Clarke ran into Peter Cook as they shared a dressing room at the Melbourne Comedy Festival. Cook said 'Are you the John Clarke who wrote this thing in the paper today?' Clarke nodded. Cook congratulated him and said, 'You should perform this interview'. Clarke hadn't thought of the interview as a performance piece, but Cook's advice made sense to him. Soon afterwards he began performing 'interviews' on radio, teaming up with a presenter called Bryan Dawe. This imaginary interview format soon became Clarke's signature comedic form, providing the framework for the mesmerising series of television interviews with politicians entitled *Clarke and Dawe* that soon followed.

When Clarke fell out with ABC radio in 1981 over the use of his work across the network, Phillip Adams, who had produced the Barry McKenzie film, invited him to work on a film script with writer and director Paul Cox. John was flattered but panic stricken, explaining anxiously to Adams that he was not suitable: 'this is very generous of you' he said, 'but you should know that I'm uniquely unqualified to be

---

5   *Times on Sunday*, 27 March 1987.

here. I've never made a movie; most of the things I've done have been relatively short – everything I've done in the last few years has been only minutes'. Undeterred, Adams encouraged Clarke, explaining that he needed Clarke to work with Cox, who Adams regarded as a brilliant filmmaker, but given to making 'gloomy Dutch interiors that need something'. Clarke felt sure Adams was making a mistake, but agreed to meet the auteur, to discuss collaborating on the script for the highly original romance *Lonely Hearts*.

As he drove to his first meeting with Paulus Henrique Benedictus "Paul" Cox, the anxious Clarke berated himself: 'what will this experienced European film maker think of me who knows nothing of cinema?' When he arrived at Cox's house, there was a creative chaos in the place that delighted Clarke – including a visiting Werner Hertzog living in the back yard shed with a dingo – and as it turned out Clarke and Cox got on famously. Cox already had the film in outline and they worked on it together, re-scripting it in parts. Clarke recalls the joy of working with Cox: 'when you collaborate with somebody you sort of become one another to a degree … your sensitivity to the other person encourages you to think in ways that will help the other person's strengths'. Incredibly, some of the most overtly comic material in *Lonely Hearts* was written by Cox and some of the more lugubrious bits were written by Clarke.

For Clarke working on *Lonely Hearts* was a revelation. He and Cox would act bits of the story out for one another to try out the script, and in the finished film Clarke appears momentarily as someone trying to work out the cables for lights, in an amusing sequence in which the characters are rehearsing for an amateur theatre production. This scene was Paul's idea. The finished film was utterly unlike other films being made in Australia at the time. It was not a masculinist comedy, or an historical story. It dealt with a couple of ordinary people in the suburbs of Melbourne. The couple are uncomfortable in themselves, awkward: 'everything about it is awkward, it's a monument to awkwardness', Clarke recalled, laughing. Initially nobody would distribute the film but it won an AFI award for Best Film, and there was a sudden flurry of interest that extended to art houses in the United States and Europe.

Sketching Pollies

Gradually Clarke drifted back into television and to his original game: sketch comedy and current affairs. *The Gillies Report* was performed in front of a live audience, reviving a form in Australia pioneered by *The Mavis Bramston Show* in the 1960s. It was broadcast weekly and centred on the actor Max Gillies, who played all the politicians of the day: Fraser, Hawke, Peacock, Menzies, Whitlam, Gorbachev, Thatcher and an alzheimic Ronald Reagan. Gillies' laconic opening lines in the first episode set the mood of the show: 'Hello, I'm Max Gillies and most of the people you'll be seeing tonight aren't'. Each episode featured a lavish musical production number with the full cast in chorus and Gillies as lead vocalist. A musical tribute to Gough Whitlam offered one of the most memorable satirical sketches ever presented on Australian television. Clarke introduced *Il Dismissale*, an opera by Gean Carlo Trimbole (an allusion to the crime boss Robert Trimbole) and said, 'In keeping with the tradition of hugely overproduced and increasingly baroque big budget versions of the dreadful, tawdry and pitifully shameful events of our recent history, we proudly present the following attempt to gloss over the facts …'. Gillies played Whitlam, Fraser and Sir John Kerr in this sketch. Gillies, with his expressive features and bulging eyes, was an extraordinarily powerful mimic. His impersonation of Bob Hawke, for instance, was remarkable, with every intonation of the man's voice, each movement of the eye, hand gesture and twitch of the lips, perfectly rendering the politician. Also memorable was Gillies' impersonation of the gargantuan and notorious Queensland Minister for Racing, Russ Hinze. Gillies, singing the hilarious 'I am Queensland', was encased in a fat suit so massive that he could barely sit down. The writing was clever, politically astute and perfectly attuned to the theatre of politics and the strutting star turns of our elected leaders. The writing time for the sketches was tight and there was only one day for rehearsals. But the pressure, which was evident in the sometimes florid acting, was part of the joy of it for John.

Clarke, who played a newsreader in the series, wrote all his news bulletins just before the program was recorded. Some of the sketches were light and whimsical, while others were dark and more biting in their satire. In the final episode, Clarke appears at intervals wearing long effeminate wigs that become bigger, and more elaborate, in each scene. These segments were collated from the earlier episodes in the series. By the end of the episode the wig is a huge black and pink beehive and in the ultimate segment it morphs into a massive white cone out of which a Christmas tree pops. This decidedly strange idea came about because the production team had wanted John to wear a wig. He wasn't keen unless the wig was funny, so each week he wore a bigger one, with increasingly bizarre features: for instance, one of the wigs lights up, and a cuckoo flies out of it.

Clarke parodied the national obsession with sport, inventing a new imaginary sport called farnarkeling and reported on Australian prowess in the sport regularly during the series. If the series favoured a hyper masculine style, offering its female actors Wendy Harmer and Tracy Harvey less opportunity to shine, it certainly recognised the problem in the culture and struck home in its parody of the super popular romantic game show *Perfect Match*. Gillies played the host, sporting wavy up-thrusting hair, white trousers and white shoes. Clarke appeared as a contestant in the civilian clothes favoured by cricketers and would-be cricketers in the 1980s: a tightly fitted jumper and trousers, with a chunky gold chain around his neck, chest hair protruding. They spoofed both the game show and the whole culture by making it about mates: 'What would you do if a mate switched to Southern Comfort and Coke?', one of the 'contestants' barked. 'What would you do if a mate brought his girlfriend?', asked another, as the audience hooted with laughter.

The series was demanding and exhausting: in some episodes Clarke played eight characters and Gillies 'anchored' the show, daring to scorch his employer as he announced with mock gravity that 'the Gillies Report shares the ABC's obsession with quality, relevance and lack of unnecessary excitement'. If the show cemented Clarke's insider status in Australia, and drew him back to his original form, it also set him thinking about a minimal style of acting that he preferred, one that was in stark contrast to that of Gillies, and relied on the actor's own facial expression, voice and gesture rather than an impersonation of the politician who was the target of the satire.

Playing Himself

Clarke carried his profound and enduring ambivalence about 'serious' acting around with him like a tortoise shell, which he retreated under at regular intervals. Yet he appeared in dramatic roles on film and television regularly. He disguised his acting by seeming to play himself, his nasal voice, laconic manner and blokey style a dimension of almost every role. It was an ingenious mask. This mask was also the way in which Clarke resolved the problem of drama as an actor, reconciling who he was through playing in a particular way. Every actor must do this and for Clarke a string of comic roles often coated with black humour provided that meeting of the actor and the acting. In the film *Death in Brunswick*, Clarke, in clothes reminiscent of Fred Dagg, played the gritty older mate, alongside Sam Neill's character, the hapless, good-looking young chef, 'Cookie', who accidentally kills the kitchen hand. The film offers a rich blend of romance and grungy social realism, with much of its humour dependent on physical comedy that satirises masculinity. The darkness and violence of the film is balanced by the ridiculous comic situations.

In a protracted, gruesome grave-yard sequence filmed in the Brighton Cemetery in Melbourne, Clarke and Sam Neill wrestle with the corpse of the kitchen hand Mustafa as they attempt to bury him in a grave that is already prepared (for someone else). During the filming, Clarke visited the office of the vast and sprawling cemetery and discovered that his great-great grandfather Edward Fox (1825–1909) is buried there near the grave of Rolf Boldrewood. In the film, by coincidence, John Ruane told Clarke and Neill to walk past Fox's unmarked grave during this strange comic sequence. Clarke quipped airily just before they shot the sequence: 'now there will be two of my family members in this film'. It was a casual throwaway line that made the others laugh, as they prepared for the shoot in the eerie stillness of the shadowy and silent burial ground. Sam Neill at this time was an experienced film actor and Clarke was much more used to television than film, but his ironic style was alive and well during the shooting.

Gina Riley, Bryan Dawe and John Clarke in *The Games*.
Courtesy of John Clarke.

While he was chronically uncertain about his life as an actor, in *The Games* Clarke proved a great deal to himself: 'The idea was to shoot a satirical drama that appears to be a documentary so it looks real, only we're monkeying with the visual grammar, we're asking people to question the way they watch things; is it true because it looks true and if it isn't, are the other things that look true actually or possibly false?' *The Games* is one of the most significant Australian comic series ever broadcast, pioneering a new form of comic drama. For Clarke it was 'delicious' to be working on an event that all the media were fixating on for years before it took place: the Sydney Olympic Games. The series satirised the politics and personalities around the staging of the Games, focusing on numerous real and imagined mishaps: the ticketing fiasco, corruption in the international movement, the ludicrous error of building the 100 meter track just 94 meters long, and the rank careerism of the planning authority officials – the show's main characters.

The Games, which is one of Clarke's major creative achievements, combined his knowledge of sport with his love of its theatre and politics. In the two series, Clarke pioneered the genre of mockumentary satire on Australian television and elevated the politics of sport to the central target. He collaborated on the script with Ross Stevenson, a popular radio host and former lawyer, and invited Bryan Dawe and Gina Riley to play his venal offsiders on the organising committee of the Sydney Olympics. Clarke particularly wanted Gina Riley to be in the series because of her strength as a comic actor, and her talent for playing big, confronting, unlikeable characters. In keeping with Clarke's style, all of the actors used their real names.

The apology delivered by the actor John Howard to the Indigenous people of Australia (never stating that is the Prime Minister) took aim at the real John Howard, who refused to make an apology during his term of office from 1996 to 2007. The speech tied up the episode's storyline while providing a stinging attack on the politics of indigenous affairs in Australia. The apology is both disarming and beguiling because it simulates the possibilities of the real so convincingly and is so pure in its subversive power. Gina points out after watching the broadcast in the office with awe-struck colleagues that if you didn't know who the prime minister of Australia was, you would be forgiven for believing this to be a real, much awaited political event. 'Nobody overseas knows what the Australian prime minister looks like', she crows triumphantly, recognising it as a PR coup, as her colleagues cheer John Howard's apology. Eight years later the real prime minister, Kevin Rudd – who succeeded John Howard in 2007, delivered the Apology to the indigenous people of Australia, demonstrating the resonance of the political sting in Clarke's writing.

In the finale of the series John, Bryan, Gina and Nicholas dress up as The Seekers to rehearse the nostalgic hit song 'The Carnival is Over' on the back of a truck in the vast and empty stadium, in preparation for the closing ceremony, because at the last minute they discover that the real Seekers are unable to participate. Their bluff and preposterous determination to portray the actual band members, with Gina flicking her long hair as she grimaces at the others, and their incessant bickering, capped off the fanciful theatricality of the series. Like so many of the intricately developed plot lines, this climax demonstrated the breadth of the satire, its raw physicality, and its whimsical magic. *The Games* was the highest rating ABC comedy series ever to screen, and the series sold to Canada, the US and New Zealand.

JOHN CLARKE

The Interview

John Clarke and Bryan Dawe began performing their mock interviews on television in 1989. *Clarke and Dawe* relies on a parody of the primary political exchange of the television age: the political interview. The focus is squarely on the television theatre of politics and the peculiarities of each politician. The mock interview is compressed into two-minute episodes, each one revealing Clarke as a highly original performer who has perfected a distinctive form of sketch comedy. In an episode broadcast in October 2013, just before the incoming parliament sat for the first time, Clarke played the new Treasurer Joe Hockey. The interview lampoons the newly elected politicians and their use of taxpayer funded allowances to attend the weddings of their colleagues. At least five coalition members were named in the scandal that erupted at this time, including former Prime Minister Tony Abbott, who repaid his expenses after a battering in the media over the issue. House Speaker Bronwyn Bishop did not and in 2015 was forced to resign after another scandal in which she hired a helicopter to travel from Melbourne to Geelong. Again *Clarke and Dawe* worried away at the theme, presenting several satirical swipes at the rorts, illustrating the extent of the problem in an episode that made the punch lines, the lines of attack, seem like throwaway lines. The thrust of the critique in the Joe Hockey interview refers to whether the new PM, Tony Abbott, will or will not be present on the first day of his parliament. The subtlety of the two scorching lines in the exchange below (in bold) are magnetic in performance:

> Dawe: Joe Hockey, thank you for your time.
> Clarke/Hockey: Always good to be with you Bryan and good evening.

Dawe: Parliament resumes in a few weeks.
Clarke/Hockey: Yes, it does, on the 12th I think.
Dawe: That will be an interesting session.
Clarke/Hockey: It will, yes, we've got a fair bit of work to get through in that parliament.
Dawe: Tony Abbott's first session as Prime Minister.
Clarke/Hockey: Yes, Tony will be there.
Dawe: Weddings permitting of course.
Clarke/Hockey: Yep, providing he's not at work.
(Without pausing Dawe presses on.)
Dawe: Now, the Opposition has a new leader. Are you worried about facing a fresh team?

With matter-of-fact certainty, Clarke as Hockey replies: 'No, you'd only be worried about facing Bill if he'd promised you his life-long loyalty, wouldn't you?' It's a withering line. Dawe doesn't blink, ploughing ahead with his questions. Within three lines, some 25 seconds, the two key politicians in the land – Prime Minister Abbott and opposition leader Bill Shorten – are lambasted. The memory of Shorten's behaviour would have been fresh in the audience's memory, after his infamous declaration of loyalty to Kevin Rudd, then Julia Gillard less than a year later, and despite having sworn loyalty to her, switching back to Rudd at the last minute.

In a later episode *Clarke and Dawe* returns to this signature moment in Australian politics, declaring that Bill Shorten's whereabouts are currently unknown, and that he 'is wanted in connection with two knifings'. The point is witty, sharp and graphic – comic gold.

Both the form and the style of the mock political interview are unique to Clarke. He does not emulate the real figure he plays in the sketch. Without the distraction of mimicry the audience focuses on the words and the interaction of the two performers. But this is not simply verbal humour. The targets are spin and political arrogance. Although it originated in radio and migrated to television, in *Clarke and Dawe* facial and vocal expression, as well as gesture, are all-important. Clarke physicalises spin; his entire body carries the posturing of a range of political figures in each confected moment. Each sketch offers an argument or a cogent observation on political hypocrisy. Compression of writing and economy of performance are the bedrock of this sketch style. There are no cheap laughs. It is referential but light in touch, and never crude. It is a highly disciplined satirical style devoid of the anarchic flourishes so beloved of other Australian satirists.

John Clarke is not the first satirist to expose the charade of political interviews. But his original style and method of satirising this dialogue through an interview is clearly admired by many. The British duo John Bird and John Fortune were so impressed by the Clarke and Dawe format that they reproduced it for their show, *The Long Johns*, broadcast on Channel 4 in 1995, in which they conducted interviews that closely resemble those of *Clarke and Dawe*. Despite admitting to a journalist that their producer Geoff Atkinson had seen Clarke and Dawe in action, there is no protection of 'format rights' in the UK and Australia, and so the comic duo had no legal case to answer. The BBC went on to produce a mock documentary entitled *Twenty Twelve* about the team of organisers working on the London Olympic Games, using an almost identical format to that developed by Clarke and Stevenson for their series on the antics of the Sydney Olympic Games organising committee. This rankled particularly because Clarke and Stevenson had pitched a series to the BBC after London was awarded the 2012 Games in 2005, and had participated in numerous meetings, phone conferences and correspondence about just such a project. But the BBC went ahead with the show without the Australian writers. Reflecting on this, Clarke told me that it had made him 'grumpy about the colonial economies being used to feed the British one'.

John Clarke and Bryan Dawe appeared together in
Clarke and Dawe from 1989 until 2017.
Courtesy of John Clarke.

Satirist

Clarke insisted that he was not an intellectual. But his interests were wide, and his knowledge of fiction, poetry and history was staggering. He recorded his ideas in lengthy online essays that should delight anyone who stumbles across them. Clarke continued to read Auden regularly and recognised the sharpness of his observations about his own time, and the desolate state of the world before the onset of World War II.

Clarke suggested that in Auden's poem dedicated to Yeats ('In Memory of W.B. Yeats') with its famous lines written in 1939 'In the nightmare of the dark/All the dogs of Europe bark ....', that Auden is 'a writer thinking aloud', explaining that 'The poet's project is himself''. Clarke, like Auden before him, was haunted by the events of a world war (Clarke by the Second World War, Auden by the First World War).

To celebrate the centenary of Auden's birth in 2007, John Clarke and Clive James, another Auden devotee, were invited to discuss the poet together in a session at the Melbourne Writers Festival. With his usual self-doubt gnawing away, Clarke told James that he thought it would work better if Clive appeared on his own in the session. James would have none of it, and insisted Clarke join him on the stage. John, still anxious, was keen to meet Clive beforehand to work out a plan for the session. They met twice but never seemed to get around to talking about the Auden event. Clarke telephoned James the day before the session, and said 'I'm going to wrestle you to the ground and force you to talk about this with me'. 'OK' said Clive, 'How shall we do it?' And John began to say something about Auden. Immediately Clive interrupted and said 'Don't tell me; don't tell me. Tell me tomorrow in the session'.

***

John's father, Ted, was not someone who frequented the theatre and never saw his son or his wife perform on stage. But in the 1980s when Barry Humphries was touring New Zealand, Humphries sought Ted out and arranged two complimentary tickets for him to come and see his show. After the show, Ted telephoned John, and gave a glowing account of Humphries' performance. He thought it was brilliant, and regaled his son with a blow-by-blow description of the jokes and the scathing hilarity of Humphries' satire. John could hardly believe what he was hearing. Ted sounded ecstatic, suddenly alive to a new world of comic drama, a world in which his son had been immersed for twenty years. It was as if he had just woken up. He said with admiration and awe: 'Do you *know* this bloke?' When John explained that he did know Humphries and had worked with him Ted was silent. After years of disinterest and hostility towards John's theatrical world, it was a transformation he would never forget.

Years later Ted visited John in Brisbane, and John invited him in to the studio where he was filming an episode of *Clarke and Dawe*. John was based in Brisbane because he was half way through the shoot of a film called *Blood Oath*. Bryan Dawe was in Melbourne, and it was late in the evening when John arrived at the studio to shoot the episode. All the staff had left for the day and John settled down in front of the camera and the monitor to prepare. Ted walked around like a child, looking at lights and equipment and asking questions. He had never been in a television studio in his life. As there was nobody else except Ted available to assist him, John asked his father to hand him a piece of paper at a certain point in the sketch, instructing him to stand at the edge of the frame. His father duly obeyed. They rehearsed the sketch twice and then filmed it. It was not the ideal way to shoot an episode, but after some conversations by phone with the editor who was also in Melbourne, Ted and John left the studio. John drove and Ted sat quietly. After a while Ted said 'I can see why that works … it's partly the rhythm'. They chatted for a moment about the sketch and Ted said 'it's easy if you understand the rhythm'. John drove on speechless. He realised that his father understood the way the sketch worked through its rhythm. Ted had been masterful in his own appreciation of rhythm in his own speech, and it was as if he acknowledged for the first time that something in himself was at play there in John's sketch. The exchange signalled something precious to John. Ted had seen his son for the first time as a writer, actor and satirist, and inheritor of something instinctive in him too, and at that moment he appreciated his son as a comic artist, just as he had appreciated those Goons on the radio so many years ago.

Like any actor or writer, and like Auden, Clarke's project was himself – his performances sometimes seemed to be a 'writer thinking aloud'. This is part of his appeal. His sketches appear organic and spontaneous. The directness Clarke discovered in his first revue is one of his strengths. But just like the poets Clarke admired, the words in his dramatic sketches were put down with discipline, skill and intense focus. His satirical wit relied on comic judgement and restraint. Clarke's writing, like his personality, was outward looking and generous, and his work is a gift both to the audience and to the larger democratic project in which satire plays a glorious and vital part.

Chapter 6

TONY SHELDON: DO YOU BELIEVE IN ANGELS?

(B. 1955)

I first met Tony Sheldon in 2008 on a rainy Friday afternoon in Sydney where he launched a book I had put together about the actor and playwright Nick Enright. He had agreed to do this in spite of his gruelling schedule at the Lyric Theatre playing Bernadette in *Priscilla Queen of the Desert*, and in spite of the fact that he did not know me at all. Tall and svelte, Tony arrived in the foyer of the NIDA theatre in Kensington for the launch. He was fresh faced and gracious and entertained the crowd with his hilarious memories of Enright who he had known since the two of them were teenagers. Tony would skive off football training to listen to records of Broadway shows in the afternoons at Nick's flat in Edgecliff. Enright died in 2002 but in his short life he had many friends. Drew Forsythe sang one of Enright's songs, *Jindyworobak*, to loud applause. At 5pm we were farewelling Sheldon as he strode out to a taxi in the teeming rain, praying that he would arrive at the theatre in time to makeup and dress for the evening performance, a process that took three hours. Tony's warmth and generosity spilled out of him that day, and later that night, sitting in my seat in the back row at the Lyric I was transfixed by his voice and his shining stage presence.

We met again in New York City in 2014 on a mild autumn evening. Tony had been rehearsing a show since the early hours of the day. He had already been on the go for 12 hours. I had fully expected him to cancel our interview because his mother Toni Lamond was to receive a Lifetime Achievement Award that week in Sydney. I felt sure he would want to be home for this event. But Tony kept our appointment and told me he didn't want to 'muck me around'. I was flabbergasted. He smiled and said: 'and it all turned out for the best. Because I stayed here, I could accept a role in a new musical at the last minute'. With a broad smile he said: 'you see how the universe works, if I'd gone back I couldn't have done *Bandwagon*'. Clearly thrilled with his role in this musical, Tony told me about it, and about his whole life over the next four hours. Tony refused food, explaining his strict diet and monkish ways. He glowed with vitality and joy.

Swinging on a Star

The boy is seven. Dressed in a dinner suit tailored to his small frame, a crisp striped shirt and bow tie, he walks on to the set of *In Melbourne Tonight*. Graham Kennedy lifts his small body onto a table, and they begin their routine. He smiles as he looks up at the suave compere, his fingers nervously tapping on his knees as he waits for his cue. The boy is angelic, with sparkling eyes and plump cheeks. He sings a duet called *Swinging on a Star*, an American war-time pop song made famous by Bing Crosby. He makes all the gestures confidently – pigs, mules and fish, for every verse. He is calm, sweet and all of Melbourne is watching him. Within days he receives a gift of three new Walt Disney LPs: *Alice in Wonderland*, *Peter Pan* and *Cinderella*. Along with the records is a letter from the head of Channel Nine, telling him that he had 'made a lot of people very happy' and offering him a regular spot on the show.

Every second Wednesday Tony would leave school just when the other children were eating their sandwiches and playing outside. He rehearsed his routines for the evening show all afternoon. The show was filmed live and so there was no room for mistakes. He always appeared in the first half hour to comply with regulations that only allowed children to perform up until 10pm, and he was the only child on television at that hour. Tony sang, danced and performed short comedy sketches. His parents, Frank Sheldon and Toni Lamond, called him 'Butch'. The nickname came from Doris Whimp, a dancer who had partnered Frank Sheldon in variety shows. Doris saw that baby Tony was dressed in a pink garment and said that this would not do: she changed him into a blue outfit, and then quipped 'Doesn't he look butch?' Sheldon at 7 looked anything but butch: he was more like a choir boy and he appealed to adults with his round face, big eyes, dimples and slight lisp. His entire family worked on the show. Frank was a producer and Toni a regular performer, appearing four nights a week. Even Tony's grandparents, Max Reddy and Stella Lamond, sometimes appeared in 'bring back the Tivoli' nights, when Frank invited in all the older stars.

Frank had been a dancer himself, and was a member of the chorus when he met Toni Lamond at the Tivoli in Melbourne, where she was the leading lady to the English comedian Tommy Trinder. Toni Lamond's parents vociferously objected to her decision to marry the tall, dark-haired Frank Sheldon, precisely because he was a chorus boy and in the hierarchy of theatre this was marrying down. There was another reason that Stella Lamond warned her daughter off Sheldon. Her own husband, Toni's father, the comedian Joe Lawman, had left Stella for a chorus girl and 'she was gravely insulted', Tony told me. But the young lovers prevailed. They married and Toni gave birth to her son, Anthony Sheldon, in Brisbane. It was 1955. Toni and Frank were on their way home from performing in a variety show in Manila.

Tony Sheldon with his mother, Toni Lamond.
Courtesy of Tony Sheldon

Tony Sheldon made his first theatrical tour as a toddler, with his parents, who were both performing in a new American musical called *The Pajama Game*. It was the first time an all-Australian cast performed a professional musical since the 1940s.[1] The producers, JC Williamsons, often imported their leading performers. Frequently these were understudies from the UK or the USA. But for some reason nobody expected this musical about a strike at a pyjama factory to run for long, and a local choreographer, Betty Pounder, was despatched to New York to document the Broadway production so that it could be replicated in Australia, although she was given permission to re-stage the dances. Pounder had danced in musical comedies with Gladys Moncrieff, and choreographed Australian musicals for some years. She favoured an all-Australian cast on principle, irrespective of the fate of the musical.[2] At the time the performers did not receive any rehearsal pay, and therefore took on evening work. Lamond performed in a floor show at the Savoy Club near Spencer Street Station in Melbourne.

The Australian production of *The Pajama Game* was a huge success: the show ran for two years. Lamond played the union leader Babe and it made her name. It also propelled Jill Perryman and Tiki Taylor to stardom. The cast frolicked in brightly coloured pyjamas on a gigantic bed atop a truck that rolled along the streets of Melbourne in the Moomba Parade. Tony, looking like a miniature Pierrot, clad in a pair of cut down pyjamas with a large diamond pattern, waved and smiled to the crowds for the duration of the two-hour parade.[3]

---

1   John West, 1995, 'Musical Theatre', in Philip Parsons (ed.) *Companion to Theatre in Australia*, Sydney: Currency Press, p. 384. West says it was an 'almost all-Australian cast'.

2   Frank Van Straten, 2012, 'Betty Mildred Pounder (1921–1990)', in *Australian Dictionary of Biography Online*, http://adb.anu.edu.au/biography/pounder-betty-mildred-15484.

3   Toni Lamond, 1990, *First Half*, Sydney: Pan, pp. 96, 110.

TONY SHELDON

The little boy had only just started talking, but he could already sing fragments of 'Hernando's Hideaway', having heard it so many times. The company travelled by train on the tour and railway porters would greet them at each town demanding to meet 'the kid' as soon as the train pulled in. They would shout out to Toni Lamond: 'Where's the kid who sings?' One of Tony's earliest memories is watching his father dance one of the big numbers of the show, called 'Steam Heat', dressed in stovepipe trousers and bowler hat – a soft shoe shuffle of considerable difficulty, with a rousing jazz tune.

Tony Sheldon with his father, Frank Sheldon.
Courtesy of Tony Sheldon

Sheldon junior was just four years old when his father took him to his first dancing lesson. It was a fiasco. The teachers tried to teach him difficult steps, one after the other, all in the first lesson, possibly nervous at having the celebrity dancer Frank Sheldon's son in their charge. The small boy was overwhelmed and left the dance studio in tears. Frank Sheldon could not disguise his irritation with his son, and that was the end of the dancing lessons. The experience of feeling as though he had failed and disappointed his father had a lasting effect on Tony. Added to this, his father did not ever allow him to go back to lessons.

Tony continued as a regular on Graham Kennedy's *In Melbourne Tonight* for two years. He enjoyed it but it set him apart from other children. One day during a rehearsal with his father he defied Frank's instructions. Frank told him to sit up on the stool properly. But Tony had other ideas. He wanted to sit with one leg on the floor like the American singer Perry Como, who was smooth and suave on television. Frank kept on at him: 'No, you're a child. Sit on the stool like a little boy'. During the performance Tony disobeyed his father and sat like Perry Como. When he walked off set his father was waiting for him: 'That was the last appearance you've ever made. You've just kissed your career goodbye. You're going back to school tomorrow and that's it'. Frank fired the nine-year-old boy on the spot. It was unusual for Tony to disobey his father, and in hindsight he thinks it was because at one level he did not want to continue on the show. He was bullied at school and had very few friends. Perhaps his behaviour reflected his own sense of anxiety about his parents also. Frank and Toni were struggling, and one day Tony walked in to find his father beating his mother. There was intense competition between his parents, and Frank wanted Toni to give up her career now that he was a well-established producer, but she refused. His jealousy of her success was corrosive. To make matters worse Tony was sent to board at Glamorgan in Toorak. It was the preparatory school for Geelong Grammar and Sheldon loathed it.

Tony's mother encouraged him to audition for *Oliver*, and he remembers his encounter with Betty Pounder vividly. Pounder enjoyed legendary status by this time, and already knew his parents from the landmark production of *The Pajama Game* in 1957. She cast Tony as one of Fagin's boys, explaining that he was too young to play Oliver or the Artful Dodger. Toni Lamond was cast as Nancy. Toni and Frank agreed that Tony could participate when the show transferred to Sydney in the spring during his school holidays. Tony's stage debut in *Oliver* in 1966 was a formative experience. He loved playing the orphan boy in this big musical, and cherished the camaraderie of the other children and the kindness of the adults in the cast. He also admired the boy who played the Artful Dodger, Andrew Sharp. The Theatre Royal was an old classic in Castlereagh Street (demolished in 1972). He recalls the thrill of walking through the classical columns of the foyer, the smell of old timber, and standing on the small stage gazing up at the three levels, marvelling at the soaring, full height flying facilities of the old theatre. You walked down a driveway to get to the stage door and a doorkeeper sat in a tiny glass office outside. For years afterwards Tony would always stop and chat to whoever was sitting there

On Tony's eleventh birthday, during the last week of the Sydney run of *Oliver*, he spent a happy day with his father. As he wasn't in the matinee he and Frank toured the sights. They had their photo taken together in one of the new automatic photo booths dotted around the city. During a rowdy cast party at their flat, Tony put himself to bed but later awoke to hear his parents arguing; in the morning he discovered his mother covered in bruises, and his father was gone. Lamond could barely move. Years later Tony found out that his mother had told Frank that she wanted a divorce. Sheldon lost his temper and bashed Toni.

A few days later Tony received a late night phone call from his father who had returned to Melbourne, and was inconsolable. Through tears he told his son that he knew he had made a terrible mistake and that he simply did not know how he would cope without Tony in his life. He revealed that Lamond had warned him that she would not allow him to see his son. Tony spoke to his father again the next evening, hoping his mother would not catch him. But Toni got up from her bed, where she had been all day because of her injuries, and snatched the phone out of the boy's hands. He heard her icy tone as she informed Frank: 'I will only speak to you through a lawyer. I repeat, you are never going to see your son again'.

Tony began to shake as he heard his mother slam down the phone. He was frightened as she loudly demanded in her next phone call that the police provide protection for her on her return to Melbourne. The arrangements were made and Tony and his mother packed up to prepare for the overnight Southern Aurora train to Melbourne. Tony lay awake as the train lurched and rattled on its slow journey south. He was restless and could hear his mother tossing and sighing on her bunk below him. It was midnight when the train arrived at Goulburn and pulled into the station. 'Why is the train stopping?' Tony whispered to his mother, hoping that she would answer. 'They take on mail', she replied reassuringly. He drifted off, only to be startled by a knock on their door. A policeman appeared and delivered the news that Frank Sheldon had taken his own life. Tony sobbed uncontrollably.

At Spencer Street Station early the next morning Tony and his mother found themselves blocked by a crush of reporters in long coats and hats pressing forwards as they tried to leave the train. They barked out questions all at once, demanding an explanation of Frank Sheldon's death. He was only 39. Tony listened, trying to hold back his tears as Lamond insisted that her husband had died of a heart attack. Within days Sheldon was marooned again at boarding school, drowning in his grief, while his mother continued the *Oliver* tour. Swamped in his own dark misery, Tony wondered at how she managed to keep on singing every night. Tony's anger and confusion about the death and the events that led up to it left him reeling, and the loss of his father cast a long shadow over his teenage and adult years.

Speculation about the real cause of the death filled the tabloids: wild rumours raged about Frank Sheldon, the well-known entertainer and television producer, claiming that he was an alcoholic, a homosexual, deeply depressed and suffering from all manner of problems. One newspaper ran a series of articles under a banner headline that screamed 'What killed Frank Sheldon?' above a photograph of Lamond dressed in a leotard, high heels and a bowler hat, dancing and singing. When she saw the photograph Lamond wept quietly and murmured to Tony: 'It looks as though I am dancing on his grave'. Tony could not find words to answer his mother and hot tears ran down his face.

The Birthday Party

With his father's assets frozen, rumours rife, an inquest still to be endured and a living to earn, Tony's mother decided that her best course of action was to leave Melbourne and to seek employment in the new large clubs of Sydney. Tony listened wide-eyed to his mother as she explained that these were new establishments called RSL'S (Returned Service League) clubs that had opened in various suburbs, and offered cabaret entertainment. Tony hoped that the move would mean that he would live with his mother at home again, but his heart sank when she announced that he would board at Cranbrook School in the eastern suburbs of Sydney.

Sheldon found the new school daunting and oppressive; he had no interest in football or in the cadets, and disliked the other boys. Worst of all he missed his mother and longed to be with her in her flat at Bellevue Hill. But at Cranbrook Sheldon met Terence Clarke, a mathematics teacher, feared by many of the boys. One day he heard Clarke calling his name in the corridor. 'Sheldon' he said 'I'm having a reading of *The Tempest*. And I would like you to come in and play Miranda'. Tony replied 'No, I'm not going to do that. I don't want to play a girl'. Next time he saw Clarke the teacher said the play would be Harold Pinter's *The Birthday Party*. 'You'll come to that, won't you?' He read the part of Meg Boles, the 60-something-year-old landlady in a seaside boarding house. Sheldon was just thirteen but he liked the play immediately, and was pleased to see Andrew Sharp who he remembered from *Oliver*. He realised slowly that he could act and Clarke encouraged him, telling him emphatically 'You know, you're good at this'. For Sheldon it was an extraordinary moment. Firstly to have someone tell him that he was good at acting, and second to realise for the first time that he didn't have to dance like his father, and that he didn't have to sing, like his mother. He glimpsed something of his own in this raw and absurdist play, and sensed that there might be a possibility that 'I could make my way in the world'. Terry Clarke had opened a door just at the right time when Sheldon was bereft, vulnerable and aimless.

Andrew Sharp was four years older than Tony and the friendship between them was discouraged at school. Handsome and popular, Sharp was a free spirit and the two of them shared a love of drama. He came from a wealthy, respectable family. Sheldon was wide eyed with admiration for the older boy and remembers his delight in Sharp and his family. He was talented, wealthy and beautiful. In retrospect, Tony imagines himself as a kind of teenaged Charles Ryder in thrall to Andrew's Sebastian Flyte, except that it was 1968 and Sharp was a hippie.

Tony only saw his mother at the weekends until without warning she left for England. He was shocked at her hasty departure, but he found her letters astonishing: she described her life in England working in clubs in Manchester and other places, sometimes with a big band, often accompanied with a dreary organ and drums, her delight in Ginger Rogers playing Mame at Drury Lane, and her awe of John Gielgud and Irene Worth in a matinee of *Oedipus Rex* at the Old Vic, performed in modern dress: brown skivvies and trousers. Lamond did not spare her son's sensibilities and regaled him with the details of Worth as Jocasta, slowly impaling herself on a sword through her vagina, and the startling finale in which the cast encircled a massive gold penis. She alluded to her relationship with a Canadian called Ed who only wanted to drink beer and watch ice hockey on television, and not long afterwards explained that Don Lane had offered to bring her back to Australia.[4]

On her return Tony persuaded his mother to let him live at home. It was difficult for the two of them as they hadn't lived together for several years and Tony had matured and had a social circle and his own views about his future: there was also an unresolved fury in him about being abandoned to boarding school when he had most needed his mother. He told me calmly, as a man of fifty-nine who had clearly spent a lifetime thinking about this, that it was a 'fractured relationship: we didn't know each other very well'. Lamond picked up shows on the club circuit and Tony secured a few spots as an extra in the Norman Lindsay Festival on the ABC. Gradually Sheldon realised his mother was not well. He suspected she was abusing tranquillisers and sleeping pills. Once more Tony was 'shuttled' back to boarding school. He didn't like the school but in compensation he always enjoyed the plays and had decided he would pursue acting as a career. One day his mother complained to him about the expense of the school fees. Without even blinking Sheldon said 'I won't go back. I won't finish'. He had one more year. Lamond cautioned him against leaving before he completed his schooling, warning him that it would not be easy for him to work as an actor. Immediately Sheldon picked up the telephone and in his most formal and haughty voice informed the receptionist at Cranbrook, as if he was the parent, that 'Tony Sheldon will not be returning to school'.

A week later he successfully auditioned for *The Fantasticks*, and moved out of his mother's house. He played Matt in the exuberant

---

4   Toni Lamond, *First Half*, p. 182.

musical, with lyrics by Tom Jones and catchy tunes such as 'Try to remember', presented at the Intimate Theatre in Neutral Bay; his appearance led to a series of invitations to perform. Sheldon was just 17: he had a large oval shaped face with generous features and high cheek bones, a broad smile and animated hands. He was now six foot tall, slim and towered over his mother, with long legs and short, cropped light brown hair. But his enthusiasm for his new life as an actor took a dive during a run of a strange new Australian play called *Goldilocks and the Three Bears R Certificate* by Robyn Moase. Sheldon was understudying the lead actor Bruce Myles. After three days Miles resigned, leaving the rather green young Sheldon to carry the production. He played Baby Bear and appeared in every scene of the play. He was nervous about working with the Ensemble crowd because of their focus on Method acting, something he'd only heard about; the actual approach to acting used by the Ensemble actors remained a complete mystery to him. Somehow he struggled through the rehearsals, but after the preview show the director John Macleod began giving the cast members copious notes. He didn't offer anything to Sheldon who sat with the others sipping a glass of beer, waiting for his notes. Ninety minutes passed with every member of the cast receiving notes but Sheldon. Finally Macleod paused and said coldly: 'And now we come to Mr Sheldon'. A chill passed over the cast who froze in their seats as he glared at the young actor. 'Never have I seen such an incompetent, outrageously indulgent, inept performance', began Macleod, who delivered a tirade of criticism and humiliating abuse. Sheldon sat dumbly, praying for the man to finish. When he finally concluded, he instructed the cast to re-assemble at ten o'clock the following morning to 'rehearse the show for Mr Sheldon's benefit'.

The cast duly assembled for the rehearsal. It was the day before opening night. On his first line, spoken to a tree as he walked across the stage carrying his suitcase, Macleod yelled 'Stop! What action are you playing? Sheldon stammered: 'I'm playing the action to talk to a tree … No, I'm playing the action to be frightened'. Macleod was irritated and bellowed 'You can't play the action to be, you have to be playing the action on the tree'. Sheldon in defeat replied: 'I don't know', at which point Macleod stood up and addressed the entire cast. 'Well, we will all sit and wait until Mr Sheldon works out what his action is.' Every time Sheldon began a new line he was interrupted by the director and ridiculed. During a short break he walked outside sobbing quietly, hoping none of the others would notice him. As they rehearsed the next act Sheldon exploded with rage in character. Baby Bear was supposed to become hysterical and Tony played it with all the energy he could summon, crying, screaming, the tears streaming down his face. After this Macleod said calmly 'That's how I want you to play every performance. This is how you do it'. Not knowing any better and determined to please the director Sheldon 'tore himself apart' every night. But he would cry all the way home because he was raw with the effort of having become hysterical night after night, without knowing how to manage the shattering outbursts of anger in performance. Late one night in the car on the way home, crossing the Sydney Harbour Bridge, Sheldon attempted to jump out of the speeding vehicle but another passenger pulled him back. Sheldon told me that he did not intend to kill himself but was hysterical. The trauma of this experience left its mark on the young actor. It also had a material effect: Sheldon was not invited back to the Ensemble Theatre for twenty years because he gained a reputation from that production, unfairly, for being 'highly strung'.

Theatre Animal

John Bell cast the 18-year-old Sheldon as Joe Cassidy in the premiere of *A Hard God*, a raw, intense play by Peter Kenna. The diminutive and passionate playwright, Kenna, had begun his career as an actor and the character of Joe was semi-autobiographical. Kenna was a devout Roman Catholic. When Sheldon first read the script he was stunned by the power of the role of the young man Joe Cassidy, and its personal resonance. It was as if the character of Cassidy had been written for him in its exploration of the struggle of a young man with his sexuality; although Sheldon had no experience of Catholicism he played Joe with an authenticity that was staggering. John Bell had an Irish Catholic background and the world of the play was his world.

Sheldon brought a vulnerability to Joe that was close to the truth of his own life. Playing opposite his school friend, Andrew Sharp, cast as Jack Shannon, meant that it was less awkward to find a way of making the intimate relationship between the two teenagers credible as they struggle with their homosexual longings, and the strictures of their faith. Another 'buffer' for Tony was Gloria Dawn who played his mother (Aggie Cassidy) with dry humour and stoic strength: 'it was like having a surrogate mother in the show', Sheldon recalled. Dawn was a star of variety and musical comedy, and Tony had known her since he was a child.

The play toured. In Melbourne one night after the performance Peter Kenna discovered the New York theatre dynamo, Stella Adler, alone in the auditorium after everyone had left the theatre. Knowing she had come to see the play he had waited for her in the foyer, too afraid to attend himself, in the presence of this celebrated acting guru. When she failed to emerge from the theatre Kenna walked in to find Adler was prone, on the floor in her fur coat, crying and shaking. When she realised Kenna was standing beside her, she looked up at him and through her sobs said 'Oh Peter, I have never been so overcome, so overpowered in all my life!'[5]

Sheldon was invited to appear in a television version of *A Hard God* to be produced by the ABC. He felt a new pang of terror about performing in front of a camera. Suddenly self-conscious, Sheldon dreaded the intimate sequences he knew had to be filmed in front of a director and crew, even though Andrew and Gloria were amongst the familiar cast members. To add to his difficulties he felt that the director Carl Schultz did not engage with the actors. His reserve and unstinting focus on the technical elements of framing shots were a stark contrast to John Bell's emotional commitment and energy during the rehearsals for the stage play.

In the television movie Tony is captivating as Joe Cassidy. With his glossy hair, full lips, long fingers and gentle demeanour he is restrained, and he conveys the fear, confusion and intensity of the young man with freshness, warmth and clarity. Vocally he is flawless in this production but physically he is slightly awkward at times. He does not look comfortable in the high waisted baggy trousers of the 1940s, or sitting stiffly beside the water in knitted box-legged full bathing suit that covered his whole torso. Tony worried about his ability to act on television, fearing that when he scaled down his dramatic expression for the camera he lost all personality. Although he had appeared on television as a boy on Graham Kennedy's variety show, and in an early episode of *Homicide*, he felt clumsy and

---

5   John Bell, 2003, *The Time of My Life*, Sydney: Allen & Unwin, p. 114.

unappealing in front of the camera. One director had barked at him 'Don't move your face so much', making him uneasy and stiff. It seemed to him that he was only capable of acting on stage where he did not have to restrain his facial expressions. He also felt more comfortable in front of a live audience, where he could make an immediate connection. If there was any doubt in his mind before this he knew now that he was 'a theatre animal'.

Although he enjoyed his new independence and his emerging career as an actor, Tony could not put his worries about his mother out of his mind. Lamond continued to work in the clubs but seemed to be sliding into a drug-fuelled darkness that was overwhelming. A phone call late one night brought all his fears for his mother and his years of grief for his father back in a rush of emotion. He learned that during a cabaret show at Wrest Point Casino in Hobart she appeared on stage slurring her words, and forgetting her lines. The manager told her to leave after one performance. On Christmas Eve, alone in her hotel room, Lamond took 50 sleeping bills with half a bottle of vodka, before taking to the bath with a razor blade where she slashed her wrists. An hour later a hotel maid delivered towels to Lamond's room, to find her comatose and bleeding profusely on the floor in the bathroom. Lamond was rushed to hospital.[6] Her close call with death was averted, and a long period of rehabilitation followed in hospital and then under the care of a devoted friend called Joan Hamm. Sheldon was despondent, having lost his father to suicide, and watching powerless as his mother deteriorated over several years. The ray of light was that Toni had been saved just in time. Sheldon marvelled at the fact that a chambermaid had arrived on Christmas

---

6   Lamond, *First Half*, p. 220.

morning, and had let herself in to the room: he consoled himself by imagining his mother with a guardian angel looking after her. His relief made him light headed and he could not think of anything else for weeks. It was the beginning of a softening in his relationship with his troubled mother, but not the end of his own difficulties.

When Terry Clarke invited Tony to join a new theatre company, the Hunter Valley Theatre Company, based in Newcastle, he leapt at the opportunity. It was not only a chance to contribute to a new venture; Clarke promised Sheldon roles that would help to extend him. Secretly he was smarting from several comments made by two people whose opinions mattered. In a conversation with John Bell, Tony had confided that he would like a break from playing 'sensitive homosexual boys'. Bell quipped 'Can you play anything else?' It was a joke, and Sheldon recognised it as that, but the words stung. Not long afterwards he played a young homosexual boy who seduces a married man in Simon Gray's play *Spoiled*. The influential critic, Katharine Brisbane, who expressed admiration for Sheldon's performance in the role, cautioned him emphatically after the show. She said 'Yes, wonderful, again … but you really should stop playing these roles'. He knew that Bell and Brisbane were right and that he should break away from the one kind of character. But their words wounded him. He wondered if he could play other roles. Unlike many of his contemporaries he had not studied acting formally. During the run of *Spoiled*, Sheldon asked Peter Carroll one day: 'Should I apply to NIDA?' Carroll thought about the question and advised Sheldon not to bother: 'You wouldn't cope with them. And they wouldn't cope with you', he said with conviction. It was a relief to hear Carroll confirm his own thoughts. Sheldon knew he would find it difficult to endure the 'breaking down' of student actors 'to rebuild them in a different image', and feared that he might not survive it. He would continue as before, learning from directors during rehearsals and bringing to each new role the 'concentrated tenacity' that Brisbane herself had observed early in his career.[7]

In the first production presented by the fledgling company Tony played the comic entertainer in John Romeril's radical new play *The Floating World*. The action takes place on a 'Women's Weekly Cherry Blossom' cruise to Japan. Sheldon appeared inside one of two large rotating funnels on stage playing a drum set. After each of his jokes he played a tune on the drums. It was an extraordinary production that enraged some audiences. In Muswellbrook some audience members were so shocked by the play that they walked out, demanding their money back.[8] Others found the raw insights into Australian xenophobia startling, and admired the portrayal of delusion triggered in the main character, Les, (played by Michael Rolfe) by wartime memories. The play is now regarded as an Australian masterpiece, with its incisive exploration of the long shadow of the war in the Pacific, its haunting satire and its quirky vaudeville elements.

Sheldon appeared in a range of roles after the Romeril play, cast by Terry Clarke as Tom in *The Glass Menagerie*, the young boy Alan in *Equus*, and other plays. It was a glorious and productive year for him; he shared a house in Newcastle with two of the other company members, Robert Alexander and Kerry Walker. Clarke, like John Bell, shepherded, bolstered and supported the actors, giving them freedom to discover a character and a role, without denting their

---

7   Katharine Brisbane writing of Sheldon in *Inner Voices, Theatre Australia*, 1978, reproduced in Brisbane, 2005, *Not Wrong Just Different: Observations on the Rise of Contemporary Australian Theatre*, Sydney: Currency Press, p. 276.
8   Robert Alexander, interview by phone, 2 June 2015.

confidence as they experimented. Both of these directors offered Sheldon rich opportunities to play a range of roles. It was these men, Tony assures me 'who taught me ... they really taught me to act'.

Carrying a Torch

Sheldon learned through experience and sometimes this was painful. But his early life in the wings and in variety served him particularly well later on. One of the valuable lessons of comedy he learned from the English comic actor Johnny Lockwood, when he appeared beside the veteran entertainer in a production of *A Funny Thing Happened on the Way to the Forum*. Although Tony felt he was miscast and did not enjoy the production, Lockwood valued Sheldon as his 'rock' in the play. He confided in Tony, explaining: 'You're the only person I can trust on this stage'. He was referring to Sheldon's ability to play the straight man for the comedian, Lockwood. It is often a problem in this play and in other comedies that actors compete to be hilarious on stage and the production loses balance. The straight man has to stay straight in order to free up the comic character. It was an important lesson for Sheldon who put it into practice with flair.

It was in this iconic production at the Sydney Opera House Drama Theatre, directed by John Bell, that Sheldon met a dark-eyed, trimly built actor called Tony Taylor who took his breath away. One critic described Tony Sheldon and Tony Taylor as 'musical theatre Wunderkinder'.[9] Taylor had a wild mass of dark curly brown hair, neat features and a serene face. He had come up through the Pram Factory in Melbourne, had appeared in the original cast of *Don's*

---

9   Julian Meyrick, 2008, '"Loved Every Minute of It": Nimrod, Enright's *The Venetian Twins* and the Invention of Popular Theatre', in *Nick Enright: An Actor's Playwright*, Anne Pender and Susan Lever (eds), Amsterdam: Rodopi, pp. 157–172, 163.

Party in 1971 (he played Simon), and the two Tony's became very close. Sheldon knew that he wanted to give this relationship with Taylor his full commitment after getting to know him for a few months. The two of them enjoyed both writing and performing: they wrote a Christmas show together for John Bell that year, and set up house together. Sheldon turned down a big opportunity to work with Jim Sharman in Adelaide, a disappointed Sharman slamming the phone down on Tony. He could not face the idea of leaving Taylor behind. It was not an easy decision but Sheldon is not one to agonise when he makes a decision. He goes with his instinct. But there was an immediate cost to his career. The following year Sheldon found himself drifting without any employment when Grundy's invited him to write for the television series *Sons and Daughters*. Sheldon, glad of the work, took up the offer and spent the next twelve months writing episodes of the program in an office day and night. He was pleased to have a salary but tired of the demands of the show after a few months, particularly the solitary life of writing, without the thrill of performing that he loved and missed.

Aware of his misery, Sheldon's good friend, Robert Alexander, encouraged Tony to audition with him for a new American set of plays called *Torch Song Trilogy*; Alexander had seen the New York premiere of the show and was excited by the prospect of playing in an Australian production of the play, with its bold exploration of homosexuality, and award-winning status. Both actors were delighted to be offered the roles of Ed (Alexander), a closeted bisexual, and Arnold Beckoff (Sheldon), the family-minded Jewish drag queen hero of the play. Sheldon was nervous about the role because it was a lead role in which the character is on stage for nearly three hours. But he was also anxious because of the conservative views of so many

Australians with regard to homosexuality, and towards homosexuals raising children. He had good reason to be apprehensive. Homosexual acts were still a criminal offence in New South Wales in 1983, the year of this Australian production (they were not decriminalised until 1984). In taking on the role of Arnold, however, Tony knew he had to assert himself both on and off the stage, and to stand up for the values espoused in Fierstein's play, by embracing the gay role with conviction and passion.

In his relationships with directors he had become more confident. The director of *Torch Song*, a Texan called Peter Pope, who had flown in from the United States especially to direct the Australian production of the show, insisted on some rather strange rehearsal exercises that included tying cast members together with phone cables attached to phones, until Alexander and Sheldon insisted he stop. Only a few years before this, Sheldon had not been confident enough to ask John Bell why he pushed Sheldon and Andrew Sharp through endless games in rehearsals, forcing them to be matadors, Spanish senoritas, gangsters and sword fighters. It was only later Bell confessed to Sheldon that he had worried the two accomplished young actors would be bored.

Torch Song Trilogy was a JC Williamson production with the potential to bring Sheldon to huge audiences, and had enjoyed success on Broadway. Peter Pope exclaimed confidently to Tony: 'this is the part that is going to make you a star'. Sheldon had his own reservations however, because of his understanding of the way in which the media 'maketh the stars'; in spite of Pope's confidence he worried constantly about how it would go. For the first time the name Tony Sheldon appeared above the title when the play opened at the York Theatre at the Seymour Centre in the spring of 1983. Critics praised the show. Harold Kippax marvelled at Sheldon's star quality: his 'exceptional stamina and virtuosity, his emotional depth and his 'comic but indomitable' humanity. Sheldon's authentic and 'irresistible' New York Jewish accent also impressed the Sydney critic.[10]

But the houses were small and the trilogy of plays that had been a major triumph on Broadway under the same director, closed after a few months. Undeterred the two young publicists on the show, John Frost and Ashley Gordon, purchased the rights and decided to produce the show in Melbourne. They transformed the marketing campaign, ditching the poster of Sheldon alone in drag, in favour of a photo that featured the couple in the show played by the golden-haired Deborah Lee Furness and Robert Alexander, alongside Sheldon and his mother in the play, the actor Myra de Groot. The new message was clear: not only is this a show about gay life but it is a show about families.

Tony and the other cast members never looked back. *Torch Song Trilogy* broke box office records for the longest running play in Melbourne. It was a major achievement for Sheldon, and a joy to be so celebrated in the city of his childhood and the place where many people remembered his parents with affection. He was given countless standing ovations during the long season. But it was exhausting answering constant questions from the media about his own sexuality, battling a recurring throat problem and performing the character of Arnold for so long each day. Sheldon also took the trouble to answer hundreds of letters from individuals who expressed distress about their sexuality and who found solace in the play, and others from the mothers of homosexual sons who shared their concerns with the actor.

---

10   Harold Kippax, *Sydney Morning Herald*, 24 October 1983.

Although he often felt unqualified to respond he always answered the letters. The production returned to Sydney 'in triumph' and, as Sheldon proudly recalls for me, 'it put me on the map'.

Tony Sheldon in *I Hate Hamlet* at the Marian Street Theatre, Sydney, 1992. Courtesy of Tony Sheldon.

Unfinished Business

Tony was approaching his 30th birthday when he telephoned his mother to tell her that he had written a cabaret show for the two of them. Lamond was living in Los Angeles, and she agreed to return to Sydney to appear with him in a musical piece he had called *Madonna and Child*. Toni and Tony played versions of themselves, a mother and son who are reunited after ten years and come back together especially to play in a show together. The 'story' was not invented: it came straight from their actual lives. In one scene Tony's character berates his mother as the two of them rehearse a show the night before it is due to open. The young man is furious as he remembers her leaving him in boarding school in order to go off on tour and pursue her career, accusing her of ruthless ambition at a time when he was grieving for his father. It was all part of the script, but as it was so close to the truth of their own lives, it presented his mother with a bitter rebuke. Lamond went along with Sheldon, playing her role willingly, saying nothing in the rehearsals about the painful material. Tony, aware of the sting in some of the dialogue, took out some of the more confronting lines, but the essence of the relationship was laid bare. For Tony it was satisfying to draw on his own life in writing and performing and to direct his own musical. He created something for the two of them about their profession out of the carnage of his childhood years. It was almost as if he wanted to test his mother by expressing his rage and his love for her in the language of musical theatre, a language that particularly belonged to them, but without the usual sentimentality of the genre. They sang together and found a harmony in their singing that they had not done since Tony was a child when they often listened to music and sang together at home. It was Sheldon's way of ridding himself of some of his demons and for Lamond, a way of making amends.

Some members of the audience, especially those who knew the protagonists, found it difficult to watch the show because of its intense and bitterly personal content. But the reviews were positive and the music, lyrics, Sheldon's witty dialogue and the performances of Lamond, Sheldon and pianist Ron Creager received high praise.[11]

A triumphant production does not guarantee that the next role will be a fulfilling one, or that there will even be a next role. Sheldon did not want for roles after his success in *Torch Song Trilogy*, but soon afterwards he lamented the fact that he had found himself back in the musical theatre, because he wanted to make his way as a 'serious actor'. In the mid-1980s, suddenly the preference in the theatre and in the cinema had moved to the musical. He was relieved that actors who could sing were invited to play the roles rather than musical comedy performers who were not necessarily actors, and appeared in several musicals, and then returned to spoken word to play with a large cast in a play called *The Sisters Rosensweig* written by the American, Wendy Wasserstein.

When the film *Muriel's Wedding* was released in 1994, Sheldon thought it was a brilliant achievement, and was stunned by the performance of Rachel Griffiths. Griffiths was a member of the cast of the Wasserstein play in which three Jewish sisters from London adapt to life in New York. Griffiths and Sheldon played alongside Ron Challinor, Judi Farr, Max Gillies, Genevieve Picot, Jacki Weaver and several others in what was a highly successful production. Griffiths

---

11   Bob Evans, *Sydney Morning Herald* 22 July 1985 p. 10; Andrew Urban, *Australian* 19 July 1985, p. 10; no byline, *Sydney Morning Herald* 20 July 1985, p. 45; Antoni Jach, *The Age* 24 August 1985, p. 12.

was young and not long out of her drama and dance training: Sheldon found her headstrong and pugnacious. But she looked after Tony, driving him to the dentist early every morning, for a few weeks, and he marvelled at her sensitivity, and her talent.

Sheldon was less enthusiastic about the musical film *Priscilla Queen of the Desert* that everyone was talking about that same year. In fact he detested the film. At Christmas he wrote a spoof cabaret, presented at the Tilbury Hotel in Woolloomooloo called *Pavlova: Queen of the Desserts*, featuring Phil Scott, Julie McGregor and Garry Scale. In spite of enjoying a variety of roles, some pantomime and some cabaret, Sheldon was unhappy. He had begun to drink and smoke heavily, and he had ballooned out. He was unfit and dreaded the constant running up and down the stairs in his next role in *Noises Off*. It seemed to him that his career was not moving on, and he felt a gnawing anxiety about his life. His doctor warned him that if he did not cut down his drinking he might die because his liver was already showing signs of damage. The diagnosis was pancreatitis. Sheldon went cold turkey, gave up smoking and drinking but failed to lose weight. One of the other cast members in the chorus of *The Witches of Eastwick* observed that he was eating bread, spaghetti and cakes all the time. Immediately he gave these up and has only eaten protein, vegetables, nuts and fruit ever since.

It was a significant moment for Sheldon who was attempting to transform his life. He acknowledged to himself for the first time that the overeating, and that the excessive drinking and smoking were part of an emotional response to his childhood loss, and his failure to resolve his sense of self doubt that plagued him ever since the death of his father. He knew that he needed to take charge. It was as if he led two lives: outwardly funny, always entertaining and gregarious but privately miserable and self-destructive, his moods swinging dangerously. Tony Taylor bore the brunt of the emotional torment in Sheldon. Taylor recognised the terrible symptoms of alcoholism, as his own father was an alcoholic. He withdrew, stepped back, and forced Sheldon to deal with his problems.

Sheldon gritted his teeth as he reluctantly accepted a role that he did not want to play, that of the flamboyant and queer theatre director Roger De Bris in *The Producers*. Quietly to himself he bemoaned his decision. Another man in a dress, another musical: he despaired of ever playing a 'straight' character in a serious play again. But he took the opportunity to work on disciplining himself, not only changing his diet but his attitude to life. In fact Sheldon did everything to avoid playing the gay director character, De Bris, turning down the role three times, and only giving in when Taylor spoke his mind. Taylor said: 'Don't you think you should reconsider when a major company is begging you to play this role?' Taylor was right, and Sheldon went on to win a Helpmann Award for his performance as De Bris.

Tony and *Priscilla, Queen of the Desert*

Before *The Producers* closed one of the actors mentioned that Simon Phillips was inviting participants for a workshop in preparation for directing an adaptation of *Priscilla* as a stage musical. Sheldon's draw dropped when the actor said 'You could play the title role'. Sheldon replied 'It's a bus. Priscilla is a bus! … And I would rather stick pins in my eyes than play another drag queen'. The idea of it made him feel physically sick as he pondered what seemed to him to be a treadmill of queer theatrical roles.

In spite of his reluctance to get involved in another musical about a party of drag queens, when the Melbourne Theatre Company telephoned and invited him to the ten-day workshop with Simon Phillips, assuring him that the script for the stage musical had nothing to do with the film, he agreed. 'It's only a workshop', he reminded himself as he set off for Melbourne in the heat of the summer, 'I have never worked with Simon Phillips and I will give it a try'. To his surprise Phillips listened when Tony suggested changes to the script. Sheldon found himself rewriting dialogue in the evenings and enjoying the renovations he was making. Phillips welcomed the contributions and Sheldon relaxed in his unofficial role as dramaturg, finding an easy rapport with the honest, hardworking, friendly director. Sheldon knew the characters portrayed in this story from life. As a boy he was surrounded by men dressing as women. The cast of *Les Girls* always came to see Toni Lamond: 'I recognised who they were ...'. The designer, Lizzie Gardiner, listened carefully to Sheldon's ideas and said, 'I'm going to make you look like Rita Hayworth'. It is this attention to an actor's interpretation of character from the director and the designer that allows the actor to excel.

At the end of the workshop the group presented a short show. Outside it was blisteringly hot January day, and Sheldon had lost all the excess weight he carried over the past year. He felt lithe and energetic as he performed, still sporting his summer beard, and unencumbered in loose cotton shorts and sneakers. He felt happy playing that character, glimpsing the possibilities of the role and his own interpretation pleased him. Just as he began to dare to hope that he might be cast as the lonely Bernadette, he realised that the role was not automatically his. In spite of his participation in the workshop he was aware that an international search was ramping up in the hope of securing a star actor to play Bernadette in the stage premiere in Sydney. Some of his friends auditioned and he had to steel himself when they phoned him requesting his guidance on how they should prepare. Phillips tried to reassure Tony, telling him to 'sit tight', and explaining that both he and the producer Garry McQuinn favoured Sheldon. Months passed while Tony waited, pondering the irony of his complete transformation over the ten day workshop, shocked at his sudden new enthusiasm to play this middle aged transsexual, in this new Australian musical.

When he was finally offered the role he was jubilant and slipped in to the rehearsals easily and happily. Simon Phillips was sensitive to the performers, but he is also a director who gives helpful signposts, once or twice reminding Sheldon of the character: 'Don't forget you're a lady', he would say when Tony was too strident, crude or manly. Phillips asked for Sheldon's opinion on all manner of aesthetic decisions, and so he felt he was a vital part of the creative process of making the stage musical. Over the next few months Sheldon was synonymous with this new major Australian production. The rehearsal schedule was extremely tight, and the cast were still trying new scenes even as the show toured New Zealand. It was evolving and changing as it rolled along. Sheldon enjoyed the touring and the ongoing work on the staging and script. As the leading member of the company he set the example for behaviour; he did everything to ensure that all the cast members enjoyed the production, and that they had every chance to succeed. He checked in with each one every day, bought birthday presents and ensured that there was time for talking and unwinding together. It was second nature to him to do these things, as he had observed in his mother and other women of the theatre he admired, such as Nancye Hayes.

The transformation Sheldon made to play Bernadette was extraordinary. Right from the beginning he knew that the whole love story of the musical hinged on his credibility in playing a woman, a once glamorous star, and that it could not work if the audience thought for a second that they were looking at a man. He also recognised that for this kind of role to work an actor needs to be fearless and not to be worrying about losing all expressions of their own masculinity. It began with the body, and his portrayal of Bernadette was flawless in that every limb, every part of his body had to be feminised. He shaved his legs, arms and chest, and kept his nails manicured, always remembering to extend his fingers on stage rather than clenching his fists as men do.

For Bernadette the facial transformation began with the eye makeup, with a thickly applied light pink eye shadow in a wide arc around and above the eye, and a strong line of black at the eyelid, exaggerating the eyes, under a thin, highly arched eyebrow line. Tony wears glasses but because he couldn't wear them to put on the outsized false eyelashes, he used a magnifying mirror, coating the curled lashes generously with black, and pushing up his cheek bones with coppery foundation and soft pink powder. He enlarged his lips in a gorgeous cupid's bow of fire engine red. With the blonde wig of wavy Mae West coiffed hair swept up from the brow, secured with clamps, for the opening funeral scene, feather-like radio microphone poking through, he felt almost complete. Sheldon practised putting on the makeup, varnishing his nails (bright red) and fitting his corsets, shimmery pantyhose and court shoes quickly. He also learned the trick of removing makeup in record time, using baby oil, soap, water and a damp flannel.

By the time the show opened in Sydney, the production was 'tight as a drum', Tony explained to me. It had a creative integrity of its own that seemed to grow out of the film but was not overly obedient to the screen version. It was clean but not chaotic, brilliant in its swirling colours but not kitsch, whimsical in its costuming without being garish, simple rather than slick. In one magical song number the performers glided around the stage in massive cupcake dresses decorated with huge smarties of purple, carmine and deep blue discs, fastened on to the stiff tulle skirts, each actor balancing a hat with a single two-foot long candle towering above their head, and a parasol in one uplifted arm. The cast was exceptional and included Michael Caton as the mechanic Bob, and Genevieve Lemon as the pub owner Shirley. Caton brought an understated laconic Australian touch to the spectacle and Lemon a bawdy and gritty charm to her character.

For Sheldon the show was demanding. The long evenings in the theatre beginning at 5pm in makeup, and never leaving the theatre before midnight, meant that he had to maintain his regimen of exercise and careful 'no carb' diet, pacing himself every day over the long season. He took magnesium tablets to help with the cramps that crept up on him, caused by dancing for so long in the 13-centimetre high heels and numerous platform boots. But it was a thrill for him and he enjoyed it in a way he could never have anticipated.

The exuberant spirit of the musical with its romance, comic dialogue and aerial Divas, spectacular with their extended feathery wings, and billowing white satin gowns (played by Danielle Barnes, Sophie Carter and Amelia Cormack), gleaming costumes and spare set design impressed critics, and they predicted it would be a hit. Some were lukewarm about the liberal use of disco and pop favourites such as *Downtown*, *Hot Stuff* and *I Will Survive*, lamenting what they saw as a missed opportunity for some original songs.[12] Bryce Hallett, theatre

---

12 Bryce Hallett, *Sydney Morning Herald*, 9 October 2006, online: https://www.smh.com.au/entertainment/art-and-design/priscilla-queen-of-the-desert-20061009-gdoif7.html.

critic on the *Sydney Morning Herald*, praised Sheldon as 'sensational' in role as 'the buoyant and brooding Bernadette. He gives the work its anchor, humour and heart', the critic wrote.

West End Wastrels

For Sheldon the invitation to join the London production of *Priscilla* was a moment he will never forget. Coming from a family of performers it represented a major achievement to be playing the lead role in a West End musical. It is a privilege very few Australian performers have enjoyed. The preparations were intense for the production. Lavish and loud, the management spared no expense to promote the show in London, and the performers were central to that message. Twelve members of the creative team were invited to travel from Australia to London to launch the West End show, including Todd McKenney and Daniel Scott, the three Divas, some ensemble members, the designers, choreographer and musical director. Tony wept as the plane taxied down the runway at Mascot and during the flight he fought tears, as he reminded himself that he was going to star in an Australian musical in the West End. It was the first time an Australian musical was to be staged in theatre-land, London. *The Boy from Oz* had won over New Yorkers on Broadway in 2003. But Nick Enright's book had been adapted for American audiences, and some of its decidedly Australian elements stripped away.[13]

Sheldon and his fellow cast members were photographed in front of the iconic London landmarks including Big Ben and the Houses

---

13   Peter Fitzpatrick, 2008, 'Life or a Cabaret? Nick Enright and The Boy from Oz', in Nick Enright: An Actor's Playwright, Anne Pender and Susan Lever (eds), Amsterdam: Rodopi, pp. 30–31.

of Parliament. In one of the photographs, Tony, looking debonair in his neat dark suit and tie, leans on a bright red telephone box as four of the characters stride through the streets in their sparkling lurex costumes, complete with massive colourful headdress arrangements of flowers and fruit. There seemed to be no end to the money that flowed in promoting the extravagant production. Each of the Australians revelled in this new-found celebration of all things Australian, and all things camp, as they paraded through the British capital ahead of the previews.

Sheldon savoured the moment. It was especially rewarding because he knew that for some of the decision makers, he had not been the first choice for the role of the veteran transsexual. Alarming, almost lurid rumours circulated about Michael Crawford appearing in drag for the producers who, realising their mistake, beat a hasty retreat. Sheldon heard that Ian McKellen was another possible Bernadette, but Simon Phillips and Garry McQuinn stood firm, continuing to champion Sheldon for the role. Eventually he was chosen to reprise the role of Bernadette, and Jason Donovan was cast as Tick (Mitzi). Sheldon and Donovan were the only Australian cast members. Donovan was known to British audiences, having become a household name in the UK because of his role in the ever-popular television series *Neighbours*, but Sheldon was not known outside Australia. A young Welshman, Oliver Thornton, trained in classical ballet, was chosen to play Adam (Felicia).

After the golden run in Australia, the West End production was not all plain sailing. Sheldon was surprised that the British cast members approached the show as though it was pantomime, 'all big and broad and comic', but took this cultural difference in his stride. The production company insisted on stripping out some of the Australian references, and at one stage attempted to insert the Queen and a corgi into the story. Toni Lamond arrived from Sydney to see her son perform on opening night in this extravagant production at the Palace Theatre in Shaftesbury Avenue, the heartland of gay London.

Several seasoned London critics praised the show, offering a profusion of enthusiastic reviews. Nicholas de Jongh remarked on the 'ingenious adaptation' with its 'brio' and 'spectacular, helter-skelter momentum of songs'.[14] 'Their low comedy gives high pleasure' the critic affirmed, observing that the production 'offers a joyful antidote to a world of hatred and violence'. It was an important statement because it identified a political dimension in the production. He prefaced his comments with a bold statement about the value of the show given the 'homophobic bullying in London schools and attacks on gay men on the dramatic rise, and a few mad, dangerous Muslims in town calling for homosexuals to be stoned to death'. Benedict Nightingale praised the 'energy, fun, tunefulness and, above all, the most outrageous swirl of costumes that I, who have seen *La Cage aux Folles* ... have yet encountered'.[15] Charles Spencer described the production as 'insanely euphoric', and its vulgarity as 'wildly contagious'. 'It's ten times more enjoyable than the screen version', he proclaimed.[16]

In almost every review Sheldon's performance was singled out for positive comments. One reviewer who was less convinced by various elements of the musical praised it as a 'glitter-strewn spectacular'. Kate Bassett found fault with the script (too thin), railed at the

---

14 The *Evening Standard* 23 March 2009.
15 The *Times* 25 March 2009.
16 The *London Telegraph* 24 March 2009.

number of disco hits belted out by three divas (the songs were likened by the critic to silicone implants and the divas to 'tongue in cheek goddesses, sheathed in swans' wings), and criticised the attempts at humour as 'strained' and 'woefully unfunny'.[17]

Every critic purred about the extravagant costumes and praised the striking choreography. There were many comparisons made with *La Cage Aux Folles*, the musical adaptation of the French play about a gay night club manager and his drag entertainers. Michael Billington was muted in his response to the Australian production of *Priscilla*, declaring the show to be 'underscored and overstated' and lacking the 'quaint charm' of the film. Several critics baulked at the crudeness of the jokes, and Billington rejected the production as 'defiantly tasteless', lamenting its overall effect. In his view it committed the greatest sin of all: 'it never touches the heart'.[18]

In spite of the reservations of some critics, and the antics of the cast, the season rolled on and the houses filled. *Priscilla* was a box office success in the West End.

Broadway Debut

In New York the experience of playing in *Priscilla* on Broadway was exhilarating. Many of the Australian references were put back into the script, some cuts were made to simplify the opening scene, and a few of the vulgar jokes were removed in an attempt to avoid offending middle American audiences. Tick's six-year old son Benji, appeared in Act 1, pleading with his father to come and see him after many years without contact, to reinforce the theme of a family reuniting. But

---

17 *Theatre Voice* 27 March 2009.
18 *Guardian* 24 march 2009, online, https://www.theguardian.com/stage/2009/mar/24/priscilla-queen-desert-palace-theatre.

the production did not lose its flamboyant style, abrasive humour or its celebration of camp excess. The casting was superb. Will Swenson won the role of Tick/Mitzi. Nick Adams played Felicia. As the rehearsals began, the 500 costumes 200 hats, 72 wigs and 150 pairs of shoes arrived from the UK.[19] In New York the headdresses were finished with feather detailing that included 295 ostrich plumes, and hundreds of new crystals and beads were sewn onto acres of satin and tulle costumes.

Tony Sheldon and Tony Taylor set themselves up in the East Village, and the show previewed in Toronto. During the preview season in Canada the cast heard that Bette Midler had been coming to see the show regularly. Without warning one day they were introduced to the tiny entertainer, known for her love of all things camp, before she disappeared. Like other wealthy entertainers in the US, Midler entered into lengthy negotiations about investing in the show. Oprah Winfrey had 'produced' a musical version of *The Colour Purple*, Whoopi Goldberg produced *Sister Act*, and eventually Tony Sheldon in character, wearing one of Bernadette's glamorous ballerina dresses, posed for a photograph with Swenson and Adams, that was published under a banner headline 'Bette Midler presents *Priscilla Queen of the Desert*'. Midler surprised everyone when she insisted that some of the 'racier' lines were excised and a second round of editing ensued.

The cast performed for the press in a studio a month before the show opened. The floor still had the tapes on it for foot placement in rehearsal, and each of the actors seemed relaxed. Without costumes or makeup they presented four of the opening song numbers (*Don't*

---

19   Barbara Hoffman, *New York Post* 17 March 2011.

Leave Me This Way, It's Raining Men, Go West and *Say a Little Prayer*) clad in their rehearsal track-suits and t-shirts. Swenson and Adams tried out their Australian accents and Sheldon appeared in black jeans, a plaid shirt with sleeves rolled up and high heeled dancing shoes over black socks. He looked calm, athletic and happy. His warm baritone voice with its soothing quality was in perfect condition. He mischievously told a reporter that he was going for a Lauren Bacall or Kathleen Turner sound.[20] The operatic strength of C. David Johnson's voice, as he flopped about playing Bob at the launch, and the gospel range and intensity in the voices of the divas (Jacqueline B. Arnold, Anastacia McCleskey and Ashley Spencer) brought new fire power and energy to the musical. Most apparent was the raw talent of all the performers, their dazzlingly strong voices, grace in movement and power as actors all the more obvious, without the elaborate costumes, lights and acrobatics of the full production on stage. It was an ingenious way to launch the show for the press.

Much of the media attention focussed on Will Swenson. Dark eyed, with glossy black hair, the good looking 37-year-old sang *Say a Little Prayer* towards the end of the launch, with the tiny boy playing Benji sitting on the floor at his feet, arms around Tick's leg in childish adoration. His voice is deep and sonorous, and as Tick in this scene, his face was open, gaze direct and serious, and his conflicted sense of his two worlds was conveyed with naturalistic restraint. Swenson had recently played Berger in *Hair* and for that role appeared naked apart from a fringed thong. His family are Mormons but Swenson left the church as a young man. He had never appeared in a role that

---

20   Cindy Adams, *New York Post* 14 March 2011.

required him to be both a man and a woman, and found walking in towering high heels difficult. Changing costumes within 30 seconds also proved a challenge for the actors but they listened to Sheldon who had by this time performed Bernadette some 1,200 times, and perfected the quick transformation for his 20 costume changes in the show. Backstage areas were divided into 'bunkers' of black cotton tents for quick changes for chorus members, each one filled with a rack of hangers for each costume. Eleven dressers, along with a large crew of stagehands assisted with the 261 costume changes, carting baskets of shiny satin outfits, boas and jewelled capes from the bunkers to the wings and back again.[21]

Priscilla opened at the magnificent Palace Theatre on Seventh Avenue and West 47th Street, on 20 March 2011. With some 1,740 red plush seats, gilded art deco features and curved balconies, the theatre had been the premiere house of vaudeville throughout the 1920s, a fitting venue for Sheldon with his family background in variety and musical theatre. The cast had to negotiate a maze of basement corridors to access the stage, often strewn with all manner of coloured wigs on mannequins, orange lizard costumes, and trollies laden with extravagant headpieces. But Sheldon's dressing room was quiet, neat and suitably glamorous, decorated with elegant rows of posters featuring actors from years of Broadway shows, all of them familiar to him after some 45 years as an avid student of American musical theatre. He was most at home in this room, and felt comfortable, contented and welcome. Toni Lamond travelled to New York for the opening in spite of her painful arthritis, and the

---

21 *New York Observer* 18 April 2011, p. 37.

two of them raced around to see as many plays as they could together during the day.

Charles Isherwood of the *New York Times* praised Sheldon's performance as 'particularly winning as the gracious lady transsexual Bernadette'; he described the show as 'hyperactively splashy' but complained that for all its 'gleaming verve' it 'feels monstrous and mechanical'.[22] Matthew Murray also found that for all its colour 'crimson, chartreuse, purple, and pink – especially pink – in this swirling spectacle' the show was devoid of *'emotional* colour'. He denounced this musical version of the book, blaming Elliott and Allan Scott for 'scrapping every nuance of plot and feeling in favour of "feel-good theatricality" that is everything *but* real'. This critic found Swenson and Adams' voices impressive but their portrayal of character unconvincing. Tony Sheldon was singled out for offering 'exactly the persona the rest of the show desperately requires'.[23] Most critics were positive about the leading male trio, with one reviewer admiring Sheldon's witty performance and steely poise, likening him to 'Uta Lemper on steroids'.[24] Even when the reviews were negative the performers were praised, especially Sheldon, of whom one said 'we really believe in both his sexuality and his search for a soulmate'.[25] Throughout the reviews, though, there were traces of puritanical objections and thinly veiled homophobia.

---

22 *New York Times*, 20 March 2011, online: https://www.nytimes.com/2011/03/21/theater/reviews/priscilla-queen-of-the-desert-on-broadway-review.html.
23 Matthew Murray, Talkin' Broadway, 20 March 2011, website: https://www.talkinbroadway.com.
24 Michael Sommers, New Jersey Newsroom, 20 March 2011, website: formerly available from http://www.newjerseynewsroom.com.
25 Martin Denton, The New York Theatre Experience, 22 March 2011, website: formerly available from nytheatre.com.

During the first six months of the Broadway season the producers became embattled with a local non-profit group dedicated to preserving live music in theatre. They objected to the minimal nine-piece band and recorded strings on offer in the pit at the Palace for *Priscilla*. But the producers defended their decision on the grounds that the 'recorded' sounds were used specifically because that was the way 1980s drag shows in Sydney sounded.[26] It was an ingenious if specious argument, but one that was difficult to refute.

Sheldon maintained his strict regimen of daily exercise and healthy eating in order to meet the demands of this highly physical production. On matinee days he left home at 10am to arrive at the theatre by 11 in time for the performance at 2pm. For the evening performances he was in his dressing room by 5pm beginning the elaborate process of dressing and applying makeup. He continued to greet the other cast members before the show and they responded warmly. Unlike his experience of the West End production, Sheldon made friends with each member of the company and keeps in touch with them. It was an affirming and rewarding experience professionally and personally.

Leading Man

When the awards season approached Sheldon felt all the signs of terror that had dogged him throughout his career: a sense of being unworthy and paralysed by the demands of the press calls, and the pressure to sell the show. He was nominated for a Drama Desk Award for Outstanding Actor in a Musical, and dreaded having to appear for an interview at the press announcement event. As he

---

26   *New York Post* 26 September 2011.

set off to walk to the venue on that spring day he found himself shaking uncontrollably. Before he entered the building he happened upon a familiar face. One of the chorus dancers from the Australian production of the show stood on the street grinning at Tony. He explained that he had picked up a job as the 'welcomer' at the event. Sheldon instantly relaxed as the young man embraced him. It made all the difference to Tony as he composed himself to face reporters from all over the world and multiple film crews. It was a gruelling month for him. But when he learned that he was amongst a dozen actors who had made their debut on Broadway, to be honoured with a Theatre World Award for his performance in *Priscilla* he felt a rush of genuine pleasure and pride.

Sheldon arrived at the awards ceremony on a summer afternoon not quite knowing what to expect. He learned that the actress Tovah Feldshuh had specifically requested to present Tony with his award: she had seen Sheldon in the first Australian production. When he rose to speak Sheldon was nervous but knew what he wanted to say. He explained that he had been an observer of Broadway for many years, from the other side of the world. Sheldon had been a keen reader of the book that is published annually by the American Theatre Wing, filled with production photographs, cast and crew lists, going back to 1944. He owns every edition and has spent countless hours studying these volumes since he was a small boy. He said 'You think that you are just doing your job for a small group of tourists who come to see your shows … but there are people paying attention, following everything you do. You are inspiring people … I have watched people move from the chorus to principal roles. I've seen stage managers become directors … and people move, get married, have kids who are now doing shows … I know everything about you'. The audience began to erupt with cheers of encouragement and applause. Some wept as Sheldon continued to explain his joy and sense of achievement in winning this particular award: 'You must never forget who you are doing this for: the little kid on the other side of the world who is reading these books and thinking one day maybe I can do that'. For Sheldon it was a moment of pure satisfaction, triumph, humility and pride all mingled together.

It wasn't quite so enjoyable being nominated for a Tony Award for Best Actor because of the stress of rehearsing for the Awards night. The full company of *Priscilla* was invited to perform at the Awards. Sheldon was dumb founded when they said he needed to perform in full costume and then return to his seat in the auditorium, wearing his dinner suit, all within four minutes. In order to accomplish this he had to rehearse it three times on the morning of the ceremony, while someone stood with a stop-watch chanting: 'You still need to cut off another 20 seconds', until they had it perfect. He suited up in full costume for Bernadette assisted by five dressers and several makeup artists, and then took it all off and put on his dinner suit, scrambled back down several flights of stairs and into his seat in the stalls of the Beacon Theatre. He prayed that he could repeat the whole procedure that night. On top of that he was convinced he wouldn't win the Award. He also had to get back home to his apartment in the East Village after the rehearsal to prepare for the awards in the evening, and make his way back uptown (some 60 blocks) again in time for the Awards night. He worried about how he would get to the awards in time, without being utterly dishevelled before he even started the charade he had rehearsed, given that he planned to get there by subway. At 4pm in the afternoon he was relieved to learn that a car would be provided to collect him and bring him to the ceremony.

Later he discovered that several of the *Priscilla* cast members had complained to management about the fact that he was expected to make his own way to the ceremony, and that if a car was not provided, they would take up a collection to pay for one, and go to the press.

As soon as he had walked along the red carpet and entered the historic theatre for the gala awards ceremony, with Tony Taylor beside him, he was ushered up to wardrobe to prepare for the song number. Sheldon was so anxious about the entire proceedings, and the scramble he knew he had to make, that he found himself in the wrong place on stage during the song number. But he made it back to his seat in the allotted time so that the camera could pan towards him when his name was read out. He had succeeded in performing this incredible transformation for the cameras in order to sell tickets to the show, and sat in his place relieved and smiling. Sheldon did not win the award but when it was all over and he recovered from the stress of the ceremony he realised that being nominated for a Tony Award for Best Actor was a superb achievement. His name would forever be prefaced with 'Tony nominee', and that, said his friends, is something every actor should treasure.

He treasures it and the fond memories of his 549 performances as Bernadette on Broadway. These days Sheldon is enjoying life as a New Yorker. After *Priscilla* he simply could not leave: 'I wanted to try to make a life here in this theatre world. I wasn't sure if it was possible for me. I certainly didn't want to die wondering', he told me. Sheldon has played in musical theatre in and out of the big apple, and taken roles where he can find them. In 2015 he returned to Sydney to play the lead in *Man of La Mancha* in a short season for a small, independent theatre company. He has always wanted to play Don Quixote, and didn't baulk at the fact that he would not be paid. We met in the foyer after his magical performance in the classic musical. He was relaxed, and cheerful in loose trousers and short-sleeved shirt. He embraced me, one hand clutching a grey plastic shopping bag with his costume in it, ready to take home so that he could wash it in time for the next performance. He seemed particularly pleased to be working with a cast of young and emerging newcomers in what was an extraordinary production put on by a non-profit musical theatre company. As we parted, I wished him well and watched him walking out of the theatre. I marvelled at this Tony Sheldon: a man who has played in Shakespearean comedy, cabaret, plays by Peter Kenna, Louis Nowra and Nick Enright, a man who has written and directed theatre in all genres, and won numerous awards. This is a theatre animal, a talented, honest, hardworking, charming and brilliant leading man.

Chapter 7

DENISE SCOTT: COMEDY IS NOT PRETTY

Standing up and Talking out Loud

(B. 1955)

I met Denise Scott, 'Scotty', to her friends, a few days after the funeral of her Uncle Len, a man whom she had admired, and who was the last of the five Scott brothers to pass on. Denise delivered the eulogy for the man whose death marked the end of the era of her father's generation. It was a grey autumn Saturday in Melbourne as we sat in a quiet booth at the Grand Hyatt Hotel overlooking blustery Russell Street. Denise was about to begin a new job as host at *Studio Ten* in Sydney as a presenter of day-time television, a role she has always wanted. Over the last ten years, I have met Denise half a dozen times, and have always come away feeling calm and happy. During our interviews, Denise has talked about her uncertain path as a performer, but says confidently that these days she enjoys performing alone, adding swiftly that in spite of this 'the days and hours leading up to a performance are sometimes torture. There is nothing lonelier than an empty dressing room', she says, 'with nothing to distract you but the clock ticking away until curtain up. There is literally nothing to do but wait'.

After years of crippling stage fright that would set in weeks before a performance, Denise now sips half a glass of Chardonnay and puts on her makeup to keep her nerves under control. Even if the show is going well, anxiety is still a bugbear. The more prepared she is for a performance, the more she can control her nerves. The commonly held belief is that 'impro' means being free and fresh in each performance. Envisaging some improvisational material beforehand eases her nerves, and if all else fails, just getting through the prepared lines is the option that takes over when for some reason it is impossible to engage with an audience.

At five foot-two inches (157 cm), with blonde wavy hair, Denise's face is unforgettably vibrant. She uses her large china blue eyes expressively on and off the stage. Her complexion is fair, creamy and smooth, and her round face quickly transforms into the expressions of a clown mid-conversation. For more than 30 years Denise has entertained audiences as a clown, in a comedy troupe, as a stand-up comedian, radio presenter, panel show personality on television and more recently as an actor in several television series. Talking about failure has become her stock in trade — and her own failures are the bedrock of all her comic material.

Over the last ten years Scott's career has taken off. With multiple sell out shows, and various appearances on television in comic roles such as *Winners and Losers*, Denise now has a following in stand-up comedy circles, and on television. Denise's new role as host on *Studio Ten* is not without controversy, with fans of the show slamming the network for its choice '… we forget how this "comedian" ripped the piss out of folk with so called "fake" conditions including autism & Asperger's …', one viewer posted on Facebook. Another lamented the choice of this 'fuddy duddy'. 'I shouldn't look at Facebook or Twitter', Denise tells me as we discuss the furore, and the fact that the events of 2011 'never go away'. 'But how do you work in this kind of public role and stay away from it?' she says. At the same time Denise remains intensely self-critical: 'Every now and then a cross woman of my age messages me and says 'I've seen you do that routine five times, I'm sick of it', and I think 'My God, you're right'.

Greensborough Girl

Where Denise grew up in Greensborough in the 1950s, each house looked exactly the same. Greensborough is situated on the leafy outer ring of north-east Melbourne, and the whole suburb was built for men who had served in the war. The Scott's house was a single-storey bungalow constructed of weatherboard, with a tile roof, a small porch at the front, and a tiny veranda at the back. There were no roads – just dirt tracks and no fences between each small house. Everyone wandered through each other's yards without worrying. 'It was magical', recalls Denise, who played with all the other kids in the street and in the paddocks nearby for hours every day, popping back to the house for 'tea' at sundown. Without a car, the family spent most of their time at home and Denise's memories are happy. It was only later when she was older that she could see that the suburb was full of suffering as a result of the war. Looking back, Denise recognises that there were a lot of damaged men in that community, and a lot of families living with the aftermath of the trauma those men suffered. The man living next door shot himself, and many of the men the Scott family knew, struggled with alcohol addiction. For the women there was a sense of camaraderie and there were lots of big families. Denise's father, Russell, 'Russ', who had served in the navy during the war, however, did not see action, and according to photographic evidence appeared to spend at least some of his time during the war years on the beaches of Queensland surrounded by women in the marvellous bathing suits of the 1940s. It seemed to Denise that for her mother, too, the war had been a rather exciting time. Margaret worked as a nurse, went to dances every week and met Denise's father at one of these events. Russ came from a Methodist family and when he informed his mother that he had become engaged to Margaret, a Roman Catholic, she ordered him to break it off. He obeyed until his younger brother, Doug, urged him to reconsider, and follow his heart.

Denise's father worked long hours, delivering smallgoods in a van and was out of the house for at least twelve hours a day. Obsessed with football (then called VFL), he could be found in the pub every night and then at the West Heidelberg Football Club where he held office. Russ's love of football still informs an occasional routine or segment of Denise's shows today; in spite of her lack of real interest in the game she can talk confidently about it and entertain an audience, somehow drawing on the awkwardness of her observations of the game in order to create the humour. Russ also worked as a cleaner at a gallery in Collins Street, belonging to Joseph Brown, a Polish-born art dealer, and would bring home glossy catalogues especially for Denise, who spent hours looking at the paintings reproduced in their pages. He drank every night too, loved being with his friends, and Denise says she never heard him say anything bad about anyone; he was positive, generous and busy all the time.

When she was four years old, Nanna Scott was making Denise a sandwich for lunch one day, and suddenly fell to the floor with a crash. She was dead. Denise stood still, staring down at her grandmother, who had just asked her what she would like in her sandwich, not knowing what had happened. Denise's grandfather rushed in from the next room, and wailed, the visceral cry he let out sending a chill through the young Denise that she has never forgotten. Crouched on the floor he held his wife and wept inconsolably. On the way home in the car with her Dad, Denise watched anxiously as her father slumped down in his seat, with his head on the steering wheel stifling his tears.

Denise and her older sister Julie were close and the household was a happy, industrious place. There wasn't much conversation, in spite of the fact that Denise's father was a good story teller and loved to tell jokes when he got together with his four brothers. Margaret reported briefly on the goings on at the old people's home where she worked, but most of the time when the four of them sat together for tea in the evenings, there was very little talking. Denise learned to fill the gaps, chatting away and asking questions, but no one else seemed very interested in conversation. In spite of this, joke telling was a feature of the Scott family gatherings. Uncle Len would disguise a joke as a personal story, reeling in his listeners, only to end up delivering a corny punch line to his joke.

Russell Scott also liked to entertain: he had a clown suit created by Margaret on her sewing machine, and would frequently perform on family occasions and at RSL picnics. He and his four brothers loved to sing whenever they got together. Uncle Ken sang solo, and would hit his head with a scone tray as a strange kind of accompaniment, and sometimes he got so carried away his head would bleed. Family stories are integral to Scott's comedy and infuse her work with warmth, colour and candour. Uncle Frank took the eleven-year-old Denise to see Joyce Grenfell perform at the Comedy Theatre in Russell Street Melbourne. Scott was captivated and from that moment onwards she knew that she wanted to perform alone on stage telling stories of her own. The Scott men entertained everyone with jokes and singing whenever the extended family gathered. The women cooked, cleaned up after the big family meals, and formed a loyal, captive audience for the performances of the men. On their own, Denise recalls, the women were hilarious too, but they kept their jokes for each other and never 'performed' them in the way the men did. Denise loved to sing and enjoyed playing around on the neighbours' piano but never thought to ask if she could learn to play. She gave up on ballet after a few lessons and took up calisthenics, enjoying the folk dancing, rhythmic exercises and singing that it offered.

Marg occasionally resented Russ's devotion to the football club and the consequent hours he spent away from the family, but most of the time she stoically accepted the situation and life was peaceful. There was one night however, when Denise was alone with her parents as Julie was at a friend's place. It was a Saturday and her father had a bit more of a session at the pub than usual. Irritated with her husband, Margaret packed her bags. No sooner was she out the door than Russ began to shout at Denise. Margaret immediately walked back inside and grabbed Denise's hand, leading her through the deserted streets to a taxi stand where they sped off to her uncle and aunt's in West Heidelberg. 'It was great fun', recalls Denise. 'They ran a milk-bar and we had a lovely time there. After a couple of hours, we got a taxi back to the house, and life went on.'

Margaret ran a tight ship at home; she was a meticulous housekeeper, revelled in domestic life and enjoyed her work as a nurse's aide at the old people's home across the road. After her night shift finished, she would walk back to the house, farewell her husband as he went off to work in the van, put the two girls in her bed with books and toys, and sleep for hours. Denise recalls how quietly the two of them played, knowing not to wake their mother. They were obedient children, and Denise loved being at home with Margaret, especially once Julie went to school. Denise did not want to leave the safety of home and her mother when it came to her turn to start school. She had never been separated from Marg, and did not like the idea of it. Margaret, still wearing her dressing gown, had to force

Denise up the road to school each day, herding her along as she cried, tapping the back of her short legs like a calf as she reluctantly trudged towards school. Throughout Denise's childhood she stuck close to her mother, enjoying her company more than anyone else's, listening intently to her conversations and to the intriguing stories her mother's friends told. When she was six, Denise's school life improved, as a gentle young teacher called Miss Mills allowed Denise to trail her in the playground, holding a large, soft ball of wool as her teacher did her playground duty, knitting her way around the school yard.

Denise attended Our Lady of Mercy College in Heidelberg. On Sundays Margaret dressed the two girls in pretty frocks, white gloves and dainty hats, and sent them on their way to Mass on their own. Denise spent hours worrying about the consequences of her mother's failure to attend Mass, terrified that Margaret would finish up in hell as the nuns warned. She prayed every night for her mother in an attempt to save her from perdition. In fact, the stories that the nuns told Denise at school kept her awake at night for hours. She suffered from intense insomnia throughout her childhood, and could not put out of her mind the possibility that if she did not behave well she would burn in hell for eternity. The image of this torture etched in her brain, and she could not forget it. As a result of the terrifying religious instruction, school was a miserable place for her in her primary years.

To add to her woes, she suffered from serious asthma and eczema, and the red welts on her skin made her self-conscious. During one particularly bad period, Russ and Marg took turns sleeping in Denise's room because of her frequent asthma attacks. Denise watched their creeping exhaustion and felt guilty about it. On Christmas morning that year she could not even summon enough energy to get out of bed to open her presents because she was so unwell. One drug she was given produced frightening hallucinations and nightmares, and another strange tablet given to her to put under tongue for her asthma turned her teeth bright yellow. After several weeks of illness, she returned to school; the other children circled her quietly and one wide-eyed girl looked her in the eye and said 'Did you nearly die?' It was her first taste of the fact that adversity creates magnetic interest from other people, and she stored it away in her mind.

Denise, aged 9, Miss Junior Watsonia.
Courtesy of Denise Scott

Insomnia dogged Denise for years, and she was an anxious child. She was scared of night time because of the dark, and because she couldn't sleep. Lying awake at night until the small hours, she imagined all sorts of horrific events that might take place, including an invasion of Australia. Denise spent hours crying in her bed at night worrying about her parents dying, a war breaking out and any number of other catastrophes. When she heard the chinking of milk bottles at dawn, she breathed a sigh of relief, knowing that day was beginning and her family would soon be moving about the house. Photographs of her at the time show a nine-year-old with black circles around her large blue eyes. She was chronically tired and sick. No-one in her house even knew that she did not sleep at night, even Julie with whom she shared a bedroom, and Denise did not dare complain.

When she was ten, Russ took Denise to his friend's house to choose a puppy. She looked down at nine tiny Labrador puppies suckling. There was one brown puppy that Denise proudly chose to come to live with her family. Prince was an extremely excitable dog and it didn't help curb his enthusiasm that the Scott family did not know how to train or look after him. Without fences or a gate, he was free to roam the neighbourhood, often following the girls to school and Mass, creating havoc in the classroom and Church with his energetic leaping and licking of faces. One day Denise arrived home and there was no Prince waiting for her. Margaret told her matter-of-factly that Prince had been put down. She offered no explanation. Devastated, Denise cried for hours alone in her room. Her parents did not express any emotion about this injustice, and taking their cue once more, Denise kept her grief to herself. Some years later Marg admitted that she had arrived home to find Prince, looking very pleased with himself, with one of the neighbour's chooks in his mouth. Denise recalls the conversation as if it was yesterday and told me: 'Turns out he'd killed quite a few and being a practical woman, there was no two ways about it, Prince had to go. The reason she never mentioned the detail to me was because she didn't ever want the neighbours to learn the truth'.

Bush Beats

In her teenage years Denise's asthma and eczema eased. She enjoyed herself more, going out to the 'Bush Beat' dances, where her friends from the convent school and from all of the local schools met and danced to the music of a different band every month. Russ was always the one who collected the teenagers from the dances at Eltham High, piling them into the back of the sausage van to take them home. There were no seats in the back of the van, and sometimes Russ would put kitchen chairs in the empty section, blissfully unaware that they fell over at the first corner. Denise recalls with a laugh her friends rolling around the back of the van, screaming with delight as they careened through the dark streets. She remembers the thrill of a band called Frame, a highly theatrical singer called Shirley Strachan and his exceptional performances at the dances; eventually this band became Skyhooks. There were boys from all over the district at the dances and at age 14, Denise became keen on a local lad, also 14, who stole a car and was chased by police, who fired gunshots at the speeding car. The boy ended up in Turana, a juvenile justice facility in Parkville, with Denise loyally visiting him every week by train. The drama enthralled Denise. Her parents encouraged her to visit the boy, seeing the good in him and supporting her in her devotion. On each visit she brought packets of Marlboro cigarettes and Morello jubes to the teenager. Looking back, she told me, by the time she was making these regular visits 'I was pretty much over him, but loved my role as Judy Moran', and her solitary expeditions to the city to see her outlaw boyfriend.

Denise, aged 15, in costume for the 'Plastics' routine at the Ashleigh Calisthenics Club in Greensborough. In other states the routine was called 'Graceful Girl'.
Courtesy of Denise Scott

As she approached her final year at high school Denise began to worry about her future. Suddenly she was impelled to work hard for her exams in order to 'get out of Greensborough'. Without good marks her prospects were limited and she wanted to go to university. Her friends continued to go out to parties and dances all the time but Denise stayed home to study. She set up the tiny spare room in her house with a blackboard. She was 17 and did not know how to study, and so invented a way of teaching herself in role as a teacher. Teaching was one of her ambitions although she yearned to be an actress. Every day after school, Denise would change out of her school uniform into a smart outfit, complete with a colourful shawl she had knitted herself, and she would pretend to teach a class, speaking everything she and 'they' needed to know for the exams. This was Denise's way of learning and remembering in order to prepare for her gruelling final examinations. She would stare straight ahead into the mirror that sat atop a large dressing table, reciting information and jotting down notes, occasionally walking around and writing prompts on the blackboard for an imaginary class of teenagers. She would ask questions and wait for the imaginary pupils to respond. No-one at home raised an eyebrow as she 'performed' this role day after day. It was an ingenious method of learning and *playing*, in the true sense of the term, that served her well, and laid down a pattern that would later enable her to create comic scripts alone by speaking out loud, before making any notes, which is a technique she still uses today. Fear of failure drove her on and there were many setbacks. Her favourite teacher committed suicide, another was sacked and a third ran off with one of the 17-year-old girls in the class. A defeated sense of abandonment and sadness gripped the students, but propelled Denise into a sense of independence in her study. Of course, her greatest fear, other than failing, was that insomnia would take over during the exam period. The night before the first exam she did not sleep for one minute, and came home the next day after the exam weeping with despair. Margaret came to the rescue with a packet of Relaxatabs that saw her through the gruelling exam season.

Improvising

Denise imagined that she would eventually become an actress, but did not have any idea about how that would happen. She enrolled in a drama teaching course at teachers college, hoping that this would be the pathway to a life on stage. Studying with the Canadian David Lander, who pioneered theatre sports in Australia, opened up the world of improvisation and taught her the rules of performing. With the other students, she formed a troupe called Mad Hat and enjoyed regular performances. The troupe included Lyn Pierse and Nadia Tass who went on to make names for themselves, and was a formative period for Denise as she explored drama of all kinds, finding her feet in comic acting and improvisation. It was her training in 'impro' that later enabled Denise to perform solo and to work as a stand-up comedian with confidence and flair. All of the techniques she used to study for her examinations at high school continued: she spoke out loud in order to work up her material and even later on when she had her two children, she would push them along in a double stroller, talking out loud as she created scripts on her walks, before going back to the desk to write them down. To this day she refuses to use a dictaphone or recorder – preferring to speak out loud and hear the words as they come. All of her stage scripts are created in this manner. Even her two books were composed by talking out loud, and writing notes later. The improvisational core of this approach provided Denise with a thrill each time she set about creating a routine or a sketch, and kept the material fresh.

Denise spent her first months as a teacher in the wheat-farming town of Wycheproof, Victoria, and in spite of her initial hesitation at leaving Melbourne she enjoyed this stint in the country. After a year teaching in Wycheproof, followed by six months at Maribyrnong Secondary College, Scott quit teaching to move to Darwin and work in a theatre company for children, the Darwin Theatre in Education group. The company toured the Northern Territory, giving performances to primary school children. Scott lived in a hippie commune with fourteen housemates and two dogs, in a house that had survived Cyclone Tracy. Most of the time everyone was nude, Denise reports to me with a grin. She hitchhiked home to Melbourne in 1979, and set off by herself for London, thinking that a career as an actor would eventually happen for her. But she had no plans, no contacts and no money. In London Denise ran into an old friend from teachers college who took pity on her, and invited her to sleep at the Divine Light Mission in Kensington for a few nights. It soon became obvious to the Maharishi followers that Denise was not at all interested in the faith and she was unceremoniously removed. She ran into another acquaintance, a puppeteer called Maeve, and together they travelled to Edinburgh, again with no plans, but met a group of actors who were performing in a cabaret stage show during the festival. Not only were they invited to participate as chorus members, but the show required a bed, and so Denise and her friend slept each night in this bed on stage in the small theatre. After this Denise and her friend decamped, Denise still imagining that one day she would land herself a great role and her career would begin. She had no concept of developing the contacts in the cabaret group and did nothing that would pave the way for her to keep performing.

When Scott returned to Australia she worked at the Arena Children's Theatre Company in Melbourne. She considered applying to acting school but felt ambivalent and nervous about taking that step. She recalls now that: 'I sort of kept making decisions that I thought would get me closer to being an actor, but they never did. They were, in fact, though, getting me closer to comedy. Eventually it was all about being yourself, and that, being entertaining'. In 1980 Denise auditioned for a clown ensemble with the Murray River Performing Group Ensemble in Albury. John Lane, who was also from Melbourne, had just accepted a role in the same troupe as a clown and street performer. They developed two clown characters: Denise was Puff and John was Drippins and the two characters loved to flirt. Denise and John have been together since that time, and have two children, Jordie and Bonnie. But sometimes anxiety took over in the troupe when they were scheduled to perform a show for which they had not worked out any material. Denise's insomnia and fitful sleep occasionally produced the solution: once she had a dream of the performers wearing dinner suits and appearing through a window sitting on chairs. They did the show in tuxedos and began by climbing in through a window.

Building on the idea in this show, Scott performed in Melbourne with Lynda Gibson who she had met in the Murray River troupe. Lynne McGranger and Sally-Anne Upton made up the other half of the satirical cabaret troupe called The Natural Normans: a sleazy moustachioed foursome of drag kings in tuxedos. Each of them was called Norman Norman: they were quads, and the act was inspired by another dream Denise had about four bald men singing in sunglasses. When she read a memoir by the American comedian Joan Rivers everything seemed clearer. Denise still did not know much about stand-up comedy – and it was only emerging in Australia at the time – but reading about the way in which opportunities were made by the comedian herself, the way in which Rivers knocked on doors, slept in her car and wrote material, and never gave up on the chase for opportunities, roused Denise from her inertia. Yet she also wavered, torn by maternal responsibility: when the troupe was invited to perform at the Edinburgh Festival in 1988, Denise stayed home in Melbourne to look after her small children.

For a few years Denise did occasional performances, making lonely forays into the world of club comedy. At home looking after her two children she began to realise that it was up to her to take the initiative. Denise knew she was funny, and knew she could tell a good story, but she didn't know anything about the lives of actors or their career paths. She appeared in her first stand-up gig at the Last Laugh in Melbourne, at the age of 34. It was 1989, and her gig was part of the La Joke event, an all-women season at the venue. She took a tram into the city on her own, sick with fear about the performance, and in fact praying she'd get a sudden appendicitis attack, anything to avoid doing the gig. Recalling the performance now, she says only a bit of the routine worked, a routine about childbirth that was new and fresh in the world of stand-up. At the end of her routine, she rushed home without speaking to anyone, relieved it was over and resumed her life at home with the children.

Saint Denise of Parramatta

When Denise took up a regular spot on *The Big Gig* for ABC television, she was forced into the discipline of writing and performing comic material for television every week, and having to deal with the stress of regular live performance. Denise and Jean Kitson appeared in a regular sketch together, playing two housewives talking over their back fences. During the season of *The Big Gig*, and before Denise had much stand-up experience, she received an invitation to appear at a large nightclub in Parramatta to sign autographs in her character from *The Big Gig*. Denise was reluctant because it seemed an improbable prospect, and she wondered what nightclub goers would make of her in her dressing gown, without her performing partner Jean Kitson. Assured by her agent that there was no performance required, Denise wavered, reasoning that this appearance could pay for some of the things they needed at home, but she feared the trip to Sydney and the idea of appearing at a large outer suburban club. Thinking it over, she reasoned that the family had very little money and desperately needed an oven. She agreed to appear. When she arrived at the club in her pink bri-nylon padded dressing gown, Denise began to feel extremely nervous. She noticed a fence on stage just like the one in her sketch on television in *The Big Gig*, and said to the organiser: 'What's that for?' 'That's for your act', he said, looking at her with surprise. Horrified, Denise replied 'I don't have an act' and she meant it: she had not prepared anything, and remonstrated with the manager, stating emphatically that the act on television included Jean Kitson and Jean was not here at the club. Elliot Goblet performed a short routine, as Denise waited in the dressing room offstage, petrified at what was coming. She concocted a short sketch, muttering some lines out loud to herself, and watching incredulously from the wings as the first performer retreated. A deafening disco tune pounded through the floor, and the dizzying glare of a spinning mirror ball cast shadows across the stage during the break between the two routines. Her worst nightmare had only just begun. Before she knew it, the music stopped, and a gigantic male security guard dressed in a mutant ninja turtle costume picked her up, and carried her onto the stage, depositing her on the floor beside the makeshift fence.

Under a dazzling spotlight, Denise tentatively began a short, hastily improvised stand-up routine beside the fence, feeling utterly ridiculous in her dressing gown in front of a crowd of distracted 20-year-olds. Shaking, she uttered a few remarks, when out of the darkness she heard a young man's voice shouting 'Suck my dick you fucking ugly mole'. Denise froze for what seemed like minutes as silence descended. Then something took over in her head: a snap of self-preserving energy surged through her. Rather than walking off stage she launched into a tirade of abuse at the man. The audience became enraged, whipped into a fury by the audacity of this female performer and her reaction. Nevertheless, after she finished with the young man she stayed on stage, finishing her improvised routine, before retreating from the stage in a stupor and collapsing on a chair. A few minutes later, a woman in the audience called Kirsty, who knew Denise from Melbourne but had never seen her perform, appeared in the dressing room, led her to a waiting car, and made sure she returned safely to her hotel. Later Kirsty presented Denise with a drawing of that night, with Denise in her dressing gown, tied to a stake, under a burnished heading that read 'Saint Denise of Parramatta'. For years the drawing was pinned to the wall above the new oven and now it is framed and hangs on the wall of Denise's living room. It took her a full year to recover from the attack and the brutal hostility of the audience in Parramatta, and she still has nightmares about it.

The Parramatta nightclub incident is one of the worst incidents Denise can recall in her entire career but it is not the only one. Heckling and interjection are part of stand-up, and Denise became used to dealing with boisterous behaviour. She would regularly remind herself that she was there to try to make people laugh, not to do battle with them, and made a decision that if she was ever heckled about being a woman, that she would simply walk off the stage and refuse payment. As her career has progressed she has become highly skilled in her interactions with the audience, and these moments have become one of the funniest elements of her act. Her exchanges with audience members can be shocking in their candour or sometimes simply conversational. She resists the temptation of insult comedy but it is a powerful version of the form, with the fear of it hanging over the audience, particularly those in the front rows.

In spite of her appearance on *The Big Gig*, Denise still didn't pursue television opportunities. In 1992 she developed a script for a one-woman stage show called *Extraordinary Encounters of a Mundane Kind*. It was the first time she had written a complete story to perform on stage for a whole show. It was based on a real event, a family breakup that took place in the lives of some friends. Looking back 'it was amazing that I kept those friends', Denise tells me, explaining to me that she now laments her naïve appropriation of the lives of her friends for the script without consultation. Sue Brooks, a film director, worked with Denise as she rehearsed. Sitting in front of Brooks on stage, Denise spoke out the words and then at night went home to write them down. Brooks helped her to constrain some of the elements of the telling of the story, allowing Denise to convey the drama and humour of the story without explicitly making it funny, and encouraging her to rely on the story to affect the audience, and not to labour the comic elements. She performed it at La Mama and at the Belvoir Street Theatre in Sydney, but realised it was impossible to make a living doing occasional one-woman shows for small audiences.

Every now and then, Denise did stand-up gigs, and quickly retreated to the safety of home and family. Looking back, she recognises that in the early years she relied on the excuse of focusing on her family, rather than tackling the intimidating world of stand-up head on, because it was simply too confronting. For years her partner John

Lane helped with sets if she needed them for her occasional shows, and by encouraging friends to come along to the gigs. Once, Denise wanted a burnt chair for a show, and John found one in an op-shop, and dutifully charred it in the back garden for her. Friends would direct for nothing, and one neighbour took on the publicity for a show one year, and did such a good job she was offered a position at a top public relations firm. In 1993, Denise took on the role of host of *Tonight Live*. It was tough and Denise found herself sick with nerves and terror every night. The absurd situations of talking to so many people on the show fuelled her stage stories later on, but at the time they were gut-wrenching experiences. Denise transformed one experience into a hilarious extended anecdote some months later on Bert Newton's show, explaining her experience:

> ... we were interviewing some people who had been in a film about being taken by aliens ... I expressed scepticism, thereby insulting the guests. And I'm supposed to be this goofball, cracking jokes and they were bad and tactless, and everyone sat there, and I got sweaty and Sophie got sweaty. And in the ad breaks Sophie was glaring at me saying "Say something funny for god's sake". I said "I have been trying". Then we had a guy come on from a sort of male bonding group. I got off on the wrong foot with him too. I cracked what I thought was a funny joke, and I don't know how he bonded but he was like a zombie – he just sat there, wouldn't talk and it was terrible – it was the longest hour of my life.[1]

Denise's forays on television did not get easier. Her experience of working as an actor on *Full Frontal* in the early 1990s was almost as traumatic as the Parramatta Club night incident, and also ended in disaster. The sketch comedy program, originally known as *Fast*

---

1   *Good Morning Australia* 21 June 1994.

Forward, featured actors such as Gina Riley, Eric Bana, Steve Vizard, Jimeoin, Jane Turner, Glenn Robbins, Marg Downey and Magda Szubanski. Unlike their dazzling success, Denise described her time on the show as 'easily forgettable'. Indeed, when I mentioned a particularly funny sketch in which Denise appeared in one of the episodes, she had no recollection of it. 'Maybe it was my attitude, maybe it was because I just wasn't great at doing comic characters. Who knows?' One thing Denise did know was that there was not enough good material being written for all five women in the cast. One sketch she was given to perform required her to 'wear an old lady's wig, say nothing, and pour a bucket of chicken fat down the sink – that was it – I snapped – went berserk – and marched into the writers' room and started shouting at them – in hindsight not the wisest of moves', she recalled. The night before the next series was to commence filming, when Denise's call sheet was couriered to her house – there was no email at the time – she read on the page: '"Unfortunately Denise is not available for this series …" – that was the way they sacked me'.

Mothering on Stage

In 1998 Denise appeared in a group show called *Mum's the Word* with Jane Clifton, Tracy Harvey and others, presenting short comic sketch pieces about motherhood and parenting. The script was written by a group of Canadian women and was a joyful and enjoyable production. Most importantly, it brought Denise huge publicity. The show attracted big audiences, in a sell-out season at the old and majestic-Athenaeum Theatre in Collins Street, Melbourne, for six months. One defining feature of the production however was that there was no opportunity to improvise, or adapt any of the script, and the role Denise played was not written to be funny. For Denise the whole experience was extraordinary because it was so different to her previous experience of performing. She brought her own style to the role and found that it did arouse laughter, and that the discipline of repeating the same lines precisely night after night with no improvisation was not a constraint, but brought a freedom to her performance that enhanced her confidence. Crafting stories takes Denise a long time and she learned through her participation in this show that you can make a story sound natural even though it has been scripted for you: in other words, she learned to act, and she learned to trust her own style of comic acting. Denise realised that the stories about the hardships of motherhood struck a chord with thousands of women who filled the theatre every night. It was this kind of material that Denise had been doing on her own, but with less sentimentality. 'Why?' she wondered, 'did it take a Canadian show to bring so many women into the theatre?' Denise recognised that her own material was in a way cruder, more potent, less deferential to social niceties than that of the Canadians. More importantly its tone was and still is stridently Australian. Her own style is raw in a way that simply refuses to sanitise the realities of life for women in the way *Mum's the Word* did. The experience propelled Denise back to her own sense of what she could do, and to creating her own stand-up routines, believing much more fervently that her own material would appeal to audiences. She knew that her audience were her own age but the audience members for comedy and stand-up were all much younger than that at the time. Building an audience of slightly older women, a broader audience, is something that Denise has achieved over the years in parallel with the development of the form in Australia.

Comedy is Not Pretty

Working alongside Judith Lucy was important for Denise. It was liberating and enjoyable to be developing material for a show with Judith and Lynda Gibson. They worked in the 'talking out loud' way Denise had always done on her own, and developed a lot of physical material in front of a mirror, including dance and fights that punctuated the performance. The three of them worked together in a dance studio to create the show. According to Denise, the audience for the most part came along to see Judith who was much better known at the time. It was 1999 and the show was ingeniously called *Comedy is not Pretty*, an expression made famous by Steve Martin twenty years earlier. It was a significant show for Denise because it was the first time she had performed in front of very large audiences. She says that she and Lynda 'rode on Judith's coat tails' in this show, and it was exhilarating. When they opened at the Lower Town Hall space in Melbourne, they broke a number of rules in comedy. Everyone had told them not to talk about comedy, not to talk about women in comedy and not to talk about their work. They did all of those things – theatrically – and the show was a massive hit. On opening night, they sold out and the next night they were moved to a theatre with double the capacity, holding 700 seats. Each night, Denise recalls with a grin: 'our show went overtime', a big no-no in comedy festival lore. Judith and Lynda both felt guilty about this but Denise was 'just so excited with the overwhelming response to the show and the experience of a large crowd loving our material, I didn't care. I was shameless. I loved it'. It was in the sequel to this show, *Comedy is Still not Pretty*, that the three performers first appeared in what were to become their 'signature' nude suits: flesh-coloured leotards with shorts that had the genitalia drawn on in black ink.

In spite of the success of this show and its sequels, Denise still suffered from nerves and the fact that performing made her physically sick. Before performing she felt bilious for hours and generally disappointed afterwards. In spite of this she persevered with stand-up, and gained a considerable following. Another difficulty for Denise was that her mother disapproved of her work and steadfastly refused to acknowledge Scott's talent and achievements. Russ and Marg had seen her perform in a group show that was nostalgic, funny and clean, called *Back to Bourke Street*. Russ was proud of Denise, but he died before she ever did stand-up. Failing in public is part of performing as a stand-up artist and Denise is now articulate in acknowledging that part of the issue is the fear of failing in front of one's family, and their corresponding fear of being present at such a moment. Margaret expressed strong disapproval of Denise's work, but looking back now, Denise recognises that this attitude was a reaction to a fear for her daughter of failing alone on stage.

One Woman Show

For many years Scott worked in stand-up, appearing at festivals and on the comedy touring circuit. Stand-up comedy is not an easy performance option. For someone who wanted to tell stories the form lent itself to the project. The late-night club scene is unforgiving, harsh and exhausting. There is no real career trajectory and when Scott started performing in comedy it was not a career at all. Scott persisted over many years and gained a considerable following. She toured and appeared at countless festivals. But she always wondered whether she was good at it. As she grew older she wanted to perfect her craft, to feel that she had achieved something of excellence before she gave it away. She had always wanted to perform in a theatre rather than in a series of stand-up venues late at night, believing that the theatre audience would be far more receptive to her style and her extended personal stories. Scott also knew enough about the industry to be certain that she needed a producer in order to progress. Self-producing her act for twenty years and trying to pitch to producers was all very well but did not allow her to develop her own material for a full show in a theatre. Twice earlier on in her career she had approached the successful comedy manager, Kevin Whyte, to request that he take her on. Twice he refused. Scott was approaching her 50th birthday and decided to give Whyte one more go. He agreed to manage Scott and since then she has not looked back. Nor has she contemplated giving the game away since that day.

It took years for Denise to let go of the shame and self-loathing she experienced after performing stand-up routines, and to understand her mother's attitude to her work. In 2009 Scott performed a show at the Comedy Theatre in Melbourne in front of an audience of one thousand people. Her dream of performing alone on that stage when she was watching Joyce Grenfell as a girl had materialised. Scott's show was called *Number 26* and was more like a play with curated scenes and lengthy stories about her immediate and extended family. After years of struggle, she had found her own form and her own adoring audience at last.

Scott's one-woman shows in the theatre allow her to range freely and fully on stage for an audience who are comfortably seated, quiet, and are ready for a complete theatrical experience. She still stands up, focuses on talking and roves with a microphone, but her performances are full productions, with music, slides and dance. In *Mother Bare* at the Sydney Opera House Playhouse in 2015, she walked into the auditorium several times to address particular audience members, and in one hilarious, raunchy dance number, she straddled a middle-aged woman in the second row as she sang. Unlike stand-up the show was directed and although no one interfered with the content or script, the performance is fully theatrical in its creation, development, choreography, rehearsal and production. Colin Batrouney directed and curated the show and produced the enormous slides that formed the backdrop and scenography for the set. There was more than a passing echo of Dame Edna in *Mother Bare*, although Scott does not play characters and her production was tight and compact, compared to Humphries' lengthy, ritualised on-stage extravaganzas.

Denise Scott, taking a break during the *Mother Bare* season at the Sydney Opera House, 2014.
Courtesy of the author.

In 2011 Scott performed in the gala opening night of the Melbourne International Comedy Festival and had her own show at the Victoria Hotel. After the gala was broadcast on television Scott's Facebook page was deluged with complaints about her offensive remarks regarding alcoholics, coeliacs and those with mild Asperger's. Her swipe had been at those who pretend to suffer from those conditions as an excuse for their own poor manners and offensive behaviour. The hate campaign continued for days as Scott sat with her mother who was dying of ovarian cancer in hospital. Mortified that she had offended children with Asperger's and their parents, Scott immediately posted an online apology. She continued to juggle her nightly festival show, filming schedule for *Winners and Losers* and keeping her vigil with Margaret.

When Denise won the Helpmann Award for her show *Regrets* she agreed to take it to the Edinburgh Festival. 'It was the most gruelling month of my life', she tells me, performing for unresponsive audiences for 29 nights straight. The audience simply did not appreciate the humour, and the reviews were savage. Denise looked out into the auditorium one night to see her producer Kevin in the audience and felt sick. She knew he would only be there if things were very bad. He told her that the show relies on the audience being familiar with Scott, and as the audience did not have that familiarity, she could not break through this barrier. Although it was demoralising, Denise says that in the long run this excruciating experience forced her to write stronger material. Scott still infuses her television chat show appearances with stories, like the ones she tells on stage; these include amusing anecdotes about herself and her family. Speaking on television to Dave Thornton on *Studio A*, Denise talked about her son as if she was performing a stage routine:

Denise Scott performing in her show *Regrets*, 2011.
MICF/Jim Lee Photo.

Jordie said to me the other day "No offence Mum but I really wanna move out". I said "No offence taken, I really want ya to go. And in fact, he begged me, he said "Please don't put in the book that I still live at home", because apparently that's not cool for a muso, a fucked-up genius muso to live at home. Oh! Are you allowed to say that? Derryn Hinch is going to shut down your show. I didn't ask, I didn't look at the contract. I only used that word to try and connect with the youth Dave. I never say it, I wanted to connect with you … I'd feel good for my own ego if I brought down a TV show but I'd feel sad for you cos what have you got going for you? Nothin'. You've got youth, you've got good looks, you've got talent, you're thin, you've got no alcohol or drug problems – you've got everything so I'm going to bring down your show and make life hard for you …[2]

---

2   *Studio A* 25 May 2009.

Disappointments

In their recent show entitled *Disappointments*, Denise Scott and Judith Lucy played to packed theatres across Australia for a full year, appearing at two Melbourne comedy festivals. On the night I attended the show the audience was 80 per cent female with most of those in the over 50 age group. The 400-strong audience was noisy before the show opened in the Playhouse at the Sydney Opera House on 8 February 2018. When the lights went down a series of gleaming Facebook images appeared on a massive screen, showing photographic portraits of the two performers, Denise and Judith looking perfect, smiling, with their own voice overs about their lives in a glittering parody of the false way in which people present their lives on social media.

After a few minutes the screen disappeared and Denise and Judith appeared lolling in two large single beds, one on each side of the upstage area. They wore floral flannelette nightgowns, and each of them was firmly tucked in under a thick doona with green William Morris style, swirling flower patterns. Beside each of them on a bedside table was an oversize half-full glass of red wine as well as a bottle of water. Judith began with a monologue about how her life is nothing like the Facebook images the audience has just watched. She explained how she just can't stand being 'mindful' all the time, confessing that she is so glad to have worked out how to lie down in bed and drink at the same time.

After the introductions from the beds, the two of them rose and stripped off the night gowns to reveal sparkling emerald jackets and black pants, and began to make their way down the stairs at the side of the stage into the auditorium. Denise took it slowly, turning sideways, left foot first on each step, joking that '... I must look like your pissed old auntie on Christmas Day'. There were a lot of noisy latecomers still arriving in the playhouse, even a few making their way into the first row in the darkness. Judith pounced on them like Dame Edna: 'Why are you late?' she asked, as the spotlight shifted to a woman in the front row. 'We've been to a funeral', she replied in a plaintive tone. Judith retorted 'Well, there's not much I can do with that', as the audience broke into laughter. When she noticed another group arriving a few rows back, Denise chimed in 'Why are you late?' Without even a pause of hesitation, a youngish woman barked back: 'We had a bottle of wine to finish'. A few minutes later another latecomer in row G said almost the same thing. It was clear that some 20 people were late because they were drinking. Their attitude struck me as brazen and shameless, bordering on hostile to the performers. Denise masked her shock effectively, but later told me that the attitude of these latecomers irritated her and put her on edge for the entire show. She said after that interaction, that she felt it was uphill all the way, and that the two of them were working very hard to get the laughs.

Judith questioned a few people about who they were, and who they've come with to the show. She asked a woman if she was associated with the man next to her, and why was she leaning away from him. She then asked a younger woman next to the couple if she was their daughter. The young woman nodded, gave her age as 32 and her name, Danielle. Denise was onto her in an instant. She said, channelling Dame Edna, 'And Danielle, what is it in your life that has you out with your parents?' The audience roared with laughter. Meanwhile, Judith seized on a young man a few rows from the front with longish hair. With a spotlight firmly on him, Judith crooned:

'Bare arms, it's not often we get bare arms on a young man in here'. She grilled him for his name: 'Aaron' he replied. 'And who is that on your t-shirt', Judith said. 'Sandy Bernhardt', he replied. Judith sniffed and said with resignation 'Yes, quite funny'. Next Denise seized on a middle-aged woman a few rows from Aaron. This was Melinda, who immediately stated that she is 'Aaron's mother'. The audience laughed with surprise. 'What are the chances?' retorted Denise, with a wide-eyed smile. Then she questioned Melinda about whether each of them knew the other was coming along to the show. 'Yes' affirmed Melinda. 'And what did you think when you found out that you were both planning to come to the show?' Denise prodded: 'Nothing' said Melinda, 'We both love the arts'. Laughter erupted all around the auditorium. Denise paused and turned to Judith on her right and said 'What about that then?' By now Aaron and Melinda are fair game for the whole show. It's Dame Edna all over again.

The humour is crude at times and nothing is off limits. There seem to be no taboos for these two performers. Denise talks blithely about her dry vagina and Judith explains about her 'four sessions of colonic irrigation with vegetable oil – enough oil to open a fish and chip shop in my arse', she declared, to gales of laughter. Stories of disappointment structure the show. Denise talks of a disappointment on her 60th birthday, 'a few years ago', reporting that she had requested no presents. Her partner of 37 years, John, however produced a large parcel, a book called *The Luminaries*. She looked out into the audience who seemed to signal their concern about this work. She thanked John for the gift, and he explained to her 'I had to get it for you because I heard someone raving about it'. Denise is bright red in the face as she delivers the punchline to her story, her fury redolent: 'Well gee John I think that someone might have been me', she bellowed: 'Because I've been lying in bed beside you for the last six months READING it'. The audience exploded with laughter.

One of the highlights of the show was a segment in which the two performers 'argued', insulting one another with breathtaking venom, under blazing red lights. They have been talking about some of their achievements, with Denise proudly explaining that the Performing Arts Museum will exhibit one of her costumes from an earlier period of her career. Judith, aghast, reminded her that the costume was worn by her too, and that the only reason the Museum has chosen Denise's outfit is because 'IT IS MUCH BIGGER', and 'people who go to museums', she snarled, 'like seeing big things like Pharlap or a woolly mammoth'. After the argument they revealed to the audience that each of them wrote the insults about themselves into the script to be delivered by the other. It's ingenious, the dramatic tension is high and the dialogue is dangerously personal. The surge of the 'argument' demonstrates the closeness of the partnership, the risk that a script like this entails, and their precision in repartee: the insults are excruciating, and then just as skilfully they resolve the tension through reconciliation and song.

As the end of the show approached, Judith and Denise stripped off again, tossing off their sparkling cocktail jackets and trousers, to reveal their now iconic beige all-in-one nude suits, cut off above the knees, with built in bra and drawn on nipples, a wonky cartoonish 'bum' crack and daubed on pubic hair. They appear as figures of pure comedy as they stand up on the beds, Denise quipping 'I can't believe at this very moment in time I'm desperately trying to hold my stomach in'. Judith replies: 'Scotty, I think that ship has well and truly sailed …'. Jumping off the beds onto the stage they began a riotous rhythmic gymnastics session, complete with dancing across the wide stage, and billowing ribbons, as the music blasts out a version of 'I am, you are, we are Australi-an'. Above the frolicking performers, the audience could see projected portrait photographs of Judith dressed in an Indian sari and Denise bedecked in a huge Australian hat, with corks dangling from it. This dance routine is a highlight of the show and a superb finale. Whimsical and hilarious, the two performers appeared as though they have suddenly found themselves in some sort of Commonwealth Games opening ceremony in their nude suits (the Commonwealth Games were in the news daily as they were being staged at the Gold Coast a couple of months later). Denise's expression was both bewildered and determined: her mouth hanging open at the end of the dance, as she comes to a stop, staring forward, goggle eyed like a mannequin.

Disappointments has a dark edge to it, as all of Scott's work and much of Lucy's does. The disappointments relating to work are real: nothing is fabricated in this show. Denise tells me later that she had been writing a television drama that was rejected after months of work. It portrayed a comedian and she was bitterly disappointed when it was rejected after so much time and effort. The disappointment of being treated badly as a female stand-up comedian is still real for Denise. The perils of performing as a woman have not disappeared in spite of her popularity, success and years of experience. Recently she accepted an invitation to do a gig for a corporate lunch for 50 men in Melbourne. She was a little reluctant but it did not appear to be a difficult one for her; they wanted a thirty-minute routine, and the two men organising the event were pleasant and 'my age' she tells me. Everything was arranged, including a driver and a car to bring Denise into the city for the gig and to take her home.

Denise arrived at the venue near Parliament House to find a large group of men ensconced on a veranda outside, all of them bearing various poses of hostility, from folded arms to tight-lipped snarling that was only partly audible. As she began her performance, they all stared blankly back at her. She thought she'd be safe with some anecdotes about adult children and the way they seemed slow to leave home. One man sitting in the front immediately dug his phone from his pocket and started using it, without any attempt to hide his actions. Feeling rage rising, Denise asked him what he was doing. He said 'I'll stop looking at my phone when you say something funny', and kept on going with the phone. The younger men looked even more hostile after this interaction, and Denise sensed a pack mentality setting in. It would be up hill from here, she told herself. The idea of bolting crossed her mind but she persevered, not wanting the situation to get the better of her. She pressed on doggedly. 'Does anyone here suffer from arthritis?' she said, looking around at the men. One bloke yelled out to her 'Oh yes, Bob here has arthritis'. Denise seized her moment: 'Oh, she said 'And you're the arsehole friend who dobs on your mate, are you?' The man looked furious and said 'Did you call me an arsehole?' Denise paused and said 'Well, yes, I suppose I did'. He said 'I could show you my arsehole if you like'. Quick as a flash, Denise retorted: 'No thanks. I'm having enough trouble looking at your face'. She made it through the long thirty minutes only by besting them in this manner, but there was no real engagement after this. It was joyless and demeaning, but better than giving up. The whole event brought back the trauma of the Parramatta Club incident so many years ago. After so long, she is bitterly disappointed that because she is a woman, men simply will not give her a chance to entertain them and see nothing wrong with abusing her and the occasion of comedy.

* * *

At 63, Denise is in her prime as a television host, comic actor, stand-up guru of the Australian circuit and avid fan of other comedians. She recognises in them and in herself a need for the love of an audience, for validation and recognition. But she is realistic about her status as an older woman and laments the lack of roles on television. She is candid about her own health, explaining to me that she has suffered bouts of arthritic pain that scared her, and meant that she could barely walk. Denise is full of joy and praise for the work of others, and is philosophical about the disastrous reception of *Disappointments* at the Soho Theatre in London. After years of performing, she is comfortable with her own style and her own material, but is both relentlessly self-critical and buoyantly optimistic. At the end of one of our leisurely conversations, she remarked: 'Performing at the Sydney Opera House in a sell-out season is a privilege, and a pleasure: I could hardly be disappointed with that'.

REFERENCES

Newspapers and Magazines

The Age, 1979, 1985.
Australian, 1979, 1984, 1985, 2000.
Blackpool Gazette, 1940.
Border Mail, 1973.
Canberra Times, 1979.
Daily Express, 1940.
Daily Sketch, 1943.
Daily Telegraph, 1943, 1976.
The Entertainer, 1976.
Evening Gazette, 1940.
Evening News, 1941.
The Evening Standard, 1950, 2009.
Guardian, 1962, 2009.
Listener in TV, 1973.
London Telegraph, 2009.
National Times, 1976, 1979.
New Idea, 1965.
New York Daily News, 1999.
New York Observer, 2011.
New York Post, 1999, 2011.
New York Times, 1941, 1999.
New Yorker, 1999.
News Chronicle, 1943.
Newsday, 1999.
Newsweek, 1999.
The Sun, 1964.
Sunday Age, 1999.
Sunday Chronicle (Manchester), 1941.
Sydney Morning Herald, 1979, 1983, 1985, 2006.
The Tatler and Bystander, 1941.
Theatre Voice, 2009.
Times, 2009.
Times on Sunday, 1987.
Wall Street Journal, 1999.
Weekend Australian, 1983.

Interviews

Alexander, Robert, phone interview conducted by the author, 2 June 2015.
Horgan, Brendan, interview with Carol Raye, *Screensound*, 28 September 2000.

Television

Clarke and Dawe, ABC TV, 2013, 2015.
Good Morning Australia, Nework Ten, 1994.
7.30, ABC TV, 20 November 2017.
The South Bank Show, London Weekend Television, 19 November 1989.
Studio A, Channel 31, 2009.

Books, Journals and Web Pages

Bell, John, 2003, *The Time of My Life*, Sydney: Allen & Unwin.
Brisbane, Katharine, 2005, *Not Wrong Just Different: Observations on the Rise of Contemporary Australian Theatre*, Sydney: Currency Press.
Brown, Noeline, 2005, *Noeline: Longterm Memoir*, Sydney: Allen & Unwin.
Clarke, John, *Neva*, 2015, available from https://mrjohnclarke.com/tinkering/page/2.
Denton, Martin, The New York Theatre Experience, 22 March 2011, website: formerly available from nytheatre.com.
Fitzpatrick, Peter, 2008, 'Life or a Cabaret? Nick Enright and *The Boy from Oz*', in *Nick Enright: An Actor's Playwright*, Anne Pender and Susan Lever (eds), Amsterdam: Rodopi.
Humphries, Barry, 2004, *My Life As Me*, Melbourne: Penguin.
Lamond, Toni, 1990, *First Half*, Sydney: Pan.
Meyrick, Julian 2008, '"Loved Every Minute of It": Nimrod, Enright's *The Venetian Twins* and the Invention of Popular Theatre', in *Nick Enright: An Actor's Playwright*, Anne Pender and Susan Lever (eds), Amsterdam: Rodopi.
McKee, Alan, 2001, *Australian Television: A Genealogy of Great Moments*, South Melbourne: Oxford University Press.
Murray, Matthew, Talkin' Broadway, 20 March 2011, website: https://www.talkinbroadway.com.
Olander, Philip, 2002, 'Edna in America: The Shtick's the Thing', *Meanjin*, vol. 61, no. 4.
Ostling, Geoffrey, 1993, 'The Pocket Playhouse 1957–1973', *Heritage*, no. 6.
Robertson, Tim, 2001 *The Pram Factory: The Australian Performing Group Recollected*, Melbourne: Melbourne University Press.
Sharkey, Michael, 1988, *The Illustrated Treasury of Australian Humour*, Melbourne: Oxford University Press.
Sommers, Michael, New Jersey Newsroom, 20 March 2011, website: formerly available from http://www.newjerseynewsroom.com.

REFERENCES

Van Straten, Frank, 2012, 'Betty Mildred Pounder (1921–1990)', in *Australian Dictionary of Biography Online*, http://adb.anu.edu.au/biography/pounder-betty-mildred-15484.

West, John, 1995, 'Musical Theatre', in *Companion to Theatre in Australia*, Philip Parsons (ed.), Sydney: Currency Press.

Williams, Margaret, 'The Pram Family Show', formerly available from https://www.pramfactory.com/family.html.

ACKNOWLEDGEMENTS

I thank the actors for their generosity and patience: Noeline Brown, John Clarke, Max Gillies, Barry Humphries, Carol Raye, Denise Scott and Tony Sheldon.

I acknowledge the help, support and advice of Robert Alexander, Tim Battin, Graham Benton, Jennie Benton, Gail Bryant, Nick Bryant, Garry Clark, Barry Clee, Debbie Clee, Kath Dougall, Simon Drake, John Fitzgerald, Libby Fitzgerald, Jane Goodall, John Gordon, Michael Humphries, Wendy James, Adrian Kiernander, Kerry Kilner, Margaret Leask, Jeenee Lee, Susan Lever, Mary Luckhurst, Rose McCarthy, Helen McDonald, Vicki McLean, Julian Meyrick, Bruce Moore, Alec Nicholson, Catherine Nicholson, Jane O'Sullivan, Howard Pender, Robyn Pender, Grace Quiddington, Louisa Quiddington, Peter Quiddington, Des Schuman, Janice Shaw, Julie Shearer, Peta Tait, Chris Upton, Wayne Upton, Fiona Utley, Aileen Young and Iain Young.

I acknowledge the Australian Research Council for the support of a Future Fellowship that made the research for this project possible.

I am grateful for the work of the publishing team: Sarah Cannon, Nathan Hollier, Joanne Mullins and Leslie Thomas.

ABOUT THE AUTHOR

Anne Pender is Professor of English and Theatre Studies at the University of New England, a recent Fulbright Senior Fellow at Harvard University, and Australian Research Council Research Fellow 2012–2016. A Menzies scholar to Harvard and graduate of the Australian National University and the University of New South Wales, Anne was Visiting Distinguished Professor in Australian Studies at the University of Copenhagen in 2011, and taught Australian Literature at King's College London in 2002–03. Anne's other books include *From a Distant Shore: Australian Writers in Britain 1820–2012* (with Bruce Bennett, 2013), *One Man Show: The Stages of Barry Humphries* (2010), *Nick Enright: An Actor's Playwright* (with Susan Lever, 2008) and *Christina Stead: Satirist* (2002).